QA

D0411167

A guide to Offa's Dyke Path

BRISTOL CITY COUNCIL
LIBRARY SERVICES
WITHDRAWN AND OFFERED FOR SALE
SOLD AS SEEN

Wales and the Marches – General Map

Liverpool

Prestatyn
Rhyl
Clwyd
Clwydians
Chester
Denbigh
Mold
Ruthin
C L W Y D
Wrexham
Vale Crucis
Dinas
Dee
Llangollen
Bran
BERWYNS
Chirk
Oswestry

Shrewsbury

Welshpool
Powis
Severn

Montgomery
Newtown
SALOP

C L U N   F O R E S T
Ludlow
Knighton
P O W Y S
RADNOR
Presteigne
FOREST
Llandrindod Wells
Kington

HEREFORD

Hay-on-Wye
Wye
Hereford
BLACK MTS
Grosmont
Llanthony
Brecon
Pandy
Monmouth
USK
White
Abergavenny
GLOS
GWENT
Tintern
Chepstow
Swansea
Newport

Cardiff
Bristol

0   10   20   30 miles
0   10 20 30 40 kilometres

● ● ● ● ● ● ● ● ● ● Offa's Dyke path
⚘△ Abbeys   ♜ Castles

A guide to
Offa's Dyke Path

Christopher John Wright

Bristol Library Service

AN 2958418 3

Constable London

First published in Great Britain 1975
by Constable & Company Ltd
10 Orange Street London WC2H 7EG

© 1975 Christopher John Wright
ISBN 0 09 460330 8

By the same author
A guide to the Pennine Way
A guide to the Pilgrims' Way

Designed by Ivor Kamlish MSIA and Associates
Set in Monophoto Apollo
Filmset and printed in England by
BAS Printers Limited, Wallop, Hampshire

A014642

AVON COUNTY LIBRARY

15 OCT 1975

Class No. 796 510142   914.29

Alloc. 3   Suppl. HJ

Contents

Plates

Symbols and abbreviations used in the maps and plans

Map scale	2½ inches	= 1 mile or 1:25000
Street plan scale	1 inch	= 400 ft or 1:5000
Building plan scale	1 inch	= 100 ft or 1 cm = 12 m
unless otherwise indicated		

— — — Official footpath

· · · · · · Recommended footpath

—·—· County boundaries

Offa's Dyke
*other earthworks shown
similarly, but indicated*

———— Other boundaries: wall
fence, hedge, etc

Stream or river (*arrow
indicates direction or flow*)

Bridge

Footbridge

Marshy ground

Wood

Buildings

Church or chapel

Canal with lock gate

△ Ordnance column

Railway

Lake or pond

Site of town gate

Quarry or cliff

Boulders scree

Orchard

☒ Mast

⊗ Cave

(4+4 ml) (70 Km) Miles/kilometres
from Chepstow
(*on official
route only*)

N
North is top of map
(*unless otherwise indicated*)

····1800···· Contours (*at 25 ft
intervals unless
impracticable*)

Abbreviations

YH   Youth Hostel

GPO   Post Office

TCB   Telephone call box

The author would like to thank the following persons and
organisations for their help and guidance whilst preparing this
book: The Oxford University Press and the British Academy,
publishers of Sir Cyril Fox's field survey of Offa's Dyke, for the
valued permission to use material therefrom; Frank Noble and
the Offa's Dyke Association, and Tom Millar, late of the
Countryside Commission, for the use of maps and other
material; The Ramblers' Association, the Youth Hostels
Association and the Offa's Dyke Association for accommodation
lists and accommodation; Farmers, inn-keepers and others for
providing accommodation, and fellow travellers for assistance
and companionship; and to Ernie Kay, Editor of the Offa's Dyke
Association's Newsletter, for checking the manuscript.

The maps photographed in this guide are reproduced from the
One Inch Seventh Series Ordnance Survey. The sketch maps are
based on the Ordnance Survey 1:25,000 ($2\frac{1}{2}$ inch) First Series
with the sanction of the Controller of HM Stationery Office.
Crown Copyright Reserved.

Long-distance footpaths or bridleways are national routes designated under the National Parks and Access to the Countryside Act of 1949 with continuous rights of way offering opportunities for walkers, horse-riders or cyclists to make extensive journeys that mostly avoid roads used by motor traffic.

The Countryside Commission have a statutory duty to plan these footpaths or bridleways and to submit proposals to the Secretary of State for the Environment, or the Secretary of State for Wales, as appropriate, for confirmation. Twelve such routes have so far been approved, and seven of them are open for their entire length. The first to be opened was the Pennine Way (435 km) on 24 April 1965. The Cleveland Way (150 km) followed on 24 May 1969, the Pembrokeshire Coast Path (269 km) on 16 May 1970, and Offa's Dyke Path (270 km) on 10 July 1971. The South Downs Way (129 km) was opened on 15 July 1972, the Cornish Coastal Path on 19 May 1973, and the Ridgeway Path on 29 Sept 1973.

Offa's Dyke Path is unique among the long-distance routes so far designated in following not a geographic feature such as a coastline or range of hills but an archaeological one, the 'dyke' or mound and ditch constructed on the orders of Offa, King of Mercia, to mark his boundary with Wales, from the Bristol Channel to the Irish Sea.

In those times, 1200 years ago, the boundary between 'England' and 'Wales' was 150 miles long and the Dyke was constructed for 80 miles of this length. There are two considerable stretches where the Dyke was never constructed, apart from short lengths at long intervals. These are from Redbrook south of Monmouth to a point north of Hereford in the wooded Herefordshire Plain where the River Wye was apparently considered an adequate boundary, and from Wrexham to the Dee Estuary where it was probably decided to accept the older, and similar, Wat's Dyke, a short distance to the east.

Following the publication of Sir Cyril Fox's great archaeological survey of Offa's Dyke in the 1930's, a long-distance footpath was planned. The Offa's Dyke Path was designated in 1955 and the original idea had been for an 'historic route', and so for most of the distance of the Dyke the Path follows it closely, the principal exceptions being in Clwyd where the line of the Dyke is badly disfigured by modern mineral working. Thus it is that the Path follows 60 miles of the 80-mile length of the Dyke.

The National Parks Commission had to rely on the help of

the rambling organisations and local authorities for suggestions of the paths to be followed and the new rights of way to be created. An opportunity was taken to increase the variety and interest of the long-distance route by traversing hill country, in one case the easternmost main ridge of the Black Mountains and in the other the line of the Clwydian Hills. Wherever possible Offa built the Dyke to give commanding views towards Wales and this greatly enhances the interest of the route.

The 'designated' route still presented local authorities with an appalling amount of work in negotiations to confirm existing rights of way and to create new ones. Twelve years after designation, in 1967, only a dozen new stiles had been built along the whole length of the path. Everyone, from the National Parks Commission to ramblers trying to find the alleged path, was disheartened.

A new surge of interest in our footpaths has been evident since 1966. The Countryside Commission took over from the National Parks Commission with more effective powers. Because of the incredibly slow progress in creating Offa's Dyke Path, and because of the almost complete lack of information available for the intending walker, a few impatient enthusiasts formed the Offa's Dyke Action Committee, which in 1969 became the Offa's Dyke Association, to secure the completion and use of the long-distance footpath and to promote the conservation, improvement and better knowledge of the Offa's Dyke Path and the Welsh Border region. The Association had a long campaign in view, and it encouraged negotiations with the many local authorities on the route who had promised to complete the Path for an official opening in 1971 and soon stiles and signposts were erected.

The official opening of the Path took place on 10 July 1971 at Knighton, Powys, midway along the course of the Path. The actual opening site was the Offa's Dyke Park, created by the local amenity group, the Tref-y-Clawydd 1970 Society, as their contribution to European Conservation Year. Lady Green-Price performed the official opening of the Park, which preceded the opening of the Path. The ceremony of opening the Path was performed by Lord Hunt, and other speakers included David Gibson-Watt, Minister of State, Welsh Office. John Cripps, chairman of the Countryside Commission, presided. Lord Hunt was living at Weir Cottage, Knighton, when he was chosen as the leader of the first successful Everest expedition, and the celebrations were preceded with an inaugural walk over

Panpunton, behind his house.

Even when the Path was declared open a few rights of way had still to be finally agreed, and a few local authorities had still to complete their stiles and signposting. Even today some stretches are inadequately marked and alternative paths are being substituted, but at least there is now a fully recognised and acceptable walking route from coast to coast.

Although the primary purpose of the Offa's Dyke Association had been achieved – the opening of the Path – many saw the continuing need for an organisation to foster harmony between those living on the route, those using it and those responsible for maintaining it and waymarking it. The Offa's Dyke Association has found continued support from ramblers, historians and archaeologists and its aims and objects are still pursued. The author has received considerable help from the Association in the preparation of this guide, and he recommends all readers to become members of this organisation. Membership confers invaluable assistance with an accommodation list and a regular newsletter, amongst other benefits. Please address your enquiries to 'The Offa's Dyke Association, Knighton, Powys' and not to the author.

We have seen, in the introduction, that the Mercian frontier was
150 miles long, and that Offa's Dyke was present throughout 80
miles of this distance. Offa's Dyke Path is 176 miles long, and the
stretches where the Path is co-incident with the Dyke can easily
be assessed from the following rough table:

Section of Path	Existence of Dyke	
	Present	Absent
Chepstow – Redbrook	13	–
Redbrook – Rushock	–	55
Rushock – Leighton	36	–
Leighton – River Dee	–	9
River Dee – Chirk	18	
Chirk – Prestatyn	–	45
Totals	67	109
Total Distance	176	

It can be seen therefore that the Dyke is followed for just
over $\frac{1}{3}$ the length of the Path, but the 67 miles of Dyke which
are followed represent nearly $\frac{3}{4}$ of the actual total length of the
Dyke and the best preserved sections of it. The 'official' length
of the Path is 168 miles, but by accurate measurement on
$2\frac{1}{2}$ inch maps this length has been found to be 5 miles short.
To this must be added about 3 miles to take into account those
several short stretches through built-up areas which are not
'designated', and the total length becomes 176 miles. Taking
further into account the recommended detours to places of
special interest near the route, and the extra miles walked in
search of accommodation, it is likely that the total mileage per
person will be in the region of 200.

Offa's Dyke and the Offa's Dyke Path begin dramatically above
Sedbury Cliffs on the Severn near Chepstow and the mouth of
the Wye. The Wye valley offers a beautiful walk through
woods along the massive rampart of the Dyke on the edge of the
high plateau above the meanders of the river. Beyond the
precipitous slopes above the Cistercian Tintern Abbey less
spectacular traces of the earthwork may be found in the jumble
of tiny fields on St Briavels Common or one can follow an
alternative route on the bank of the Wye.

The earthwork vanishes from the landscape on the N edge of

the Forest of Dean plateau, and the Path drops down from the Kymin, with its Naval Temple, to Monmouth.

Beyond Monmouth you leave the rugged beauty of the Wye behind and pass through rolling countryside past White Castle to the Black Mountains in the Brecon Beacons National Park.

The Hatterall ridge of the Black Mountains is typical mountain moorland, and given good weather there are views over to the Brecon Beacons and the Herefordshire Plain. From Hay Bluff you descend steeply to Hay-on-Wye, then you are away from the mountains and back into quiet rolling farmland.

Disgwylfa and the Hergest ridge are two pleasant hills crossed on the way to Kington, where the Dyke is rejoined on Rushock Hill behind the town. Beyond there is typical border country, a long succession of breezy uplands, remote and sparsely populated, intersected by a succession of valleys draining down into England.

The most magnificent stretches of the earthwork are now followed, crossing the broad sheep pastures of Clun Forest in the Shropshire Hills Area of Outstanding Natural Beauty. The Dyke is most spectacular in the vicinity of Newcastle and Churchtown, but it diminishes in size as it reaches the Montgomeryshire lowland at Mellington Hall, not far from the county town.

The route from Montgomery to Llanymynech is an anti-climax to that just followed and to that ahead. It is a walk through flat agricultural land, but the journey is varied by the climb up Long Mountain to Beacon Ring and through Leighton and Lymore Parks. You cross the Severn near Welshpool and continue along its flood-banks for miles, and you also follow a stretch of the old Montgomery Canal. It makes a change to walk along the flat, but too much of the way is on roads, and busy ones at that.

The main road through Llanymynech is on the line of the Dyke, and on one side of the village street you are in England and on the other in Wales.

North of Llanymynech you are in rolling border country again, the eastern foothills of the Berwyn Mountains, with views over the great Shropshire plain. Some stretches of the Dyke are massive and these are the last fragments you will see, for at the Llangollen Canal you leave the Dyke for good.

You cross the Dee in the Vale of Llangollen beside the spectacular Pontcysyllte Aqueduct, Thomas Telford's magnificent monument of industrial architecture. North of the river you follow the limestone escarpment of Eglwyseg, which gives views of the mountains to westward. The path continues through the hills north of Llangollen below cliffs and over a wild and trackless moor beyond World's End, but there is an alternative route from Llangollen via the Horseshoe Pass to Llandegla. By following the latter route you can climb up to the ruins of Castell Dinas Bran and visit the Valle Crucis Abbey, the best preserved abbey in Wales.

After crossing the infant River Alyn at Llandegla you reach the Clwydian Range, and the Path follows over a succession of heather-clad hills, several of which are topped with Iron Age hill-forts – Foel Fenlli, Moel Arthur and Pen-y-cloddiau. Moel Famau, which is the highest, has a jubilee tower with a mountain indicator, and there are wide views over the Dee estuary to the east and Snowdonia to the west.

Following the escarpment edge you can see the distant sea, and there are a few minor hills to cross before you can look down on Prestatyn and Rhyl and the glorious sands of the Clwyd coast. Before your rapid descent into the town you can see the final hill, Gop Hill, the most northern point reached by Offa's Dyke, and you know then that you have followed Offa from coast to coast.

The whole Path takes about 10 days to walk at 17 miles per day or 15 days at 12 miles per day, and the guide has been divided into sections of approximately a day's journey each.

Those content in following the Path for its own sake can easily walk the whole length in two weeks, but the historical student is advised to allow 3 weeks. Within a mile or two of the route one can visit the substantial remains of more than a dozen castles and sites of 15 more which played their part in medieval border history. Across north Gwent the official Path passes White Castle, but you may prefer to spend some extra time on the 'Castles Variation' route, a route devised by Frank Noble of the Offa's Dyke Association, and originally intended to be the official route, sweeping farther north-east into an area of greater historic interest, as it passes the ruins of border castles at Skenfrith, Grosmont and Longtown. One may also wish to take time off for visiting and exploring Chepstow, Monmouth, Hay, Knighton, Clun, Bishops Castle, Montgomery, Welshpool, Llangollen, Ruthin and Denbigh – although several are on the route the others are not far away.

Your first day can be spent in looking around Chepstow and getting acclimatised to the Dyke by walking out to Sedbury and back. If you have arrived at mid-day then spend the afternoon in Chepstow. The walk out to Sedbury Cliffs and back the following morning will only add a couple of hours and miles to your second day, and if you want to make that a short one then stay at Tintern or St Briavels. Otherwise Monmouth is within easy reach.

One cannot begin to understand the history of the building of
Offa's Dyke without first having some idea of the political
development of this Welsh border country where the valleys of
the Wye, Severn and Dee widen into the Midland plain.

The Roman conquest of Wales between AD 48–84 was the
first political action to define the borderland character of this
region. More than six centuries elapsed between the withdrawal
of Roman rule and the first of three important events which were
to mark a stage in the territorial evolution of Wales.

The first of these occurrences was the establishment of
Offa's Dyke between 778–796 – 'the boundary line of Cymru.'

The second was the Edwardian conquest and subsequent
settlement of Wales in and after 1282, a settlement whose
terminology we still use when referring to Wales as the
'Principality.'

Thirdly, there were the Tudor Acts of Union in 1536 and
1542, these last being the events which shaped the present-day
political map of the country.

Each of these occurrences was of outstanding importance in
the evolution and development of the territory which was to
become Wales, but we need only study the first.

The marchland character of the territory between Severn and
Dee became sharply drawn after the removal of the Romans,
and the period between 400–600 saw the emergence of the
Welsh language and the spread of Christianity through the Celtic
west. At its widest extent historical Powys, the central province
of Wales, covered the area of the middle Dee with the lands to
the north and the greater part of Montgomeryshire and
Radnorshire, together with that part of Breconshire north of the
Mynydd Epynt. (Montgomeryshire, Radnorshire and Breconshire
are now new districts of the new county of Powys, as created
under the Local Government Act, 1972.) In the early medieval
period, from 5c to 9c, this area was divided into two parts.
Northern Powys was called Gwynedd and Southern Powys was
known as the Deheubarth, but it was not until the reign of
Henry II that these two states united to preserve the Welsh
culture and religion from the expansion of the English.

The Anglo-Saxons had not found Britain easy to conquer. The
first English kings began to establish bases along the Mercian
border with Wales, a border zone where two societies – Welsh
and English – met, mingled and came into conflict.

Not until 577 at the Battle of Deorham were the English able to extend their rule to the west coast, by dividing the North Welsh in Wales from the West Welsh in Devon and Cornwall. In the early 7c they drove a further wedge deep into British territory, separating the North Welsh from their compatriots in Cumbria and Strathclyde. The Northumbrian King Aethelfrith had penetrated as far as Chester to win a great victory over the North Welsh at Bangor-on-Dee in 616, and thus the Welsh-speaking people in that portion west of a line drawn between Chester and Gloucester became a separate people. Henceforth they were to be known as 'Cymry' – 'fellow countrymen.'

After the failure of the Welsh to hold these two vital points a process of unification came under way in Anglo-Saxon England as gradually many minor kingdoms declined, but in the 7c and 8c the Anglo-Saxons were solidly organised in the kingdoms that successively competed for the overlordship of the island.

Edwin, heir of Deira (East Yorkshire) was placed on the throne of Northumbria after the battle in 616 with the help of the East Angles, and he headed the greatest confederation which England had yet seen. In the latter half of his reign he invaded North Wales and attacked Cadwallon, King of Gwynedd, an error which spawned an alliance which was fatal to Edwin.

Cadwallon, who was British and a Christian, joined up with Penda, an Anglo-Saxon pagan nobleman. Together they marched against Edwin and, having killed him, set about the devastation of Northumbria in 632. Only in 633 was Cadwallon killed and Northumbria saved.

Although his ally was dead, Penda was far from finished. As King of Mercia (622–645) he invaded Northumbria, and in 642 Oswald, the new king of the aggressive armies of Northumbria, was killed and martyred at Oswestry (Oswald's Tree). Penda was finally beaten in 654 by the Northumbrians, led by Oswald's brother Oswin.

Politically Northumbria was never to fulfil this early promise of victory over Mercia, for it was weakened by internal dissensions and by raiding Picts and Scots.

Meanwhile, Penda's son Wulfhere (652–675) managed to make himself supreme in southern England. He failed to beat the Northumbrians but they no longer posed a threat to southern kingdoms.

The English were established in Shropshire and Herefordshire and they threatened the Welsh. The border had moved steadily westwards. Yet the closer it came to the hill country, the slower became the advance. The Welsh had been driven back to their unassailable strongholds in the mountains, and these they held – stubbornly, desperately and successfully.

The growth and westward expansion of Mercia continued into 8c. In the northern march, where the Welsh mountains frown on the plains of Severn and Dee, an earthwork, Wat's Dyke, was built from Oswestry to Holywell, soon after 700. It probably represents the western limit of Mercian expansion at that time.

During the half century after Wulfhere minor kings rose and fell in a period of much fighting, but Aethelbald maintained his ascendency as King of Mercia for 30 years, a reign longer than any other king, by controlling England south of the Humber, until he was murdered by his own bodyguard in 757.

In the ensuing civil war in Mercia, Offa emerged as king and he achieved unprecedented power in southern England. Offa occupied the throne for a period of no less than 39 years between 757 and 796, and in order to define the boundary of the western limit of his unwieldy kingdom he constructed the remarkable and celebrated Dyke which stretches from the mouth of the Wye to the high hills above the Dee.

Offa brought all the southern English kingdoms under his power. He made his influence felt with Charlemagne and the Pope, and he obtained an archbishop for his own kingdom at Lichfield. His coinage – the finest since Roman times – and a few surviving letters and charters of his reign indicate a competent administration. The concept and layout of the Dyke confirms this: it probably dates from the period of supremacy and comparative peace he enjoyed in the latter part of his reign after the last great Welsh attack in 784 to his death in 796.

It is said that Offa died at Rhuddlan in 796 in his last battle against the Welsh, trying to establish the final course of the Dyke to the sea – the Dyke is unfinished at the northern end. Offa's son died in the following year, but the Mercians maintained their supremacy until 825 when they suffered a serious defeat by Egbert, King of Wessex, at the Battle of Ellendum (near Swindon). Four years later Mercia itself was taken over by Egbert, and Northumbria also accepted his overlordship. Although he failed to maintain control of Mercia the history of Anglo-Saxon England from then on rested on the fortunes of the royal house of Wessex. The kingdom declined in power until it was completely crushed by the invasions of the Vikings, and the realisation of a united England was put back still further.

Offa's Dyke has several principal characteristics. Apart from its period of origin, political nature and purpose and as a boundary between two cultures the Dyke has recognisable standards of construction, and each of these aspects are examined below.

Time of Construction

There is no record of the construction of the Dyke: in fact the Dyke itself provides more evidence about the Mercian kingdom than any of the surviving documents of Offa's reign.

There had been a great battle with the Welsh at Hereford in 760 and Offa was again in conflict with this old enemy in 778 and 784 – his two great campaigns against the Welsh, the first against the Kingdom of Gwent and the second against the Kingdom of Powys – and it seems that the Dyke was probably built after this time, during a period of dominance over his enemy and relative stability. The Welsh and English churches had been reconciled in 768, and it seems that Offa's ambitions in his later years tended towards the domination of the richer lands of southern England, rather than towards any conquests from the Welsh, which were unlikely to produce much profit.

The building of the Dyke reflects a degree of political and economic organisation which was perhaps matched by a massive growth of settlement in the marchland between the Severn and the western frontier of the kingdom.

The Dyke must have been intended to provide a complete barrier within a space of a few years. In the first year or two the entire line must have been marked out, with such great engineering skill which cunningly used every natural feature of the terrain that it arouses the admiration of all who follow it across the borderland. In subsequent years people of all the Mercian villages within 40 miles or more of the frontier must have been sent to dig a stretch which had been marked out for them.

Political

Sir Cyril Fox, in his great survey between 1926 and 1931, indicated that the Dyke marked a negotiated boundary, and it is no longer believed that the Dyke was intended as a military frontier, imposed by a conquering Mercian upon the various principalities of Wales.

Fox has shown by a detailed and systematic study of the Dyke that it was a frontier based on compromise between the negotiators and that it was more fitting to regard it as a

'boundary defined by treaty and agreement between the men of
the hills and then men of the lowlands,' rather than a post-
conquest military barrier.

Although drawn in the strategic favour of the Mercian, who
was clearly the dominant partner in the arrangement, it was not
forced on his Welsh neighbour, and although Fox's views were
criticised – it was considered too optimistic a view to believe
the Welsh would have a fixed boundary forced upon them, or
that the Saxon would have consulted them in the matter – the
Dyke was, nevertheless, the original political or territorial
manifestation of the then still present cultural division between
the English and Welsh. It was a natural boundary in that it was
established after the development of the cultural and settlement
pattern of the region, and it was built in response to the
recognition of the cultural frontier zone.

The eastern margin of the central Welsh uplands, with its
extensions into Shropshire and Herefordshire and its recessions
along the Vales of Llangollen, Powys and Wye, together with
the coastal plains, is topographically a transition zone between
the highland and lowland. The character of the Dyke is con-
firmed by the general siting in relation to this relief, for in the
north it lies east of the Clwydians and the Berwyn. In the middle
borderland the Dyke swings west not only into the Vale of
Powys, but also up the minor streams which drain to the Teme,
the Arrow and the Lugg – streams whose dissection of the
upland provided always a comparatively easy routeway for
invaders from the south-east.

Between certain fixed points on the frontier the Dyke was
constructed by the Mercians to give them the advantage of the
ground   the inclusion of Gop Hill, Selattyn Hill and Bakers
Hill, for example, within the Dyke enabled visual control over
Welsh territory – but at some points the line taken by the
Dyke leaves tactical advantages on the Welsh side; for example,
the strategically valuable hill top of Ffridd Faldwyn near
Montgomery abruptly closes the view from the Dyke to the
west. Much wider views could have been obtained for military
purposes, but obviously the Power occupying the lowlands
desired and was content to include within its territory key
positions giving visual control in the mountainous borderlands.

Although the earthwork equals the frontier of Hadrian in
concept and design it does not appear to have been a completely
defended or defensible barrier, although it must have been
difficult to cross. Maybe penalties would have been inflicted

on anyone found on the wrong side of it, although the theory that any Welshman found to the east of it would have had his hand cut off seems to date from the 12c chronicles. There is no doubt, however, that the Dyke was accepted by both sides as a firm demarcation line, a frontier for all time.

Alignment

There is no doubt that Offa planned the whole work. The course was laid out by him, and the dimensions and the character of the work in general terms defined by him. Fox thinks it possible that each landowner on the Border was made responsible for a certain length of the Dyke, this length being proportionate to the resources at his command or to the extent of his estates. He inferred that the scale of the work (within the limits laid down) was dependent on the resources of the locality and the energy of, and command of techniques possessed by, the gangers in charge of the actual work of digging.

The course of the Dyke in general, though sinuous, is remarkably direct for long distances. In the hill country it swings from side to side to take advantage of dominant features within reasonable distance or to accommodate itself to changes in level. In some sections the engineer has determined to take advantage of all commanding westward facing slopes: they are skilfully selected and utilised – views to the west are normal, to the east rare, although the tilt of the land is largely to the east. Every effort is made to keep to these dominant slopes – Craig Forda and the hills of Selattyn, Whitehaven, Llynclys and Llanymynech are prime examples.

South of the Dee the Dyke swings westwards to include the spurs of the Berwyns, over very broken and mountainous country intersected by deep river valleys. Where the country is deeply indented the Dyke does not zig-zag in and out but leaves the scarp and takes a straight course across upland, though the field of view from the Dyke is thus very limited. This striking characteristic is well seen on Llanvair Hill, Cwm Sanaham, Panpunton and on the Hawthorn Hill-Farrow Hill range.

The unity of the design is shown by the use of lateral re-entrants in the east-west valleys. The side of the re-entrant which faces west is made use of in the alignment – such as are chosen from Chirk Park to the River Ceiriog, and from the Selattyn Hill to the Morlas Brook.

Right-angled corners are a novel feature of the Dyke design – such as on Rushock, Cwm Sanaham and probably Llanvair Hills.

It seems probable that it was agreed by the Powers concerned in the delineation of the frontier that it should pass over the highest point of the hill in these places. The engineer of the Dyke fulfilled the letter of the law, but did not allow it to interfere more than was absolutely necessary with what he regarded as a suitable alignment.

For some reason not satisfactorily explained only short sections of the Dyke were built in the Herefordshire Plain, perhaps at road crossings in the forest. The course is indefinite and erratic between the Wye at Redbrook and Rushock Hill and there are considerable gaps which appear never to have been artificially strengthened. Fox explains this as thinly populated, impenetrable 'damp oakwood', and this woodland would have formed a natural barrier. It seems equally likely that western Herefordshire was occupied by Welsh tribes who were no threat to an English king. Indeed, the land of Archenfield – the ground between the Wye and the Black Mountains – became Anglicised earlier and more thoroughly than any other land west of Offa's boundary.

Without the Dyke the Wye gorge would still be the finest natural frontier. It is built on a massive scale where no-one would dream of crossing as the cliffs are sufficient discouragement. Fox considered that the Dyke above the tidal Wye must have been both a concession or admission of Welsh rights to traffic on that river, or an attempt to control any invasion of the Forest of Dean. It seems more likely however to have been built as a show of force against the powerful Kingdom of Gwent.

In the alignment of the Dyke the skilful use of westward facing slopes and re-entrants is especially noteworthy, and the route has several principal physical characteristics.

1 The Dyke is sent straight down small valleys – i.e. south of Middle Knuck.
2 It traverses diagonally down large steep-sided ravines, as at Mainstone.
3 Lateral re-entrants are found and chosen when crossing main valleys – e.g. the south side of the Clun valley. A rare exception occurs at Herrock where a very steep hill is ascended direct.
4 A crossing point in a valley is chosen at a point where two streams meet – e.g. on both the River Unk and the Mainstone brook, N and S of Edenhope Hill respectively; the Wilcom Brook and the River Teme at Knighton; the Cascob Brook in the Lugg valley; and the Hindwell and Knobley Brooks below Herrock Hill.

5 Advantage is taken of rivers and streams, either their natural
  or canalised courses.
6 Direct alignment is chosen across a valley from a point high
  enough up the side to secure visual control of the whole of the
  valley floor.
    There are several instances where these characteristics are
evident and it is reasonably easy to conjecture the line of the
Dyke in those sections where it is not visible.

Size

Local differences in layout and construction are held to result
either from the different 'gangs' and different supervisors, or
from differences in vegetation resulting in
– straight massive works across cleared and cultivated land,
– wavering lines through scrub,
– and only a boundary bank, or no surviving trace, through
dense forest.
    Structurally the Dyke is a boundary-type bank and only
slight military considerations influenced its construction. The
builders were obviously practised in the art of defensive
earthworks and they modified their style to suit. They must
have been recruited from a wide area of Mercia: the massive
earthworks above Tintern perhaps represent the mining skill of
the men of the Forest of Dean, who were in demand throughout
the Middle Ages for digging the ditches of new castles.
    There is usually a ditch (or the equivalent) on the Welsh side
of the Dyke, and a bank thrown up from it on the Mercian side.
    The Dyke consistently shows a ditch on the west side in
level or fairly level country. On gentle westward facing slopes,
or even on level ground, material for the bank is frequently
obtained from spoil holes on the east side as well as from the
western ditch. Occasionally a definite east ditch is present in
addition to the west ditch. On steep westward facing slopes it
may have been impracticable to throw earth or stone upwards
and the bank was omitted. The Dyke may then be represented
by a shelf or berm only, or by a shelf with a western ditch, or
by a low bank with eastern hollow and slight western ditch.
All these examples appear on Craig Forda.
    A change in the character of the Dyke does not necessarily
mean a change in design or designers, but that the builders
constructed various types to suit the variations of contour on
the mountainous alignment.
    In some exceptional places the ramparts of the bank still

stand 10–12 feet high and the ditch is correspondingly deep; remarkable dimensions for a boundary bank. The overall width of the earthwork varies between 50–77 feet, and in many places the parapet is still broad and level enough to walk upon. The average height of the bank is 6 feet and the average overall width is nearly 60 feet.

In some stretches where there was a low 'boundary bank' it may have been topped by timber palisades, and the whole earthwork was probably reinforced with timber and with gates at the crossing points, but no traces of these features has been recognised.

Gaps

There are numerous gaps in the Dyke, both original, where the Dyke crosses rivers, streams or brooks, and 'artificial' crossing points of roads and tracks or access to fields.

Skilful use was made by the engineer of bends in the rivers, but gaps necessitated by the existence and crossing of watercourses were made as narrow as possible – for example, the Morlas Brook and Nant Eris are only a few yards wide, as are those at Middle Knuck, Garbett Hall and between Spoad and Llanvair Hills.

In the valleys of the larger tributaries and rivers – the Clun, Lugg, Ceiriog and Vrynwy, for example – winter floods have made the gaps wider than they were originally. Any construction offering a barrier to the waters would have been planed down or swept away.

The Dyke was intended to present a barrier almost complete, legitimate traffic between the two peoples concerned being confined to defined routes few in number. Openings for traffic are less numerous in the thinly populated upland country than in the lowlands. Some of the hill tracks, anciently important, cross the Dyke by well-worn and broad gaps, as at Hergan, Ffridd Hill and Newcastle Hill, and these gaps are probably Offan – they show no obvious intention of modern origin as they are not reinforced at the point of passage as are the entrances to defensive constructions such as hill forts. There are openings, now little used or disused, on Edenhope Hill and Knuck Bank, which almost certainly permitted the passage of ancient ridgeways.

Place names and Language

Generally the earthwork marks a transition zone between the

two cultures of English and Welsh, and wherever it was built the language frontier, a serious barrier to intercourse until modern times, remained close to it. Where the Dyke was not built the language frontier moved westwards in the south and eastwards in the north. Old English place-names such as 'ham' and 'ton' are found to the west of the Dyke and many Welsh names like 'tre' and 'llan' to the east, while cultural fusion appears in a variety of translated, dual and adapted types of place-names on each side.

In three areas English names notably over-step the Dyke to the west;

1 In the Severn valley, around Welshpool, a line of early English settlements lies beyond the earthwork, represented by such names as Buttington, Leighton, Edderton and Forden. It seems likely that these places record the expansion of Mercia into the Welsh borderland between AD 650–750. The later frontier of Offa was probably a political compromise to secure the whole of the corridor of the Severn in this district of Powys.

2 Another cluster of English names appears west of the Dyke in the fertile Radnor Basin where the Summergill Brook gathers most of the streams from the southern flank of Radnor Forest. Here are Kinnerton, Evenjobb, Walton and Harpton. The green ridge of the Dyke courses up and down across the spurs and valleys close to the eastern side of the basin. Here, too, it seems likely that the building of the Dyke represents a retreat from the furthest limit of settlement achieved 100 years before.

3 Another scattering of early English names to the west of the Wye in the land of Gwent suggests that Saxon settlements were left beyond the frontier when Offa consolidated his kingdom. They include Itton, among the wooded hills on the outskirts of Chepstow, and Ifton. Goldcliff and Nash, English place-names amid the salt-marshes at the mouth of the Usk, point to a tentative early settlement across the Severn estuary from Somerset.

The abundance and persistence of both Celtic and English place-name elements in the borderland also indicate that it is doubtful that either Offa's Dyke or the political boundary of 1536 served as clearcut lines of linguistic demarcation.

The route of Offa's Dyke Path is a distance of about 170 miles –
a journey of between 10–15 days. Finding the route is not
always easy, even with the help of current editions of 1:50,000
or 2½ inch maps. The Dyke has been lost in many places and it
is often difficult or impossible to locate it. It has been obliterated
in several places by mining, industry and farming, and in other
places its line is purely conjectural.

The main difficulties of travellers on Offa's Dyke Path are
concerned not with the nature of the terrain but with finding
and following the approved route – not with walking but
navigation over the border hills and negotiation of the maze
of hedges and fences in the valleys. Navigation, the following
of the designated route exactly, is the major problem. The
Offa's Dyke Path is a continuous footpath in name only: often
there is no recognisable path at all, but regular use is being
made of the Path and a route is being beaten out.

No less than 12 different highway authorities have been
concerned in the creation of the Path and they have had
16 years since the approval by the Minister of Housing and
Local Government in October 1955 to the official opening in
July 1971 – to clear the way, restore stiles and bridges, set up
signposts and other indications, and create new rights of way.
Much has been done, but the job is still not completed.

The most perplexing sections are in the valleys and the
lowlands, among the fields and farms, where a wrong stile can
lead one badly astray. Not all farmers, understandably, are in
sympathy with the long-distance footpath, and may direct one
off-course where the route is not sufficiently marked.

The route is marked by special signposts, concrete posts,
acorn symbols or waymarked arrows, but these are insufficient
and irregular. Unfortunately they are often in places where
they are really least needed – in the Wye Valley – and rarely
where they would be most appreciated – NW of Monmouth,
for example.

The waymarking is basically one of two types, usually
according to the kind of country the path traverses. The route
is identified either by a signpost in oak, with the lettering
raised or incised – some bear the name in English 'Offa's Dyke
Path', some in Welsh 'Llwybr Clawdd Offa', whilst others are
bi-lingual – or a low concrete plinth with the name of the route
as part of the casting. Another waymark at points where the
walker might be in doubt is an acorn symbol, either a metal
plaque attached to gateposts, stiles or fences, or a stencil mark

on stone walls, trees or boulders.

The highway authorities have erected many stiles of a uniform pattern, the exceptions being in Shropshire and Flintshire where they are of different styles, and the sight of one of these helps confirm the route of the path. Most of the stiles are wide, with a double rail at the bottom. Shropshire stiles have one tall post, Flintshire stiles are usually narrow and with metal rails. They are substantial affairs and quite high, and walkers carrying the popular high-rise pack frames and rucksacks will often find their baggage caught up in the overhanging branches of some hedgerow hawthorn. By the end of the journey one has become quite an expert at climbing stiles.

Early summer is the best time of the year for walking Offa's Dyke Path in its entirety; in the months of April, May and June there is a better chance of settled weather, the hours of daylight are long, and accommodation is easier to find. In high summer and autumn one has to cope with nettles, thistles, brambles and bracken, and the occurrence of such undergrowth can spoil the day's pleasure.

For the walker the countryside is at its best in these early months. One can see magnificent stretches of the extraordinary and remote earthwork striding across border hills, its ditch or bank growing hedgerows and its banks bedecked with wild flowers. Offa's Dyke country is not so extensively cultivated – indeed, the Dyke often forms the boundary of cultivation – and one can walk for miles along its crest unhindered by plough or wire. One may also walk for miles without meeting a soul and from a hundred vantage points see some of the most breathtaking views in the Welsh Border Country.

Offa's Dyke Path follows a course lying between two terminal points, one (Prestatyn) north of the other (Chepstow) and either may be regarded as the start of the Path and the other the end.

One guide – Noble's Shell Guide – refers to Sedbury as the starting point, but Fox, the archaeological authority, starts at Prestatyn. The descriptive leaflets issued by the Ramblers' Association and the Countryside Commission also start at opposite ends of the Path. There is no valid logical reason for this, and either end is acceptable, but this Guide is based on the assumption that the walker using it will start at Chepstow and finish at Prestatyn, and the text is written accordingly. There is no reason of course why the walk should not be done from north to south, and some people may prefer to do so. There is evidence, however, that the majority walk from south to north, and therefore this Guide has been designed for those people.

The book has been divided into four main parts, to correspond with the route between the Bristol Channel and Liverpool Bay which is divided into four parts by the main rivers of Wye, Severn and Dee. Each of these parts is again divided into sections corresponding to the lengths usually covered in a day's walk. There are thirteen chapters covering an average two-weeks journey, and there are eight chapters to describe the major towns along the route.

One of the principal objects of this Guide is to enable walkers to follow Offa's Dyke Path without going seriously astray, or trespassing or losing valuable time on false trails. Offa's Dyke Path has been specially surveyed for this book, and it is hoped that the Guide gives useful and detailed assistance in clearly defining the route on the map, though more waymarking is required on the ground.

It became clear to the author after hearing reports from ramblers and readers of his other books that any guide to our long-distance footpaths should concentrate on making manifestly obvious the correct route through complicated country. The The new HMSO guides to the Cleveland Way and the Pembrokeshire Coast Paths recognise this and have full-colour reproductions of the 1:25,000 scale Ordnance Survey maps, but even these official maps are out of date on some matters of detail.

The method which has been adopted for this Guide is to show a continuous strip map at a scale of 1:25,000 (approximately $2\frac{1}{2}$ inches to 1 mile) – a scale large enough to present all the information and detail necessary to follow the Path exactly.

In order to show field boundaries, contours, woods, farms,

tracks, paths, the Dyke, etc., the features of the countryside off-route have had to be omitted from the strip-maps, but this deficiency has been remedied by the use of relevant extracts from the Ordnance Survey maps. These indicate the location of the larger-scale map sections in relation to each other and the immediate district. The 1 : 25,000 strip map will tell you which field you are in, the 1 : 50,000 map where the nearest village is.

Symbols and abbreviations used in the maps are shown in the key panel, but some not indicated are self-explanatory, e.g. TCB = telephone call box; GPO or PO = post office; Tck of old Rly = track of old railway. Abbreviations are also used in the text – N, S, E, W, = north, south, east, west; RHS = right hand side; L = left; 8c = eighth century; c1120 = circa 1120; ECD = early closing day; MD = market day.

The strip maps are drawn, unless otherwise indicated, with grid north at the top of the map, so anyone travelling from S to N will therefore read from the bottom of the map to the top, or from R to L. When you walk off the top of one page the map continues on the next at the bottom or R. N to S walkers will read the maps back to front and from top to bottom with equal facility, but the run of the text will be a source of annoyance, for which apologies are presented.

Of course, one of the advantages of such detailed maps in this Guide is that they avoid the need to purchase the official Ordnance Survey publications, and they also avoid unnecessary weight and bulk in your pack. If you really want to know what 1/50,000 and $2\frac{1}{2}$ inch scale maps cover Offa's Dyke Path they are listed below. (The 1 inch Seventh Series was replaced on 7 March 1974 by a new series at 1 : 50,000 scale, or approximately $1\frac{1}{4}$ inches to 1 mile). Complete they will occupy a parcel measuring $10\frac{1}{2} \times 9\frac{1}{2} \times 2\frac{1}{2}$ inches (26 × 24 × 6 cm), weigh 2 lb 12 oz (1 kg 220 gm), and cost over £12.00.

1 : 50,000 Maps First Series

116 *Denbigh and Colwyn Bay*
117 *Chester*
126 *Shrewsbury*
137 *Ludlow and Wenlock Edge*
148 *Presteigne and Hay-on-Wye*
161 *Abergavenny and The Black Mountains*
162 *Gloucester and Forest of Dean*

1 : 25,000 Maps Provisional Edition

SJ 07 *St Asaph*
SJ 08 *Rhyll*
SJ 15 *Ruthin*
SJ 16 *Cilcain*
SJ 20 *Welshpool*
SJ 21 *Ardleen*
SJ 22 *Oswestry (South)*
SJ 23 *Chirk*
SJ 24 *Llangollen*
SJ 25 *Treuddyn*
SO 22 *Llanthony*
SO 23 *Black Hill (Hereford)*
SO24 *Hay-on-Wye*
SO 25 *Kington (Hereford)*
SO 26 *New Radnor*
SO27 *Knighton (Rads)*
SO 28 *Newcastle (Salop)*
SO 29 *Montgomery*
SO 31 *Abergavenny (East)*
SO 32 *Longtown (Hereford)*
SO 41 *Rockfield (Monmouth)*
SO 50 *St Briavels*
SO 51 *Monmouth*
SO 59 *Chepstow*

Maps are listed in numerical order, and are not necessarily in
the order in which they are used for walking the route.

The Countryside Commission have prepared the Country Code as a guide to visitors, some of whom are perhaps unaccustomed to country ways. Please remember to observe the following standards of good manners when you go to enjoy the beauties and the pleasures of the garden that is Britain's countryside.

1 Guard against all risks of fire
Don't drop lighted matches or cigarette ends, particularly near crops, plantations, woods, heaths and hay ricks. A fire, once started, is difficult to put out.

2 Fasten all gates
Fasten all gates, unless they are obviously intended to be left open. Animals can do great damage to crops and to themselves if they stray. They may be injured by traffic or be the cause of accidents.

3 Keep dogs under proper control
Animals are easily frightened by strange dogs, so do not let them disturb cattle, hens or sheep; keep your dog on its lead when near other animals or walking along the road.

4 Keep to paths across farm land
Avoid damaging crops in any way. Corn, grass and hay that have been trampled flat are difficult to harvest. Do not trespass.

5 Avoid damaging fences, hedges and walls
Where a man can go, an animal will follow, and damage to crops will result. Use gates and stiles where they are provided.

6 Do not leave litter
Take your litter home, including bottles and tins. All litter is not only unsightly but dangerous. Broken glass, opened tins and plastic bags can very easily harm livestock and damage farm machinery.

7 Safeguard water supplies
A stream, brook or well may be the only water supply for a farmer and his animals. Water is precious in the country. Do not pollute it in any way.

8 Protect wild life, plants and trees
Never dig up plants and flowers, carve on trees, and please

do not take birds' eggs. Wild flowers, birds and trees give more pleasure to more people if left alone.

9 Go carefully on country roads

Blind corners, hump-back bridges, slow-moving farm vehicles and herds of cattle are all hazards for the motorist, cyclist and walker. Careless car parking may block the entrance to fields or farmyards.

10 Respect the life of the countryside

Enjoy the countryside, but do not hinder the work of the country-man. Roads and paths run through the farmer's land, and animals, machinery and buildings are the raw materials from which he earns his living. You, the public, are on trust. Be considerate.

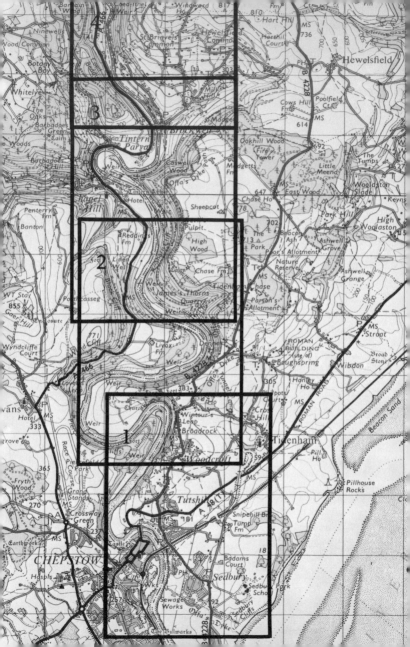

1 Chepstow

Chepstow is an important crossing at the lowest bridgehead of the River Wye, 4 miles above its meeting with the River Severn in the Bristol Channel. Easily accessible by road and rail from London and the Midlands, South Wales and the South West, it is a natural starting point for our journey and deserves more than a passing inspection (ECD Wednesday.)

Brief History
The Romans forded the River Wye here on their way to Isca Silurum, the modern Caerleon, and Offa may have set his Dyke to control traffic at the point where the Roman road crossed the river north of Chepstow Castle. Unfortunately there is no recognisable section of the Dyke here or at the later crossing point by the present bridge.

The Saxons called this place Ceapstow or Cheapstow (Chepe = market, stow — town) and the very existence of the name has led some people to argue that Offa must have had a bridgehead settlement on the Welsh side of the river.

The Normans recognised the importance of the crossing, and the first known reference to the place is in the Domesday Book of 1086. It was called Striguil (probably from the Welsh 'Ystraigl' = the bend) until the 14c, but it was the Saxon name which survived.

William Fitz Osbern, who was one of the leading figures of the Conquest and was made Earl of Hereford in 1067 by the Conqueror, established his castle on the site of the present imposing structure, and he or his son Roger set up a borough. Roger's downfall in 1075 brought the town into the hands of the king, where it remained for 40 years. From 1115–76 it was held by Walter Fitz Richard of the great Clare family who used it as a port for their conquests of Ireland as well as the centre for the whole of Gwent. It retained its importance in the time of the Marshals, 1189–1245, but its hinterland was diminished when their estates were divided among five co-heiresses in 1245, and the lordship became an outlying possession of the Earls of Norfolk, Roger Bigod II being the son of the eldest sister.

In common with other towns, Chepstow was formerly defended by a wall, and it was Roger Bigod, the Third Earl of Norfolk, who is credited with the building of the great 'Port Wall' between 1272–8. It extended for 1200 yds from the

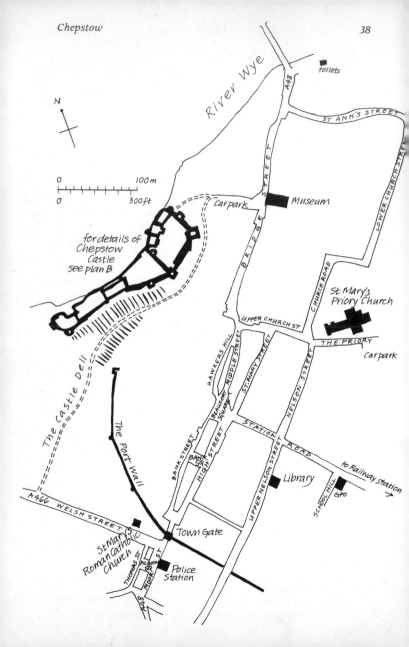

W end of the Castle in a westerly circuit back to the river. It was 15 ft high, 5 ft thick at the level of the rampart walk; the river formed an adequate defence to the east. The wall had 10 projecting semi-circular towers (of which 7 still survive) as well as the great Town Gate, which defends the town to landward. There are not more than half-a-dozen towns in Britain with surviving walls to compare with them.

Viewed from the heights above the town the Port Wall is a striking feature, marking the extent of the medieval borough. The defences are still visible for most of its length, and particularly well-preserved stretches can be seen in The Dell near the Castle and at Hardwick Village.

The wall was severely damaged during the Civil War, but most remains intact, except where removals have been made for the construction of the railway, the building of the shipyards and the extension of a new road in the town centre, all insensitive operations reflecting the 'development' of the town.

The Town Gate was rebuilt in 1524 by the Earl of Worcester and for many years it was used as a prison. The battlements and windows are modern, and the room over the archway now houses the small museum of the Chepstow Society.

The walls saved Chepstow from Glyndwr and his French allies between 1402–6, but its powerful position as a semi-independent Marcher Lordship seems to have restored its opportunities for trade. When the Marcher Lordships were abolished by the Acts of Union in 1536 it was Monmouth that gained privileges as head of the new county. Chepstow remained tightly under the control of the Earls of Worcester, who in Charles II's reign managed to deprive it of the Charter which their ancestors had granted in 1524, through a dispute with the all-powerful Duke of Beaufort.

Chepstow had been a duty-free port and it was an important and prosperous place, more important than Bristol or Newport. The town had a setback when Henry VIII, with his customary eye to the main chance, abolished the Marcher Lordships and gave his revenue officers the legal right to collect dues. In spite of this the town flourished. Even as late as Victorian times, the river bank was a long wharf stacked with timber, and warehouses were filled with corn and oak bark, cider and building stone, and wines in large quantities were imported from France and Portugal.

However, with the rise in importance of Newport, Cardiff and

Bristol, Chepstow's trade declined to them, and by 1881, assisted by the coming of the railway, Chepstow ceased to be a custom's port.

During the 1914–18 War there was a brief revival of ship-building, and National Shipyards were constructed at Beachley. In 1920 the yards were de-nationalised, and factories connected with engineering, asphalt-making, quarrying and brush-making were developed.

Chepstow is a fascinating old town, with its magnificent castle set high on a rock overlooking the winding river, its stately priory church, and the west gate of the town wall still spanning the main street. The town is a glorious start to our journey. Perched on a steep hillside it has a wonderful panorama over the high cliffs to the north and the estuaries of the Wye and Severn to the south. A steep road leads up into the town from the river, and it is well worth exploring this place before we commence our journey along Offa's Dyke.

The road bridge over the Wye, now the main entrance to the town, is one of the earliest cast-iron bridges in Britain. It was built by John Rennie in 1816 and underwent extensive repairs in 1968. From it one can obtain the best general view of the Castle, which is all the more impressive when the tide is in.

Bridge Street leads up from the Wye Bridge and delivers us straight away to the Castle.

Chepstow Castle
Owned and occupied by the Department of the Environment.

Open daily throughout the year	*Weekdays*	*Sundays*
March, April and October	*09.30–17.30*	*14.00–17.30*
May to September	*09.30–19.00*	*09.30–19.00*
November to February	*09.30–16.00*	*14.00–16.00*

Small charge for admission.

Site
The Castle is the principal object of interest in the town, a fine and extensive ruin illustrating the development of the stone castle in Britain. It stands on the end of a narrow spur which slopes down to the tidal Wye from a mass of high ground to the W. This narrow ridge has the river and its cliff making a magnificent defence on the N side, and a broad deep gully, known as 'The Dell' divides the spur from the town and the

*B *Chepstow Castle*

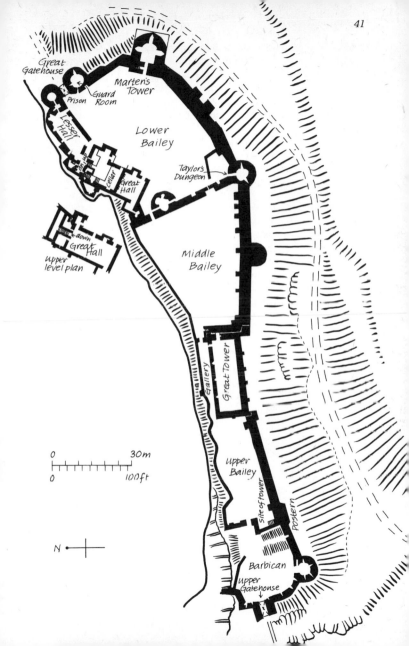

Great
Gatehouse

Marten's
Tower

Prison

Guard
Room

Lesser
Hall

Pantry

Cellar

Great
Hall

Lower
Bailey

Taylor's
Dungeon

down

Great Hall

Upper
level plan

Middle
Bailey

0   30m
0   100ft

N

Gallery

Great Tower

Upper Bailey

Site of Tower

Postern

Barbican

Upper
Gatehouse

low-lying ground to the S. The spur thus formed is about 250 yds long by 30–70 yds broad, a natural defensive site.

The site therefore dictates the layout of the castle. It consists of four courts or baileys, not concentric, but placed end to end along the ridge. From the main entrance at the E'ern end they are the lower bailey, the middle bailey, the upper bailey and the barbican. Between the middle and upper baileys, at the narrowest point in the ridge, stands the Great Tower or keep, the earliest part of the castle and one of the finest structures of its type in the country.

History

The castle was begun by William Fitz Osbern, one of the most influential followers of William the Conqueror. He devoted his energies until his death in 1071 to pushing his boundary westwards, and his castle at Chepstow was just behind his frontier. Much of this castle still survives: it is the Great Tower on the narrowest part of the ridge.

Walter Fitz Richard, a member of the great family of Clare, was granted the castle by Henry I in 1115, but there is no evidence that Walter made any additions to the castle. On his death in 1138 the king re-granted it to his nephew Gilbert

Strongbow, succeeded by his son Richard Strongbow in 1148. Henry II held the castle in wardship for Richard's daughter between 1176–89 until she married the great William Marshall, Earl of Pembroke.

He extended the castle by the building of the curtain wall which divided the middle from the lower bailey. When he died in 1219 he was succeeded in turn by his five sons, and the castle was greatly enlarged and strengthened by them in the following 25 years. The Great Tower was remodelled, the middle bailey was strengthened by the addition of a flanking tower to its south curtain wall, and the wall itself was largely rebuilt. The upper bailey was rebuilt with a fine rectangular tower to command its western gateway, and later the barbican was built.

The Marshalls also added a larger and stronger outer bailey, the lower bailey, with the double-towered gatehouse, and one may suppose that a tower was also built at this time in the position later occupied by Marten's Tower.

The castle passed subsequently by marriage of the Marshall's sister to Roger Bigod, Second Earl of Norfolk, and on his death in 1270 to his son, Roger Bigod III, who made important additions to the castle.

Bigod first tidied up the gatehouse to the barbican, and then built the Port Wall. Between 1278–1285 he built a completely new range of domestic buildings to replace the Great Tower. These occupy the north side of the lower bailey. His next task was the rebuilding of the south-east tower, now known as Marten's Tower, which was not completed until 1293. In the next 7 years he built the remaining part of the upper storey of the Great Tower. On Roger Bigod's death in 1306 the king took possession. The form of the castle was retained unaltered until Tudor times, and is essentially the form we see today.

The most striking days of the castle's history occurred during the Civil War because, like others on the banks of the Wye, it was of great importance to both parties. On the outbreak of the first Civil War it was held for the king, as Henry, Fifth Earl and First Marquis of Worcester, was a devoted Royalist. The town might have been lost to 1,300 Parliamentarians from the garrison at Monmouth in November, 1644, had not an attack on that town distracted them. On 6 October, 1645, by which time the royal cause was hopeless, Colonel Morgan of Gloucester with 300 cavalry and 400 infantry laid siege for 4 days and the garrison of 64 of all ranks surrendered.

Chepstow Castle

On the outbreak of the second Civil War in April, 1647, the castle was once more secured for the king by Sir Nicholas Kemeys. Cromwell called for its surrender, and on this being refused the Roundheads laid siege in May, 1648. The regiment, under Colonel Ewer breached the walls by cannon in the vicinity of Marten's Tower. Sir Nicholas was killed and the garrison of 120 men surrendered.

Unlike the majority of English castles, Chepstow was neither slighted nor allowed to fall into ruin after the defeat of the royal cause. At the Restoration in 1660 Charles II handed the castle back to Lord Herbert, son of the rightful owner. The castle was garrisoned and used as a prison for both political and military prisoners, of whom the most distinguished were Jeremy Taylor, a royalist bishop and chaplain to Charles I, and Sir Henry Marten, the regicide. Marten spent 20 years in captivity in Bigod's great drum-tower, which has now assumed his name.

In 1690 the castle was partly dismantled and allowed to fall into decay. In 1682 Henry, Marquis of Worcester, was created Duke of Beaufort, and his successors continued to hold the castle until its sale in 1914; subsequently the Ministry of Public Buildings and Works (now the Department of the Environment) was invested with the permanent guardianship of the castle and the town wall.

A Tour of the Castle

The Gatehouse, at which admission is obtained, dates from about 1225. The arched entrance is between two huge round towers, and is guarded by a massive nail-studded oaken door which stands between two portcullises. Any attempt to force the entrance could be repelled by archers using the slit in the S. Tower, or missiles could be hurled down through holes in the parapet wall between the towers. The gatehouse was three storeys high. At ground level the N Tower contained a prison, while the S Tower contained the guardroom. The gatehouse adjoining the S Tower has been destroyed, but that on the N has been incorporated in the living quarters of the castle.

The whole of the N side of the lower bailey is occupied by a large and magnificent range of domestic buildings, erected about 1280. It consists mainly of two halls, placed end to end and sharing a common entrance passage. Both halls were at ground level, but the ground slopes from west to east to such an extent that the western or Great Hall extends over part of the eastern or Lesser Hall.

As you enter the passage a doorway on your right leads into the Lesser Hall, a single-storey building. Beyond this entrance and the serving hatch is a doorway giving access to a double latrine discharging into the river, and immediately beyond that doorway are two cupboards built into the thickness of the wall.

At the end of the passageway, stairs lead down to a great cellar, rib-vaulted in 3 bays. It is now very damp, but it lies beneath the Great Hall, and when that was roofed would have provided extensive dry-storage space. A large opening in the NW wall would be used as a landing space for stores hoisted up from boats on the river, and it was from here that some defenders probably made their escape when the castle was captured on 25 May 1648.

Returning from the cellar into the main passageway are 3 doorways on your RHS. The small room at the head of the cellar stairs, and the room nearest the courtyard were used as pantry or buttery to the Lesser Hall. The doorway in the middle is at the foot of a broad flight of stone steps leading up into the Great Hall. This would be the servants entrance, for the main entrance to the Great Hall was the tower-like porch which projects into the lower bailey. The buttery and pantry of the Great Hall were immediately above those of the Lower Hall.

Leave the Great Hall by the modern entrance in its SE corner and re enter the Lower Bailey. The curtain wall which divides the Middle from the Lower Bailey dates from the end of the 12c and was originally fronted by a ditch on the E side. At the N end of this wall is a semi-circular Guard Tower, and we pass into the Middle Bailey by way of an archway on the R.

The N wall of the Middle Bailey is slight, right on the edge of the cliffs, and there is a splendid view of the river.

Beyond the Middle Bailey are the remarkable remains of the Great Tower, William Fitz Osbern's great hall built between 1067–72. This impressive ruin is one of the finest Norman castle buildings in the country. It measures a little over 100 ft long, is 40 ft wide and 40 ft high, and is two-thirds the size of the Conqueror's own Tower of London.

As originally built it had a sloping cellar with two storeys above it. The Marshalls, Earls of Pembroke, remodelled the original upper-storey between 1225–1245, and added a second storey at the W'ern end. In 1290 Roger Bigod, Earl of Norfolk, completed the remaining two-thirds of the second storey.

The three periods of work can easily be distinguished by their different masonry and architectural detail. Osbern's work contains large blocks of yellow stone, and built into the walls can be seen a few courses of Roman bricks and tiles, probably brought from nearby Caerwent. The detail is plain – small round-headed windows – and only the main doorway in the E wall shows any attempt at ornament.

The Marshall's work in the W'ern third of the top storey is of rough limestone, similar to the great Gatehouse. All the windows and doorways have pointed heads, and the mouldings and carved detail are elaborately beautiful. Bigod's work is different again, and shows the same materials as used in the domestic buildings and Marten's Tower.

On the N side of the Great Tower is a narrow pathway or gallery, leading into the Upper Bailey, which has a rectangular turret at its far corner, and the wall running N from this tower towards the cliff has a single arch gateway leading into the Barbican. This outer defence is separated from the castle proper by a ditch, partly man-made, which is crossed by a bridge. At the bottom of the ditch a postern gate pierces the curtain wall. The Barbican has a strong, three-storey, SW tower, and the castle wall runs N to the cliffs again. The Upper Gatehouse was built about 1270, and defended the W'ern approach to the castle. A deep ditch was dug right through the rocky ridge from the castle ditch to the river cliffs.

Return to the Middle Bailey and ascend the steps leading to the battlements, which can be followed to the large round tower which projects boldly from the SE corner of the castle wall at its most exposed point. The S curtain wall of the Lower Bailey is exceptionally thick, comprising in fact two walls with an earth filling between them, which, through settlement or removal, has sunk many feet below its original level.

Bigod's great tower, built between 1285–93, is now known as Marten's Tower, because after the restoration of the monarchy it was, for 20 years, the prison of Sir Henry Marten, one of those who signed the death warrant of Charles I. Marten died at the age of 78 and was buried in the Parish Church. In connection with this captivity lovers of Southey will recall the poet's 'Inscription for an Appartment in Chepstow Castle.'

The tower was designed to provide a self-contained lodging for the lord, whose hall was on the first and chamber on the second floor, conveniently close to the chapel, on the third

floor. On each side, where the tower joins the curtain, is an
attached square turret, solid up to second-floor level.

The tower is entered from the curtain wall by the S'ern
turret at second-floor level. The turret is small and serves only
to provide for a portcullis and a door, with a latrine above that
in the floor below. The chamber was originally lit by two
lancet windows but, like the room below, a large window was
inserted into the inside wall in the 16c. The N turret also has a
portcullis and door, and a small winding stair leads up to a
small chapel, with much beautiful carving. In each of the N and
S walls is a lancet window with a seat for a priest. The
battlements of the tower and turret are complete above.

The hall on the first floor was originally lit by arrowslits,
but it too has an inserted 16c window. The room has two
fireplaces side by side in the S wall, the larger of early 16c date
and the smaller a later 16c insertion. There is a latrine in the S
turret, and a circular stair, which serves the full height of the
tower, occupies the N tower.

We leave the tower through a doorway defended by a
portcullis, and into the courtyard.

Before leaving the castle there are three items of interest on
the inner face of the S curtain wall. To the L of Marten's
Tower can first be seen the masons' marks in the form of a
set-square, arrowhead, etc. About halfway along the wall will
be seen a plaque. It was erected by members of the Kemeys
family in 1935 to mark the assumed spot where, on 25 May
1648, Cromwell's men breached the wall, and Sir Nicholas
Kemeys, High Sheriff for the counties of Gwent and Glamorgan,
was slain defending the castle for Charles I.

Still further along the wall will be found, in the corner
tower of the Middle Bailey, the entrance to the tower where
royalist Bishop Jeremy Taylor was imprisoned. Bishop Taylor,
author of *Holy Living* and *Holy Dying* and other religious
works was detained as a political prisoner for a few months
during the Commonwealth.

A Tour of the Town

Before continuing your tour of the town take a walk up the
Castle Dell. The castle seems to be impregnably sited on its
limestone cliffs. The remarkable survival of Osbern's great hall
and the subsequent embellishments and defences by drum
towers and gatehouses by the Marshalls and Roger Bigod
illustrate the development of the stone castle in Britain.

On your re-entry into Bridge Street turn R, uphill past early 19c bow-windowed houses. At the turn at the top are the Powys Almshouses, endowed in 1716. In nearby Upper Church Street are the gabled Montague Almshouses dating from 1613.

In the centre of the town lies Beaufort Square laid out, like everything else in Chepstow, on a slope. Nearby is a gun from a captured German submarine presented as a memorial to Chepstow's vc, William Charles William, a sailor killed at Gallipoli.

The parish church of St Mary stands at the top of Church Street, which runs parallel to Bridge Street, in the lower part of the town. It was originally the church of a Benedictine priory, founded in 1076 by William Fitz Osbern and associated with the Abbey of Cormeilles in Normandy. Unhappily little is left of the ancient structure, except the shell of the nave and the W front, in which the door is a beautiful specimen of the Norman period. The building has a central tower, which was built about 1706. In 1841 the original work suffered much damage at the hands of Wyatt and his 'restorers.' Later, a large chancel was erected and the S transept was rebuilt.

The church has preserved some interesting monuments in spite of the drastic restorations. There is a Norman font, but the one now in use dates from the 15c. On the N side of the nave is a canopied tomb and the reclining figures of Henry, Second Earl of Worcester, who died in 1549, and his wife Elizabeth. On the floor of the nave, just inside the W door, is the gravestone of Henry Marten, 1602–80, who died a prisoner in Chepstow Castle. It is inscribed with his own epitaph, in the form of an acrostic:

> *Here or elsewhere (all's one to you and me),*
> *Earth, air, or water gripes my ghostless dust,*
> *None knows how soon to be by fire set free,*
> *Reader, if you are oft try'd rule will thrust,*
> *You'll gladly do and suffer what you must.*
> *My time was spent in serving you, and you,*
> *And death's my pay, it seems, and welcome too;*
> *Revenge destroying but itself, but I*
> *To birds of prey leave my old cage and fly;*
> *Examples preach to the eye – care then (mine says)*
> *Not how you end, but how you spend your days.*

Whilst in Chepstow, and before beginning your walk along the Dyke, have a look at two bridges – one a railway bridge, one a road bridge: one crossing the Wye, and the other crossing both the Wye and the Severn.

The railway suspension bridge over the Wye represents a fine piece of railway history. It was originally built by Brunel between 1849–52, with a main span of 300 ft. The weight of the span was carried by two enormous tubes, a daring idea at the time. The tubes were removed when the bridge was reconstructed in 1962, but they will be remembered by engineers for the ingenious way in which Brunel harnessed the exceptionally high tides of the Wye to lift the tubes into place.

It was Brunel's need to solve the difficult problem of bridging the Wye that led to the establishing of the 'Shipyard', now the Fairfield constructional engineering works. Fairfield's continued their long tradition of building camions, dock gates and bridges when they assembled and launched the deck sections of the Severn Bridge. These were floated out into the river estuary in a manner of which Brunel would surely have approved.

The united Severn and Wye road bridges are probably the finest architectural and engineering achievement in the Britain of our time. The site survey and design work were carried out between 1945–9. The work on the site began in the Spring of 1961 and the whole structure was opened by Her Majesty The Queen on 8 September 1966.

The Wye Bridge has a main span of 770 ft and side spans each of 285 ft. It is of the stayed-girder type – applying the cantilever in cable form – and the first to be built in Britain. The two 100 ft towers are placed in the centreline of the bridge. The stays consist of two cables that pass over the tops of the towers, and their ends are anchored to the deck of the centre and side spans at a distance of 225 ft from the towers.

This daringly constructed bridge joins a viaduct across the narrow Beachley peninsular – the neck of land which separates the Wye from the Severn – and then joins the main bridge over the Severn.

The Severn Bridge is carried on two tall graceful towers of steel that rise 400 ft above the water. The main span is 3,240 ft long, the seventh largest in the world at its time of construction. The two side spans are each 1,000 ft. The main cables are about 20 inches in diameter; each cable consists of 8,322 wires, all lying parallel, and each take a load of 6,600 tons. The suspender cables are also unusual: they are not vertical, as has been usual in suspension bridges, but are inclined, forming a triangulated system with the main cables to give extra rigidity to the platform, unique in modern bridge design.

The roadway is formed of torsionally stiff hollow steel boxes, 10 ft deep and 75 ft wide. The sides of the boxes are tapered to give a streamlined shape for winds blowing across the decks. The boxes were made in Chepstow and then floated down the Wye and into the Severn, to be lifted into position at high tide.

The revolutionary conception was designed by Sir Gilbert Roberts, and gives a lightness to the deck structure incomparable for its length and loading. All the new concepts of bridge-building embodied in the design of this bridge were thoroughly tested at the National Physical Laboratory at Teddington, Middlesex.

The Severn is over one mile wide at the bridge site, and the tidal range, one of the largest in the world, sometimes reaches 46 ft at this point. The tide comes in at an impressive speed, and the currents run up to 9 knots.

This gloriously elegant bridge is easily the most magnificent entry-point into Wales, leading directly to Chepstow and the start of our walk along Offa's Dyke.

As Chepstow is likely to be the most southerly starting point of our journey, and as Sedbury Cliffs lie some 2 miles south of Chepstow, it will be convenient for the purposes of this Guide to describe the route of this section in the direction north to south. One can then return to Chepstow, and continue the journey from south to north.

The tree-clad limestone cliff opposite Chepstow, the base of which is washed by the swift tides of the lower Wye, undoubtedly represents the Mercian frontier. The cliffs were considered to be an adequate boundary, and only when they abruptly end does the Dyke appear.

From Chepstow then, cross Rennie's narrow bridge over the Wye and climb the steep path opposite to join Offa's Dyke Path. This path turns R and runs into the end of a private road, which soon joins the main road B 4228. The Severn road bridge comes into view.

Beyond the railway line suburban sprawl has engulfed the fields, and builders rubble still obstructs the Path in the unfinished bungalow estate. The Path follows along the brink of the riverside cliffs, and it may be difficult to find as it is behind the back gardens of the bungalows. If the Path is obstructed keep along the estate road.

The estate soon ends, and beyond a field we come to the point where the Dyke recommences. The earthwork no longer follows the Wye but cuts across the promontory formed by the confluence of that river and the Severn. On the Severn side of the promontory a cliff of Triassic sandstone ends as abruptly as that of the limestone on the Wye, and provides an equally suitable flank for the frontier Dyke. The Dyke connects these two cliffs in a straight line 1,200 yds long: it is of military character in structure as well as siting, having a ditch consistently on the S side.

The Dyke begins at a re-entrant on the Wye bank at Tallard's Marsh, which was formerly a pill or creek, and which is still flooded in part at spring tides. Small boats used to come to the creek as late as the 1880's and there was a sawmill where is now the sewage works. That this creek was of importance in Offa's time is rendered probable by the presence of a small circular earthwork on a knoll – an isolated spur of the limestone plateau which marks the terminal portion of the Wye cliffs. A house now occupies this small earthwork camp.

The Start and Finish of Offa's Dyke in Sedbury Park

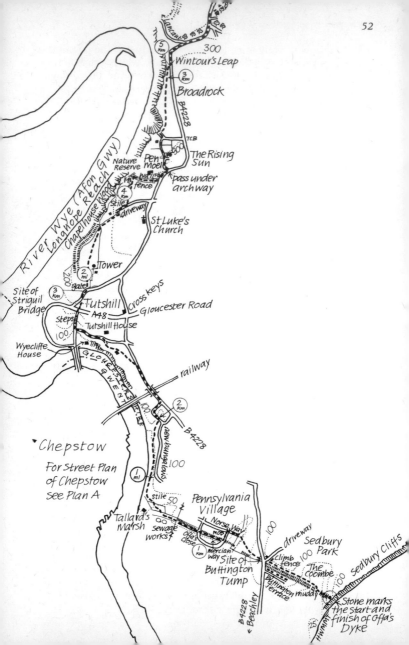

River Wye (Afon Gwy)

Longhope Reach

Chapelhouse Road

5 Km

300
Wintour's Leap

3 Km

Broadrock

B4228

TCB

300

The Rising Sun

Pen Moel

Nature Reserve

pass under archway

well
fence

4 Km

stile

driveway

St Luke's Church

Tower

200

2 ml

gate

3 Km

Site of Striguil Bridge

Tutshill

Cross Keys

Gloucester Road

steps

A48

100

Tutshill House

Wyecliffe House

GLOUCESTERSHIRE GWENT

railway

100

2 Km

B4228

new bungalows

100

Chepstow

For Street Plan
of Chepstow
See Plan A

1 ml

stile
50

Pennsylvania
Village

Norse Way

100

driveway

Sedbury
Park

Tallard's
Marsh

sewage
works

Offa's
close

Mercian
Way

1

Site of
Buttington
Tump

Buttington
terrace

muddy

100

climb
fence

100

The
Coombe

100

Sedbury Cliffs

B4228 Beachley

H.W.M.

25

Stone marks
the start and
finish of Offa's
Dyke

The bank of the Dyke, gapped and damaged, is clearly traceable through the Pennsylvania Village council estate. The streets called 'Offa's Close' and 'Mercian Way' occupy the ditch. The Dyke crosses a little valley beyond the 'new' village, the bank being well-marked on the descending slope, obliterated on the floor, and traceable – though almost completely levelled – on the rising slope beyond the embankment of the old light railway: here the ditch is very plain, and indeed, overdeepened.

At the top of the rise is Buttington Tump, an unusually large portion of the earthwork, but badly mutilated by road widening where the B 4228 passes through to Beachley. On the Tump was set a standing stone, a roughly shaped mass of conglomerate with stone slabs grouped around its base, but only one stone remains, and that is fallen.

Between Buttington Tump and Sedbury Cliffs lies a good stretch of Dyke on the major scale. Though it is neglected in condition and overgrown it is little altered. Scattered trees line that portion included in Sedbury Park; here there is a long, even slope on the N side, probably the result of ploughing down the bank. Behind Buttington Terrace the Dyke bank is much narrower and higher.

Passing into The Combe (formerly wooded and known as Buttington Wood) the Dyke forms a broad rounded bank, ditched on the S and with spoil ditch on the N, as is usual on steep slopes. These ditches become watercourses in wet weather, and are overdeepened near the foot of the slope. On the floor a 20 ft gap – which, though narrow, is evidently wider than it was originally – admits passage of the brooklet draining the little valley. After skirting this marshy hollow the Dyke is again gapped, closed by a modern trackway.

On the rising slope the character of the Dyke is resumed as a broad bank, overgrown with gorse: it is sheared off abruptly by the cliff edge. The ground falls steeply to both W and S, as well as 100 ft vertically to the E, thus rendering the position exceptionally dominant.

Fox found this point extraordinarily impressive. From it there are wide views over both land and sea, and practically the whole of the Beachley peninsula is visible. At low tide a great expanse of sandbanks is revealed. The dirty brown river below is backed by the Cotswolds, while close at hand the Severn Bridge is a fascinating sight.

1 *Sedbury Cliffs to Wintours Leap*

It was on the top of these cliffs that Fox completed his six-year survey (1925–31): a large stone of conglomerate marks the end of Offa's Dyke. Fox was so moved by this place that he wrote . . . *On this now silent and deserted spot at the south-western limit of his Mercian domain, King Offa ought to be commemorated.*

That the Dyke was governed by the one dominant idea – the visual control of enemy country – is manifest in this place, as it is to an unusual degree characteristic of the Mercian frontier line as a whole. As a vantage point and a historic site it is certainly too important to be left in its present overgrown state.

Starting from Chepstow Bridge again climb the steep lane opposite, up the steps and at the top cross the A48 Gloucester road into Tutshill.

In the fields across the B4228 St Briavels road stand the prominent ivy-clad ruins of a tower, Tutshill Tower, probably a 16c beacon. Nearby a small fragment of the Dyke can be found, on the 200 ft contour on the edge of Chapelhouse Wood, W of St Lukes church. The Dyke is a bank of moderate size, degenerating here and there to a hedge-bank near Castleford House Farm, and it gradually disappears in a strip of woodland 50 ft above the river. The purpose of the alignment is clear: the Dyke is making for the river bank, striking the river above the site of the Roman road from Glevum and the site of the Roman bridge. St David's Chapel and Striguil Bridge mark the former crossing of the river, and Offa may have set his Dyke here to control traffic at this crucial point. The apparent absence of any recognisable section of the Dyke at the river crossing and the English name Cheapstow (market place) has led some people to argue that Offa must have established a bridgehead settlement on the Welsh side of the river.

The gentle slopes of Tutshill rise by easy gradations to steep slopes, varied by rocky outcrops at the 100 ft level, at Chapelhouse Wood, and the plateau level rises from 200 ft to 370 ft by cliffs to Lancaut. The traces of the Dyke along this stretch are scarcely recognisable, and the Path follows a complicated course W of B4228. The Path in this section was waymarked by the Tidenham Parish Council with yellow arrows before the county council added the official acorns and white arrows.

Across the parkland to the R is the church of St Luke, built in 1853 by Henry Woodyer, very similar to his other church in neighbouring Tidenham.

From the top of the disused Lancaut Quarries at Woodcroft you emerge through an opening at Broadrock to the breath-taking viewpoint of Wintour's Leap. It is impossible to imagine how the Civil War escape of Sir John Wintour in 1642 from pursuing Parliamentarians by jumping with his horse and swimming the river could have come to be linked with this 200 ft precipice plunging sheer from the roadside: no horse or rider could have survived such a leap. Wintour had his manor at Lydney, up the road towards Gloucester, and was the local Royalist commander. When the Royalist cause was lost he burnt his house and fled to Chepstow, there to catch a boat to

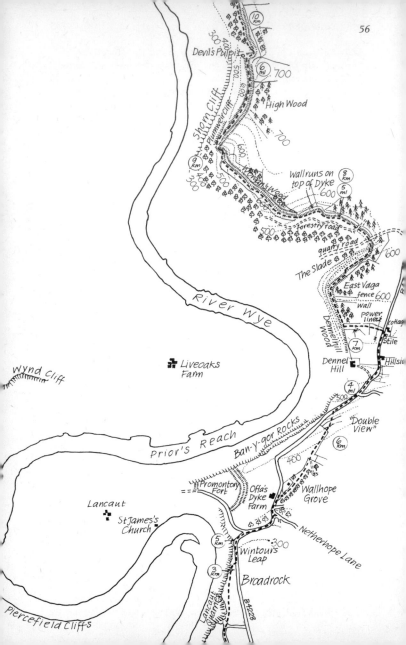

Devil's Pulpit

High Wood

Shorn Cliff

Plumwercliff

Wallruns on
top of Dyke

Forestry road

quarry road

The Slade

East Vaga
fence

wall
power lines

cottage

Dennehill
Wood

Stile

Dennel
Hill

Hillside

River Wye

Liveoaks
Farm

Wynd Cliff

"Double
View"

Prior's Reach

Ban-y-gor Rocks

Promontory
Fort

Offa's
Dyke
Farm

Wallhope
Grove

Lancaut

St James's
Church

Netherhope Lane

Wintour's
Leap

Broadrock

Piercefield Cliffs

Lancaut Quarry

B4228

France to join Henrietta, Charles I's queen, whose secretary he was.

Just N of Wintour's Leap a lane bears off to Lancaut, a peninsula formed by a loop of the Wye. Extending across the neck of the level top of the peninsula are the remains of an Iron Age promontory fort. The main defences on Spital Meend seem to have been adopted by Offa as his boundary: it is marked on OS maps, but the earthwork is certainly not Offan, which never shows a work of military type facing E. Below the fort, on the banks of the Wye, can be seen the ruins of the small Norman church of St James.

The Wye winds round the peninsula in a huge meander loop and is backed on the W or R bank by the wooded cliffs of Wyndcliff and Piercefield. The Piercefield Cliffs have twelve projecting masses of rock known as the Twelve Apostles, while a smaller mass is called St Peter's Thumb.

The famous Wyndcliff is a steep limestone mass, rising to nearly 800 ft above the river. The view from the top is well-known, though not strictly comparable with the view from Symonds Yat. The prospect is one of the grandest in England: the eye roams over the counties of Gloucester, Hereford, Worcester, Wiltshire, Avon, Somerset, Devon, Glamorgan, Gwent and Powys. The Sugar Loaf, Black Mountains and Malvern Hills bound the distant horizon, while the foreground is filled by the reaches of the 'winding silvery Wye.' Woods, rocks, rivers and sea, plains and hills combine to make a picture of rare loveliness: the beauty and colour of the river, too, vary with the height of the tide.

There is no adequate footpath beyond Lancaut above the Ban-y-gor Rocks, which form a stupendous wall of cliff, but at their northern end is the famous Double View of both Wye and Severn. The river cliffs are very steep, vertical in places, where the Wye carves its way through the limestone plateau, and these fine views along the lower Wye form, not surprisingly, such a scenic attraction for the tourist.

Within the meander loops of the river the spurs have been planed off to form a broad bench at about 250 ft above the present river level. Those of Liveoaks Farm and Lancaut are remarkably flat when seen from above. The impression of a planed-off flat is considerably enhanced by the fact that their broad open arable acres contrast so remarkably with the wooded cliffs that reach down to the river.

2 *Wintours Leap to Devils Pulpit*

Beyond the Ban-y-gor Rocks there is no trace of the Dyke although one would expect to find it: the slopes to the Wye, though very steep, are in places climbable. The Dyke may possibly have been destroyed to improve the views from 'Bough Cliffe' and 'Dennel Hill', but it reappears at a rocky scarp just to the N of the house.

The earthwork, gradually getting larger, is joined by the Path which now leaves the B4228. There are quarries beside the Dyke, sometimes large and in places it is revetted on the inner side with a modern stone wall. The Dyke follows the edge of the plateau, crosses the sharp tip of a spur, and as it descends the spur which defines The Slade on the S it is of moderate size.

The Dyke drops suddenly on a new path to a quarry road at the head of the hollow and then crosses a forestry road. Where the Dyke crosses the ravine it is seen as a low ridge, but as it ascends the slope on the far side it becomes larger. For a mile or more of tangled badger-haunted woodland the Dyke winds round The Slade and Worgan's Wood, gradually climbing up to the plateau again. The Dyke is an enormous bank and ends suddenly where the hillside becomes very steep. It begins again 70 yds away, on an easy slope: beyond a lateral re-entrant of the coombe a stone wall and old yew trees appear on the Dyke.

The plateau is regained at about 630 ft, through Worgan's Wood on an easy slope. There is no lower ditch – other than a modern drainage ditch – and the bank is of moderate size. Soon the Dyke makes a steady descent and crosses the head of an adjacent ravine as a rounded bank.

At the elbow formed by Plumweir Cliff the Dyke makes an acute angle, corresponding exactly with the contour of the precipitous scarp – a curious example of the determination shown by the builders to maintain complete visual control of the Wye valley.

A definite change in scale, though not in type, is now manifest, the Dyke becoming larger immediately N of the elbow. The Dyke runs along the edge of the plateau for three magnificent miles, through the woods, with fine views high above the river, which include the Shorncliff and the Devil's Pulpit.

The first magnificent viewpoint is the rocky outcrop of the Shorncliff, or more correctly the Plumweir Cliff.

Wintour's Leap

Beyond Plumweir Cliff the earthwork is broad and flat-topped like a causeway and without lower berm or ditch, being on the edge of the very steep scarp. Along the border of Shorncliff Wood it can be seen that the Dyke is built up from quarries on the E side with its reverse (E) slope frequently revetted with dry-stone walling. The broad, flat-floored quarries still have limestone blocks lying about. These quarries are always shallow and flat-floored, frequently continuous, elsewhere forming isolated pockets: in places they seem too extensive for the bulk of the Dyke, and may have been exploited at a later date for dry-walling. At the 700 ft contour the Dyke reaches its highest point in this section. The views along this high stretch are commanding, for the river is some 670 ft directly below.

The Devil's Pulpit – a jutting crag of limestone immediately below the line of the Dyke – affords a magnificent view of the Wye valley and Tintern Abbey 600 ft below. From this commanding rocky platform the Devil is supposed to have preached to the monks below in the Abbey grounds, hoping to entice them from their work.

At this point you can pause to try to puzzle out the purpose of Offa's work – built on such a massive scale at a point where the natural strength of the frontier formed by dangerous tidal river is most apparent. It hardly seems realistic of Fox to have argued that this was a concession to Welsh shipmen trading up the Wye, thereby giving them the use of both banks of the Wye river. The Dyke in these stretches is most massively built at precisely the point where it made a dramatic feature on the landscape, and it could therefore be an element of personal display of Offa.

At this point in the valley the floor becomes wider as the river winds from side to side and leaves behind flat terraces within the meander loops. It was on one of these flats that the Cistercian Abbey of Tintern was founded. A visit to these impressive ruins is essential, for they have often been described as the most beautifully situated monastic ruins in the world.

From the Devil's Pulpit a path leads down across the steeply wooded slopes to the old railway bridge which crosses the river just north of the Abbey. The path is a little hard to find at first, but there is another leading off a short way to the N.

Description of route continues on p 67.

Tintern Abbey

Owned and occupied by the Department of the Environment.

Open daily throughout the year	*Weekdays*	*Sundays*
March, April and October	*09.30–17.30*	*14.00–17.30*
May to September	*09.30–19.00*	*09.30–19.00*
November to February	*09.30–16.00*	*14.00–16.00*

Small charge for admission.

Site

Famed for the beauty of its natural setting, Tintern Abbey
stands in green fields on the R bank of the River Wye, 5 miles
N of Chepstow and 11 miles S of Monmouth. It was founded
as an abbey for monks of the Cistercian Order and built
according to their Rule, in what the Welsh called 'yr
anghyfanedd' – uninhabited places, away from the turmoil of
the Norman towns. Tintern has preserved its beauty in this
remote and isolated spot, and will be forever associated with
Wordsworth's famous poem 'Lines Above Tintern Abbey.'
Although one of the loveliest scenes in the Wye valley, its
beauty is indescribable, for even Wordsworth could only
manage to write:

> *To those who know thee not no words can paint*
> *And those who know thee know all words are feint.*

History

The Abbey was founded in the year 1131 in the reign of
Henry I (the fourth son of William the Conqueror) by Walter
de Clare, the Marcher Lord of Chepstow. The original Norman
buildings were largely rebuilt during the 13c and the abbey
church itself was entirely rebuilt between 1270 and 1301.

Attention was first given in 1220 to the enlargement of the
monastic buildings and when these had been made suitable for
the needs of the brethren the rebuilding of the church was
begun. This work was undertaken in 1270 by Roger Bigod,
second Earl of Norfolk, who had inherited Chepstow Castle.
That the daily services might be interrupted as little as possible,
the Earl began to erect the choir of the new church to the S
and E of the existing building. The services were transferred to
the new choir in 1287 and the new high altar was first used
on 2 October 1288. The rebuilding of the rest of the church
went forward in a more leisurely manner in the later style
called Decorated, uniform in design and consistent in style.

In 1469 new cloisters of great magnificence were begun, but

the work came to an end when the S walk and part of the E
walk had been erected. Sacristy, Chapter House and parlour
still exist as reminders of the monks' sacred duties and the
place where they met in community. Kitchen and dining-hall,
or refectory, also survive, and the quarters where the brothers
who were laymen and not in orders – those who did the
business the Abbey demanded – lived.

Henry VIII's Act for the Dissolution of the Monasteries led to
the supression of Tintern in 1536. The king needed money to
support the strong central government that the Tudors had set
up; the lead off the roofs was melted down and Tintern
became famous for its brass, iron and wire works. These works
used the waterpower from the brook that runs into the Wye
just N of the Abbey precinct, and many cottages were built in
and around the ruins.

The remains of the Abbey were granted to Henry, Earl of Worcester, in 1537 and his estates were handed down to his descendant, the Beaufort family. The Duke of Beaufort sold the Abbey and several thousand acres adjoining to the Crown in 1901. Since then, thanks to much careful restoration by the Department of the Environment, almost the entire layout of the Abbey can be traced. The precincts of the Abbey occupy 27 acres and the remains, in some cases considerable, hold many features of interest.

A Tour of the Abbey

The ticket office stands in the outer parlour of the Abbey, a place where conversation between monks and laymen was permitted, and probably the limit for the public in medieval times.

Turning R you pass the remains of the stair by which the laybrothers came down from their dormitory to the church for night-time services. Like them, you enter the church through the doorway set in the NW corner.

The church is remarkably complete, an excellent specimen of Gothic architecture. The church has no roof now, but the shell is entire. The steep pitch of the gables of nave, chancel and transepts is in harmony with the Decorated window-heads, and balance is struck by the level line of corbelled wall-tops. All the pillars are standing except those which divided the nave from the N aisle, but their situation is marked by the remains of their bases. The arches and pillars of the transepts are complete, the height of the central arches being 70 ft and the smaller arches 40 ft. The frame of the great seven-light W window, 42 ft high, is in perfect preservation. The design of the tracery is extremely elegant and when decorated with painted glass must have produced a brilliant effect.

The whole of the church had stone-vaulted ceilings, and the roof spaces above them were lit by the great windows that survive in all four gables of the church. These attics and the roofs themselves were reached by circular stairs in the arches of the transepts.

The length of the church is 228 ft and its breadth is 150 ft. The great E window, 64 ft high, is said to have been the finest Gothic window ever produced in Britain – many visitors consider that the lovely windows, framing views of steeply wooded hills, are among the chief delights of Tintern, and
Tintern Abbey

Wordsworth saw

> *. . . these steep and lofty cliffs,*
> *That on a wild secluded scene impress,*
> *Thoughts of a more deep seclusion. . . .*

As was customary in Cistercian churches the nave was
divided from the aisles by solid screen walls. The lay-brothers
attended services in the nave, and their altar stood in front of a
screen between the fourth pair of pillars from the W. The

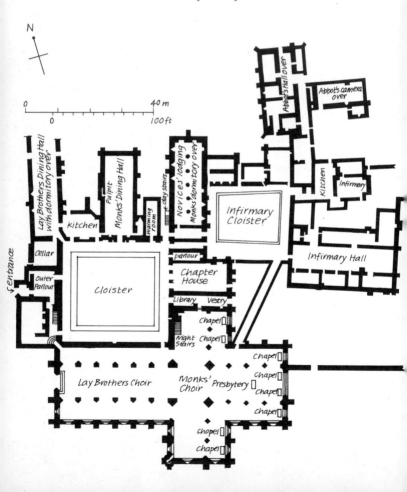

monks choir occupied the remainder of the nave and the crossing. The high altar was in a line with the last pair of piers at the E end. Behind it were two chapels and the processional way. Each aisle had a chapel at its E end, and on the E side of each transept were two chapels separated by a screen wall.

There are several interesting tombs in the church. One of these is a flat slab in the S aisle, inscribed with a cross, the early Christian emblem of the fish, and part of an inscription in Gothic characters. The only tomb in its original position is that of Nicholas of Llandaff, treasurer of the cathedral between 1191–1218, lying under the N arch of the crossing.

From the N aisle, at a point just E of the transept, ran a passage NE communicating with the Infirmary, which stood apart from the other buildings and was occupied by aged members of the community as well as by the sick. Another passage running W from the Infirmary communicated with the other monastic buildings.

A good impression of the layout of the various domestic buildings can be obtained with the aid of the plan from such a viewpoint as the top of the stairway in the N Transept. This staircase, for night use only, communicated with the monks dormitory, a sleeping-hall 164 ft long which extended over the Chapter House and buildings N'wards, including the novices lodgings.

In daytime the monks entered the church through the richly decorated processional doorway in the N aisle of the nave, leading from the cloister into the church.

The cloister consisted of four passageways covered by lean-to roofs built around a rectangular open court. It provided not only covered access between the various parts of the monastery, but was also used by the monks as a place for study – on the E side is the monks library and next to it, in the wall, two cupboards for books. Normally the cloister was placed on the S side of the church to catch the sun, but at Tintern it is on the N side.

The first doorway down the E side of the cloister leads into the library, and behind it is the vestry, entered from the church.

Adjoining the library was the Chapter House, where the monks met daily to hear a chapter of the Rule of the Order read, and where they discussed the business of the house. The vaulted roof was supported by the pillars of which only the bases remain.

*C *Tintern Abbey*

Immediately N of the Chapter House was the monks parlour where necessary conversation was allowed, and next to that a narrow chamber which probably contained the original day-stair to the dormitory above. N of this again is the passage leading from the cloister to the Infirmary.

On the N side of this passage, and completing the E range, was the large hall of the novices lodgings. Here new entrants to the monastery lived for a probationary period before graduating as monks.

The NE corner of the cloister contained the doorway into the novices lodging, and also the day-stairs to the monks dormitory above.

The first chamber on the N side of the cloister is the Warming House, the only place, apart from the kitchen and Infirmary, where a fire was allowed. The rooms above were reached from the dormitory.

In the centre of the N cloister walk a large doorway opens into the monks dining hall, 84 ft long and 29 ft wide. On either side of the doorway are two recesses: the larger once contained basins in which the monks washed before meals, and the smaller held towels. In the S wall to the R of the entrance are also two recesses – the one on the L with a drain was for washing plates and cutlery, the other contained a cupboard where they were stored. In the SE corner is a door leading to a pantry or storeroom. On the W wall of the hall was the pulpit from which the Scriptures were read aloud during meals. In the SW corner of the hall is the serving hatch from the kitchen.

The kitchen occupies the remainder of the N range. It served both the monks and the lay-brothers: the latters' dining room was in the W range. Their dormitory was above, and the stairs to it led from the parlour in the SW corner of the cloister, where we began our tour of the Abbey.

A good distant view of Tintern can be obtained from the Devil's Pulpit up beside Offa's Dyke, but the best view of it is from St Mary at Hill, a little church, itself semi-derelict, on the hillside above the ruins. Take local advice and do not miss a visit to Tintern in the September and October full moons, for then the moon, crossing the E window of the Abbey church, just below the rose, floods the church with a light which no painter can transmit to canvas.

Offa's Dyke at Devil's Pulpit (p 67)

Tintern to Bigsweir Bridge

If you have visited Tintern and wish to avoid an unnecessary climb and descent you can follow the River Wye at a low level to Brockweir, and then continue along the E bank on an official alternative path as far as Bigsweir. In so doing, however, you miss a stretch of massive Dyke above Caswell Wood, and are not so well placed for a visit to St Briavels.

Beyond the Devil's Pulpit the character of the earthwork again changes: it has a high ridge of massive Dyke. It is a remarkable structure with an unusually steep scarp exactly on the edge of the plateau. At the spur of the hill in Lippets Grove the scarp measures 27 ft and, though on a steep slope, there is a definite lower ditch 15 ft across, cleanly cut out of the limestone rock. This lower ditch is continuous from the Devil's Pulpit for over $\frac{1}{2}$ mile. Again, in Lippets Grove, the earthwork has a lower berm 10 ft broad and a scarp 31 ft on the slope.

No more perfect or impressive stretch of Offa's Dyke exists. If a few trees on the W side were cut down it would look most striking from the R bank of the Wye near Tintern, situated as it is on the crest of very steep and, in places, precipitous

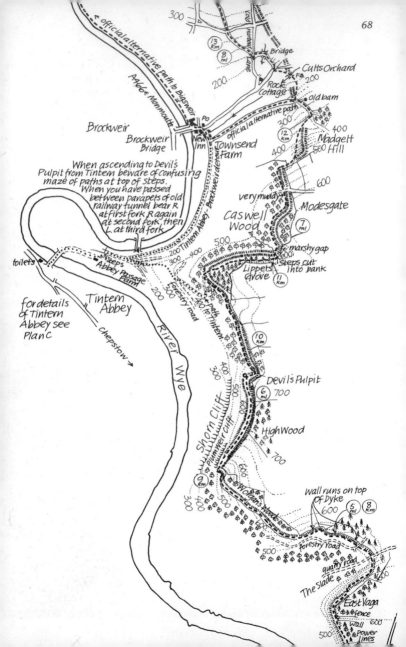

A663 Monmouth →

← official alternative path to Bigsweir

300

Bridge

13 Km

8 ml

Cutts Orchard

200

FB

Rock cottage

old barn

200

400

Brockweir

Brockweir Bridge

Po

official alternative path

New Inn

Townsend Farm

300

12 Km

Madgett Hill

400

500

When ascending to Devil's Pulpit from Tintem beware of confusing maze of paths at top of steps. When you have passed between parapets of old railway tunnel bear R at first fork R again at second fork, then L at third fork.

600

very muddy

Modesgate

Caswell Wood

7 ml

marshy gap

toilets

Steps

Abbey Passage Farm

200

400

500

Lippets Grove

Steps cut into bank

11 Km

200

300

Forestry road

path to Tintem

Tintem Abbey: Brockweir detour

for details of Tintem Abbey see Plan C

Tintem Abbey

200

10 Km

← Chepstow

River Wye

400

300

Devil's Pulpit

6 ml

700

500

600

High Wood

500

Shorn Cliff

Plumweir Cliff

600

700

9 Km

400

600

Wall runs on top of Dyke

600

Wolfan Wood

300

500

5 ml

8 Km

forestry road

500

quarry road

The Slade

400

East Vaga

fence

Wall

500

600

power lines

slopes, 600 ft high. The Dyke itself commands magnificent prospects when gaps in the woodland permit a view over the Wye valley, one being the same view as celebrated in Wordsworth's 'Lines.' Old yews and hollies mark its course, though the woodland generally is young.

Through the Lippets Grove stretch there is a shallow hollow on the upper (E) side, from which much of the material for the bank was obtained; it is not clearly defined and is in no sense a ditch.

Beyond Lippets Grove the Dyke still keeps a level course following the contours of the hill; it dips slightly to cross a narrow ravine and a brooklet, and is gapped.

The Dyke leaves the plateau edge by Modesgate as a very large bank descending the steep scarp. This high and broad rampart has a deep W ditch cut in the limestone, and is also built up to some extent from the upper (E) side: the scarp has an average measurement of 22 ft 6 ins.

The Dyke is then hardly traceable for a few yards, but beyond the cross-track the Dyke is seen as a small bank thrown up from the SE side, turning NE along the margin of a short but steep wooded limestone scarp. The Dyke descends this to the pasture, at the 500 ft level, then only a trace can be seen as it crosses the field diagonally, a small low grassy ridge preserved in the ploughed field on the slopes of Madgett Hill, but it cannot be traced in the arable field beyond.

The Madgett Hill/Brockweir trackway cuts through the Dyke. From here one can follow alternative routes: the proper way is tracing fragments of the Dyke along the tangled narrow lanes of St Briavels Common and The Hudnalls to Bigsweir, but a more leisurely and attractive way is along the delightful riverside paths and pastures from Brockweir. If you have visited Tintern you may have followed the river up to Brockweir, and if so this alternative route avoids unnecessary climb and descent.

North of the Madgett Hill/Brockweir trackway the Dyke crosses rough pasture, becoming larger. As soon as the easy slope becomes steep – at about 220 ft – it is for a few yards very large: a broad rounded bank, 66 ft overall, with a well-defined W ditch and spoil ditch on the E side. The S flank of the little Brockweir valley is very steep for a few yards and the Dyke is then present as a small ridge. On the narrow floor, in Cutts Orchard, a broad, high bank is seen revetted

3 *Devils Pulpit to Brockweir*

with stone walling, which suggests that the Dyke has been at some time enlarged and utilised as a mill dam.

There is a very sharp ascent through scrub from the Brockweir brook, then a gradual ascent from this lateral valley to St Briavels Common. Although straight alignments would seem to have been possible over this extensive upland mass, the line of the Dyke is uncertain and sinuous, and it can hardly be doubted that the hill was forest in the 8c. The whole of the hill has been subjected for a long period to small scale and intensive cultivation, and the Dyke, though its course is hardly ever in doubt, has suffered much damage. Where perfect it is a bank of moderate size, consistently ditched on the E, and without any trace of a W ditch. It was known to the peasantry as the 'Devil's Rudge' (i.e. ridge).

Near Spring Farm at 700 ft the Dyke begins a level course around the easy W slope of The Hudnalls. The chosen alignment commands magnificent views over the Wye valley. The view looking S down the gorge of the Wye along the line of the frontier is magnificent.

The lane continuing beyond Birchfield House runs to Coldharbour and St Briavels, but we will not visit this village until we have reached Bigsweir Bridge.

The topography N of The Hudnalls is interesting. The Mork Brook lateral valley separates The Hudnalls from Wyegate Hill, the Dyke's next objective. Lindors Farm occupies a knoll on the intervening ground: around it is low boggy ground, source of many streamlets which is an abandoned ox-bow of the Wye. The steep slopes around the meander loop represent the former river cliff of the Wye, and the present site of Lindors Farm was once the slip-off slope within the meander loop. The flat bench on which the farm is situated lies about 100 ft above the main Wye valley. Small streams have cut deeply into the floor of the armchair-shaped embayment left by the river. The whole setting of wooded slopes and the cleared fields can be seen at advantage from the road just below St Briavels.

The Dyke is present on the steep N scarp of The Hudnalls, here dense woodland, and it descends the slope directly to Bigsweir House. (The earthwork marked 'Offa's Dyke' on OS maps which extends from Red Hill Grove to the riverside near Bigsweir House was built c1740 in a fine situation overlooking river-crossing, a holloway for the most of its course, and unconnected with Offa's Dyke).

Bigsweir House was built c1740 in a fine situation overlooking

the Wye, and just beyond it the main Path is joined by the
alternative riverside route. The course of the Dyke across the
Mork Brook cannot now be followed, so follow the Bigsweir
House drive to the road A466 at Bigsweir Bridge. This bridge,
having a fine single span of 160 ft, links the counties of Gwent
and Gloucester, and crosses the river at the highest point to
which ordinary tides flow.

The Path rejoins the Dyke $\frac{1}{2}$ ml up the St Briavels road, and
it is well worth paying a visit to this interesting village before
we continue on our journey.

Description of route continues on p 75

St Briavels

This village, standing high above a wooded valley of the Wye,
is understandably a favourite halting place for visitors in the
Wye valley and the Forest of Dean – one of the greatest primeval
forests in the kingdom – and has a castle and church of interest.

The Castle was built in 1131 by Milo Fitz Walter, Earl of
Hereford, possibly as a border defence against the Welsh,
although it has no military history. The existing remains date
probably from about 1250. The Normans' establishment of a
castle here changed the political geography of the Forest of
Dean. St Briavels castle became the centre of administration for
the royal forest. The Constable of the Castle always held the
post of the Warden of the Forest of Dean, and it became a
favourite place for Norman kings to hold hunting parties. Not
only was the castle the administrative centre of the Forest, but
it was also close to much iron-smelting industry – cross-bow
arrowheads called 'quarrels' were manufactured at the castle
in the Middle Ages – Henry III ordered 6,000 in 1223, King
John had 2,000, and in 1333 Edward III ordered 500 iron clubs
for his troops to quell riots in Ireland.

Today only a fragment of the castle remains, the chief
remnant being the great gateway and its two flanking round-
towers. The walls of local red sandstone are 9 ft thick, and the
towers were used as a debtors' prison between 1670–1720.
Graffiti of that time still shows on the walls of the cells. The
gateway was defended by three main portcullises, and even
the doorways from the passageway into the porter's lodges
were defended by smaller portcullises. The keep collapsed in
ruins in the middle 18c, and the rest of the castle has since
been altered to suit the various uses – today it is a youth

Bigsweir Bridge and Wyegate Hill (p 72)

hostel. Objects of interest are the dog-turning spit wheel in the kitchen, a hunting horn carved on the outside chimney, and the jury and court rooms.

A wide but dry, deep moat surrounds the castle, being nearly in the form of a complete circle. The moat has been destroyed near the castle gateway where it has been cut by the village street, which separates the castle from the church.

The church of St Mary was built in 1089 to a cruciform plan, and although much of it was restored and rebuilt in 1861 some early work remains – five simple Norman arches survive in the S aisle, while the equally narrow N aisle has four bays and is Early English. Prior to the restoration the original central tower was taken down, but the fine Transitional arches of the crossing remain. A new tower was built over the S porch in *c*1830. The chancel is Early English and although it was rebuilt in the restoration its remains are exceptionally beautiful.

On Whit Sundays a quaint ceremony is commemorated when the villagers of St Briavels are given bread and cheese. Milo Fitz Walter, Earl of Hereford, granted the villagers the right to

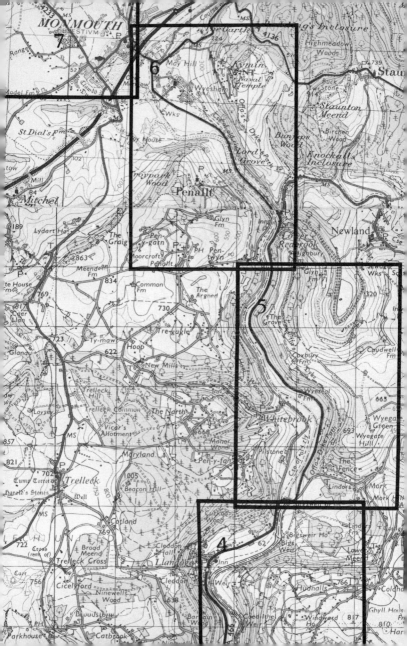

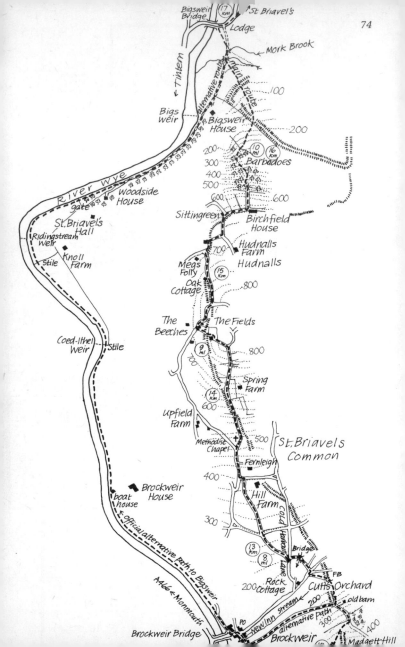

collect firewood from The Hudnalls, and the custom has been observed, in its present modified form, in this ceremony ever since.

Bigsweir Bridge to Redbrook

The official main and alternative routes unite at Bigsweir Bridge, and the Path rejoins the Dyke a little way up the St Briavels road. The Dyke ascends to the 550 ft level on the shoulder of Wyegate Hill, climbing 350 ft within $\frac{1}{4}$ ml of the road, then descending 250 ft on the far side. This curious course seems to be due to a determination on the part of the engineer to maintain wherever possible a commanding alignment above the Wye. The sweeping curve of the alignment so noticeable on the map is dictated by the contours of the hillside.

On the easy slope of the diagonal ascent the Dyke is clearly visible with a W ditch. At the highest level reached – where the slopes are almost precipitous – it is small and much obscured by stone quarries, and the W ditch has become a berm. In the diagonal descent the Dyke maintains for some distance the

large scale, and the work is similar to that seen on the ascent –
a very large bank built of limestone rubble with lower ditch
or berm and upper spoil trench.

The Path ignores this interesting stretch of Dyke on
Wyegate Hill and follows a lower line below the boulder-
strewn slopes, only joining the earthwork for a short stretch
at the far end of the wood before coming out into the open.

Beyond the woodland the Dyke is not obvious and in parts
it is non-existent. Instead of an artificial construction the
natural scarps of the valley were used. The scarp now reached
is wooded, while the gentle slope above is occupied by pasture
fields; cultivation has accentuated the sharpness of the transition
by causing silt to accumulate along the lower edge of the
fields.

The skill in the layout of this stretch is striking: an almost
straight alignment on easy gradients for $\frac{1}{2}$ ml above a
precipitous slope, followed by a steep ascent into Oaken Grove,
a woodland newly felled and replanted. Here the limestone
reappears, and the Dyke, a broad bank, is but little altered. In
the field beyond the Dyke is represented by a steep scarp, but
still no ditch is evident. Trending uphill across rough pasture
the Dyke is seen as a broad, low, lynchet-like bank, aligned on
the knoll of Coxbury Farm. The W boundary of the farmstead
is on the line of the Dyke and the ridge is well-marked in the
orchard near the farm. It is only faintly traceable on the
boundary of the next two fields, and then its continuity is
broken by boggy ground.

A new course is now taken, the Dyke being aligned for the
climb up the steep scarp to the Highbury Plain. A broad bank,
with a holloway on its W side and a spoil ditch on its E side,
climbs to Coxbury Lane: beyond the Dyke ascends through
woodland, the steep climb above the easy slope being partly
bridged by a broad rounded bank. The Dyke then fades out,
but the gap is a narrow one: it gains the plateau where it
narrows to a ridge at its S end. The scarp is steep, and the
Dyke is a high rounded bank, with no lower berm.

The profile of the Dyke varies from point to point along the
plateau of Highbury Plain, the W edge of which it consistently
follows: its form depends on the angle which the scarp makes
with the plateau. It is a very large work – a broad bank with

4 *Brockweir to Bigsweir (p 74)*
  St Briavels Castle (p 75)
5 *Bigsweir to Highbury (p 77)*

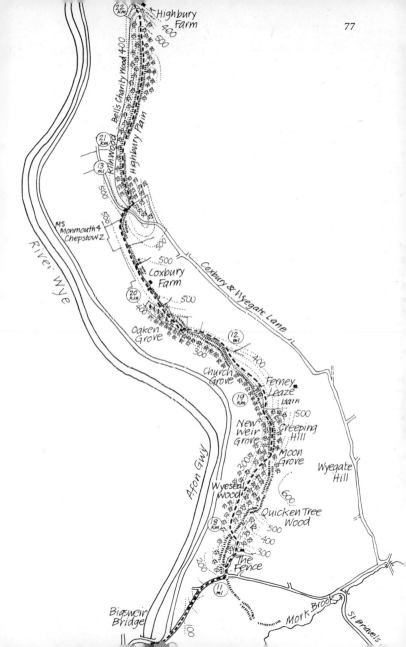

berm, and with upper spoil trench, on the very edge of the steep W slope. The plateau is well wooded and the undergrowth sometimes dense.

Fox found this area impenetrable 40 years ago: it had been abandoned as farming land at the turn of the century and had reverted to scrub woodland. Now the saplings have grown high enough to shade out the undergrowth and it is no more difficult than any other woodland stretch. This casts some doubt on Fox's explanation that no Dyke was built for 30 mls N of Redbrook because of impenetrable 'primeval damp oakwood' on the marls of the Herefordshire plain. Old oakwood is seldom impenetrable on foot.

The flat-topped spur of Highbury Plain projects a long narrow tongue, defined on the E by a ravine, in which flows the tributary stream which gives its name to the hamlet of Lower Redbrook, and it is here that the most southerly stretch of the Dyke ends.

Its ending in Highbury Wood is an original feature: the Dyke shows a slight downward trend and fades into the slope, which here becomes more acute. The continuation to the N is a more modern work – it does not link up with the ridge of the Dyke, and it is a stony bank, probably a collapsed dry-stone wall.

The Dyke has extended for $13\frac{1}{2}$ miles with but few gaps from the sea at Sedbury to the Wye at Redbrook, and we will not see it again until we have covered another 55 miles. The Dyke reappears on Rushock Hill above Kington, so for the intervening distance we take a scenic diversion over the Black Mountains.

Description of the route continues on p 82.

Redbrook

The small, formerly industrial, villages of Upper and Lower Redbrook were the N'ern terminus for the old Wye Valley Railway. The rails were taken up during the 1914–18 War and sent to France, and the line was never reopened.

It is at Redbrook that the second of the old and now abandoned meander loops of the Wye occurs. The former meander left the present river valley near the Bush Inn and followed the line now taken by the B4231 road through Upper Redbrook as far as Newland. From here it ran S'wards for about 1 ml before bending back to rejoin the present valley

6 *Highbury to Monmouth*

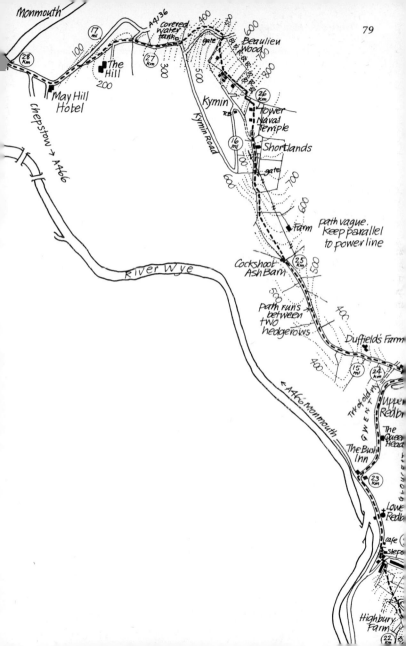

at Lower Redbrook. At its highest point on the loop the land rises to just over 400 ft near Newland. This means that this loop could only have been occupied by the Wye when it was flowing at a much higher level in the past, before the down-cutting took place to form the present river valley. This loop is much higher than the corresponding loop at St Briavels, which means that it was abandoned at an earlier date. The cut-off had the effect of shortening the river's course by almost 5 miles.

Since the time when the loop was abandoned, small streams have cut short deep valleys along parts of the former course, and the Valley Brook between Newland and Lower Redbrook is particularly noticeable. These short but active streams have succeeded in cutting back deeply into the margins of the limestone plateau to form deep coombe-like valleys.

These valleys and their streams were turned to good advantage when the iron industry came to the Forest of Dean. In places the limestone plateau contains rich pockets of haematite, and for centuries it was mined in shallow pits. The greatest exploitation came in medieval times. From the plateau top where

it was worked the iron ore had to be taken to the valleys where there was water available for the smelting and the forging. Here ponds were built to store water and also create the necessary fall to turn the water wheel which was to provide the power for the blast in the furnace and the hammers in the forge. In many valleys there was a 'hammer pond' and a 'furnace pond', each associated with the distinct processes of iron-making.

The Lower Redbrook valley was particularly well-suited for the building of these ponds. Today the furnaces have gone, but the ponds still remain as the last surviving link with this once prosperous industry. A great stone dam formed of huge limestone blocks is now broken and the pond overgrown with rushes and reeds on its margins. One of the mills in the valley was lately used as a brewery and one is today a paper mill.

Newland

Newland is an attractive old village, founded by Robert de Wakering about 1219 after having been created by a clearing in the forest. In the church of All Saints, sometimes called the 'Cathedral of the Forest' because of its size and proportions, there is the richest collection of early monuments in the district, objects that remind one of the history of the region.

In the S aisle is the tomb-chest of Sir John Joce, 1344, and his lady, 1362. The knight is in armour similar to that of the Black Prince at Canterbury, and the lady wears a square head-dress. In the S chancel chapel are the effigies of two priests, one the founder, Robert de Wakering. To the W of the font is the tomb of 1457 to John Wyrall, who was a forester of the Forest of Dean. He is shown in the hunting costume of the period, with his hunting horn, sword and knife. At the E end of the S aisle is a 17c slab showing a bowman, complete with horn, bow and dagger, and in the S chancel chapel there is a unique brass, the figure shown in relief, of a medieval free-miner, carrying a wooden hod on his back, a pick in one hand and a candlestick in his mouth. He is wearing what appears to be a thick flannel jacket and leather breeches tied with thongs.

The church stands on the shoulder of a little hill, and its flat rectangular churchyard is surrounded on all sides by houses, including the Grammar School, 1639, Almshouses, 1615, and The Ostrich Inn.

Redbrook

Redbrook to Monmouth

Offa's Dyke reappears in continuous form at Rushock Hill above Kington, and it is probable that the Wye formed the Anglo-Cymric boundary. Throughout Herefordshire the Dyke is intermittent, although there are good stretches. This is partly due to the fact that, in Fox's opinion, the area was thickly wooded in 8c, and it was only necessary to defend the valley tracks along which incursions in force were feared.

Offa's Dyke Path therefore follows a scenic alternative to the route across the Herefordshire plain. From Monmouth the Path runs NW to traverse the Black Mountains to Hay-on-Wye, so joining the Dyke again at Kington.

The Path leaves the Wye just beyond the Early Decorated style church (1873) of St Saviour, Redbrook, and follows the valley road to Upper Redbrook. From here it climbs steadily to the top of a hill, over 800 ft high, called Kymin, which overlooks Monmouth town. Nine acres of this hill were acquired by the National Trust in 1902, and it commands a fine view over nine counties, including the Black Mountains and the Brecon Beacons, and the Wye and the Monnow valleys, but of more immediate interest are two curious buildings – the Round House and the Naval Temple.

The many-windowed tower known as the Round House was built by a group of gentlemen of Monmouth in 1794 for their weekly dining club meetings. It contained a kitchen and an upper banqueting hall, with a flat roof for observing the view. It proved so popular that a bowling green was added, and the Duke of Beaufort provided extra dining accommodation (now in ruins) and stables. A carriage road was constructed to the summit, and the hill top was laid out with walks, seats and vistas.

The club built the Naval Temple in 1800 on the second anniversary of the Battle of the Nile in honour of the Royal Navy. It was dedicated to the Duchess of Beaufort, Admiral Boscawen's daughter, and was opened on 20 June 1801 with a public breakfast and dancing on the hill.

The original temple was an elaborate affair, crowned by a statue of Britannia seated on a rock. On its pedestal were two paintings, one representing 'The Standard of Great Britain waving triumphant over the fallen and captive Flags of France, Spain and Holland,' and the other 'The Glorious and ever memorable Battle of the Nile.' The frieze around the paintings

The Naval Temple on The Kymin

carried the words 'Glorious Victories' and 'Britain's Glory'.

The walled enclosure contained four cannon and was entered by fine gates 10 ft high. The temple has been 'restored' many times – the statue, cannon and gates have gone and the temple has been turned into a shelter with a verandah. A tablet on the building says:

'This Naval Temple was erected August 1st, 1800, to perpetuate the names of those Noble Admirals who distinguished themselves by their Glorious Victories for England in the last and present Wars.'

Sixteen medallions commemorate the following admirals and their victories:

18 Aug 1759	Boscawen	*Defeat of French at Lagos Bay.*
20 Nov 1759	Hawke	*Defeat of French at Quiberon Bay.*
12 Apr 1782	Rodney	*Defeat of French at Battle of the Saintes.*
11 Dec 1793	Gell	*Capture of the Spanish treasure ship 'Santiago'.*
18 Dec 1793	Hood	*Blockade and capture of Toulon.*
1 Jun 1794	Howe	*Defeat of French off Ushant.*
16 Jun 1795	Cornwallis	*Encounter with French off Brest.*
23 Jun 1795	Bridport	*Capture of 3 French ships of L'Orient.*

14 Feb 1797	Vincent	*Destruction of Spanish fleet off Cape St Vincent.*
14 Feb 1797	Thompson	*Second in Command to Sir John Jervis at defeat of Spanish, Cape St Vincent.*
11 Oct 1797	Duncan	*Defeat of Dutch off Camperdown.*
1 Aug 1798	Nelson	*Battle of the Nile.*
12 Oct 1798	Warren	*Capture of a French force off Ireland.*
18 Jun 1799	Kieth	*Surrender of Dutch expedition against the Cape at Saldanha Bay.*
28 Aug 1799	Mitchell	*Defeat of Dutch in the New Deep off Texel.*
2 Apr 1801	Parker	*Commander at Copenhagen when Nelson destroyed Danish fleet.*

In 1802 Nelson, Lady Emma and Sir William Hamilton were entertained here at a public breakfast on the occasion of a visit to Monmouth, having boated down the Wye from Ross. Nelson congratulated Monmouth on having in the Temple 'the only monument of this kind erected to the English Navy in the whole kingdom.'

Nelson was made a Freeman of the Town and he is commemorated in Monmouth in the Nelson Museum, the finest collection of relics in the world, left to the Borough under the will of Lady Llangattock.

There are a variety of ways off the Kymin into the town, but the recognised one for us is to continue forward in the same line as the Temple and Tower to the corner of the grounds, where rustic steps lead to a sunken path, and follow a path down beside a fence on your LHS through scrub woodland to the main path in Beaulieu Wood. The remainder of the path into Monmouth is straightforward.

Description of route continues on p 97.

The Round House on The Kymin, built 1794

The Wye flows in a series of large meander loops in its wanderings across the Herefordshire Plain and at the foot of the Forest of Dean plateau. Each meander loop has a similar form, with a steep river cliff on the outer side and a more gently-sloping slip-off slope within the loop.

Around Monmouth, where the tributary Monnow (Afon Mynwy) joins the Wye, the valley is so open that it forms a small basin surrounded on all sides by wooded hills. It was in the centre of this basin, within the loop formed by the two rivers, that the town of Monmouth grew up. Thomas Gray wrote: 'It lies in a vale that is the delight of my eyes and the very seat of pleasure' and few will disagree with him.

The site occupies a strategic position and the natural line of defence also influenced the siting and growth of a town at this point. It holds the lower hills between the moorland heart of Wales and the wide fields of the Midlands; it masters the outfall of the rivers whose upper reaches lead to the central passes between Severn and Dovey, and whoever held it could control the whole Deheubarth, or South Wales.

Although there was a crossing point of the river here when the Romans had their camp, and a small chapel was built by the Saxons, the town did not really begin to develop until the years following the Norman conquest. The borough was probably established when William Fitz Osbern, Earl of Hereford, built the castle in 1067–68. After the rebellion and dispossession of his son, Earl Roger, in 1075 the lordship was granted to Withenoc, the Breton. He built a 'Church within a castle' to supplement the existing church of St Cadoc (probably St Thomas of Over Monnow) and endowed a priory of the Benedictine Abbey of St Florent from Saumur-en-Loire. The original settlement grew up round the castle and the church of St Mary, built by the monks in 1101, and was sited on a river terrace where it was free from flooding.

Withenoc's successors remained firm 'King's Men' even through the reigns of John and Henry III. John of Monmouth's men were defeated by the rebel Richard Marshall, Earl of Pembroke, in 1233, when the castle and town were taken and the whole lordship pillaged and burnt.

In 1256 the Lordship came by exchange to Henry III's eldest son, the future Edward I. This was the occasion for a royal charter of privileges to the burgesses, one of which was the right to hold fairs. The market place, now the open square in

D *Monmouth*

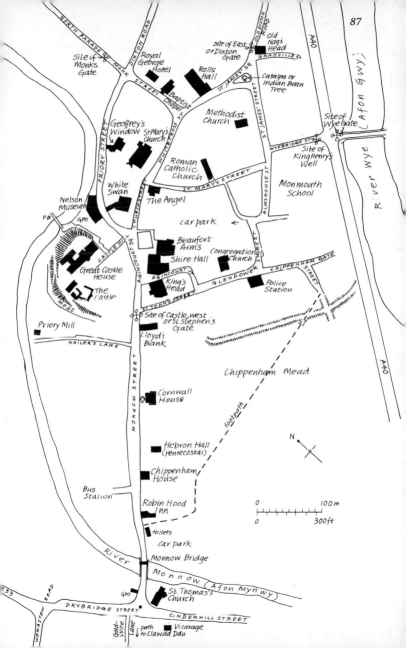

the centre of the town (Agincourt Square), was sited on the very edge of the river terrace before the land dropped away to the damp and often flooded meadows of the river plain.

In June 1267, after having been captured by Simon de Montfort, it passed, along with the adjoining Lordship of the Three Castles, to Henry's second son Edmund 'Crouchback' on the occasion of his creation as Earl of Lancaster. The settlement then consisted of the walled and moated town of Monmouth, covering an area of 20 acres, and the suburb of Over Monnow across the river. They were connected by the 'Great Road', the broad street running down to the river (Monnow Street), where the Monnow Bridge was built in 1272.

After the fall of the last native Prince of Wales Edward I of England took Gwent, alone among the territories administered by the Lords Marcher, into the kingdom of England, as a recognition of the extreme military importance of the area. At first the burgesses were headed by a Reeve, appointed by the Lord, but after the Charter of 1447 they had a mayor, though the town was not fully incorporated as a Royal Borough until 1549, after the Acts of Union of 1536–42. Although Monmouth had been royal property since Henry of Lancaster came to the throne in 1399 (Henry V was born in Monmouth Castle) it was a Marcher Lordship, not part of the realm, until the County was set up by that Act.

Before the Acts of Union Monmouth and its county were in Wales, but when the principality was divided into counties by Henry VIII the shire was added to England. At the same time it was ordered that two knights should be chosen to represent the county in Parliament, and one burgess the borough.

The legislation of Westminster has increasingly had to refer to Wales and Monmouthshire, because so far as Parliamentary matters, educational purposes and local government is concerned, and for recruitment of the Welsh Guards, Monmouth is included in Wales. Although for civil purposes the county is part of England it can be truthfully said that Wales has recovered at least one of its lost provinces.

The route of Offa's Dyke Path is not defined through the built-up parts of Monmouth, so we will take a tour through the town on the most convenient through-route, visiting some of the places of interest on the way.

Monmouth. The Shire Hall, built 1724, with Rolls statue

A Tour of Monmouth

The Wye Bridge was built in 1617 and was widened in 19c after the construction of the railway, which caused additional traffic across the river.

Wyebridge Street opposite leads into the town. On the L is Monmouth School, founded in 1614 by a great benefactor of the town one William Jones, a man, according to his own account, who was born at Newland in the Forest of Dean 'of high parentage but without pride'. Most of the buildings here date from 1865–95. On the R is the Queen's Head, a half-timbered inn with a good plaster ceiling in the bar.

Turn L into St James's Street, then R into St Mary's Street. Halfway along on the R is the Roman Catholic Church. It began as a small room deliberately hidden behind houses in the street soon after the Reformation and, as restrictions on public worship were relaxed, it extended towards the street, the later part dating from 1792–1820. Inside may be seen relics of Blessed Father John Kemble, the Hereford priest who was executed in 1679 when aged 80 years, one of the victims of the Titus Oates Troubles. The church also possesses two early crosses, one of which belonged to Evesham Abbey.

Continue along the street, past The Angel which derives its name from the fact that it was once the Church Brew House. It became an inn in 1726.

Opposite stands St Mary's Church, whose well-proportioned slender spire, rising to a height of 200 ft, is the dominant feature of the town and the valley. The S gates of the church-yard were erected by the parish on ground given by the corporation in the 1750's. They are all that remain of the surroundings of the Georgian church built by Smith of Warwick.

The original medieval church was dedicated in 1102 and was attached to a priory, the inmates of which used the choir, while the nave formed the parish church. On the suppression of the monastery the choir was allowed to become ruined, but the nave continued to be used by the parishioners until 18c, when the building was demolished, with the exception of the Norman W wall and the 14c tower.

The building which replaced it was designed and built in a Classical style by Francis Smith of Warwick in 1732, except the medieval tower which was retained and given a tall and slender spire by Nathaniel Wilkinson. This church lasted only until 1881–2, when it was rebuilt in its present Gothic style to the design of G E Street.

A few objects from the original priory church have been preserved, the most interesting being a cresset stone (a stone with cup-shaped hollows for holding grease to be burnt for light).

The bells were recast in 1706. One of them retains an old inscription 'Habeo nomen Gabrielis missa de Coelis'. Misreading Coelis, local legend has it that Henry V, displeased at hearing the bells of Calais ringing joyfully after he had put to sea, caused them to be brought to his native town.

North of the church are the remains of the Priory, c1500. It was probably a prior's lodging over the gate into Monmouth Priory itself. The priory's connection with St Florent was broken in 1399 and it was dissolved in 1536. One portion of the building, used as a school since 1770, incorporates a picturesque projecting Perpendicular window which faces on to Priory Street. This is commonly called Geoffrey's Window, taking its name from Geoffrey de Monmouth, the celebrated chronicler and ecclesiastic who lived about 300 years earlier.

The details of Geoffrey's connection with Monmouth are obscure. He probably spent his early life in the town as a monk in the priory before moving to Oxford, and in the last

two years of his life he was Bishop of St Asaph. His fame rests
on his fabulous 'History of the Britons' written between
1130–40 and compiled from the writings of early chroniclers,
interwoven with current legends and creations of his own
fertile imagination, the whole professing to be a translation of a
chronicle found in Brittany. This remarkable work is the source
of the stories of King Lear, Cymbeline, Merlin and of King
Arthur and his knights as they have since appeared in English
literature.

When you leave St Mary's go along Priory Street, leading to
the banks of the River Monnow. The Castle Field across the
river here was the scene of the Battle of Monmouth in 1233.
The street was built in 1837–9 by George V Maddox, a local
man, to take mail coaches out of Church Street where they
caused congestion. This road was the first major alteration to
the town plan since 1450. Before the street was built Maddox
erected slaughterhouses along the bank of the river to support
it, and a Market Hall was placed on top of them. The
slaughterhouses can still be seen, but the Market Hall was
burnt down in 1963 and the new building erected on the site
in 1969 now accommodates the Post Office, Nelson Museum
and Local History Centre.

The Nelson Museum (small charge for admission) contains a
comprehensive and magnificent collection of material
associated with the great admiral. Bequeathed by Lady
Llangattock, the collection includes Nelson's fighting sword,
models of his ships and a great working model of the Battle
of Trafalgar, many letters, miniatures, much plate and numerous
objects intimately connected with him.

The Local History Museum (admission free) has a most
interesting exhibition of the town's history. There are displayed
collections of antiquities, photographs, prints, maps and
models of the town, and specimens of the local butterflies,
flowers and grasses (changed according to season).

Continue along Priory Street until opposite the end of
Church Street, then turn R up the Castle Hill. The restaurant
on the corner was once the home of Charles Heath, the
Monmouth printer and historian. Here he received Nelson and
Lady Hamilton when they came to the town in 1802. As you
near the top of the rise of Castle Hill you will be entering the
inner bailey of the former Monmouth Castle.

Monmouth Castle stands on a cliff where a steep scarp rises
above the flats of the River Monnow, but there are scant

remains. The castle was founded in 1068 by William Fitz Osbern, as the link in the line from Clifford (near Hay-on-Wye) to Chepstow. The most imposing part of the ruin, and the principal building remaining, is a massive rectangular two-storey block of the mid-12c Great Tower, containing the hall of the Norman castle. The upper storeys were built in 1340, and considerable elaborate alterations were made by the first Duke of Lancaster in the mid-15c. The stronghold is notable as the birthplace, on 16 September, 1387, of Henry of Monmouth, later to become Henry V. His father, Henry of Bollingbroke succeeded John of Gaunt as Duke of Lancaster and by his accession to the throne as Henry IV in 1399 brought the Lancaster inheritance into the same line of succession as the Crown.

The castle was destroyed by the Parliamentarian army in the Civil War and was surrendered to Fairfax by the Marquis of Worcester on 19 August 1646. The castle has changed hands several times since. The last private owner was the Duke of Beaufort, but it now belongs to the Department of the Environment. The castle enclosure – a grassy square with crumbling walls – is kept locked. There is free access at all

reasonable times, and the key may be obtained from the
Great Castle House.

The handsome Great Castle House stands to the R of the
Castle. It was built in 1673 by the 3rd Marquis of Worcester,
(later to become in 1682 the 1st Duke of Beaufort) for his
daughter-in-law, in order that she 'might lie in of her first
child near the Spot of Ground and Space of Air where our
Great Hero, King Henry V, was born.'

It is an interesting Renaissance building. The perfectly
symmetrical façade, with a flight of steps to give dignity to
the ground floor rooms, the central feature of superimposed
pilasters, the projecting wings with corresponding breaks in the
hipped roof and the marked eaves projection, and the heavy
moulded string-courses above the windows, all illustrate the
insular development of the Italian tradition brought in earlier
by Inigo Jones. As might be expected of its builder the house
contains good woodwork, a fine roof, an elaborate overmantle
and magnificently ornate plaster ceilings.

This house served as a temporary assize hall until the Town
Hall was built. The ranges on either side were added at the
beginning of the present century. The house is now owned by
the Department of the Environment and is occupied by the
Royal Monmouthshire Royal Engineers and the Monmouth
County Territorial Association. There is free admission to the
principal rooms at the discretion of the military, usually
weekday afternoons between May and September. Apply to the
Adjutant, RMRE.

Return down the hill and turn R into the old market place,
lying originally in the outer bailey of the castle. It is now in the
centre of the town and has been given the romantic name of
Agincourt Square in honour of Henry V.

The Square is dominated by the fine Georgian Shire Hall,
built in 1724 on the site of an Elizabethan market hall. The
interior was destroyed in the 1830's to make a more impressive
staircase for the judges, for the assize courts were held here
until 1939. The influence of the Assizes on Monmouth's
domestic architecture has been considerable, many of the
better 18c houses having been built by prosperous lawyers.
An ungainly statue of Henry V graces the alcove below the
clock. It was installed in 1792 at a time when his cult was
being encouraged by the many diarists, poets and other
travellers making the Wye Tour.

Monmouth. The Great Castle House, built 1673

Standing in front of the Shire Hall is a bronze statue by Sir William Goscombe John commemorating another local boy who made good, Lady Llangattock's son, the Hon. Charles Stuart Rolls. Charles Rolls, the pioneer of aviation and motoring, was born in 1877, and was closely associated with the Wright Brothers, whom he first met in 1896. He bought his first car in 1895, when only three other people in the kingdom owned cars. He began manufacturing his own motor cars a few years later, and in 1904 Mr Royce joined him to found the firm Rolls Royce Ltd. Rolls was a successful racing motorist, and in 1907 a Rolls Royce car created a world's record for reliability, and many other triumphs followed.

Rolls also made 170 balloon ascents, filling his own balloons at the family home 'The Hendre' by special arrangement with the Monmouth Gasworks. In 1910, a year after Bleriot's flight, he crossed the English Channel in an aeroplane in 95 minutes, then a record, and he was the first person to fly the Channel in both directions without landing. Rolls was killed a few months after his record flight through the collapse of the tail-plane of his machine when flying at Bournemouth. He is buried in Llangattock church.

Flanking the Shire Hall on the N side is the Beaufort Arms, an old coaching inn with Regency-styled charm and cobbled approach, famous for Nelson's sleeping here when he visited Monmouth. Occupying the S side of Agincourt Square is the King's Head, a 17c inn, enlarged in the coaching era. In the bar are plaster ceilings and a plaster overmantle with a portrait of Charles II, put up as a memorial in about 1670 after the Reformation, and closely comparable with the contemporary plasterwork in the Great Castle House.

Exiting from Agincourt Square out of the town to the Monnow Bridge is Monnow Street, the chief thoroughfare, narrow at the top where stood St Stephen's Gate, and wider lower down to accommodate the market stalls. All the most interesting buildings are on the S side of the street, and although there are other pleasant buildings the following are probably the most rewarding – Lloyd's Bank, Cornwall House, Chippenham House and the Robin Hood Inn.

First comes Lloyd's Bank, one of the best 18c buildings in the street. It has a fine fanlight over the door, and at the back a summer house commemorates Nelson's visit to the garden. Cornwall House beyond is one of the most important houses in *Monmouth. Monnow Bridge gatehouse, built 1270*

the town – at one time home of the Duke of Beaufort's agent, a despot to be feared. Chippenham House further on set an example for other small houses in this street, and just beyond it is the Robin Hood Inn, one of Monmouth's oldest inns, with its doorway dating from 15c.

At the end of the street is the Monnow Bridge, a unique fortification which, though no part of the walled town, seems to have been designed primarily as an outer defence. It is the only specimen left in Britain of a fortified gateway actually standing on a bridge. The only comparable work is at Warkworth, Northumberland, where the tower is at the end of the 14c bridge over the River Coquet.

This fortified gatehouse was built in 1270 on an ancient and narrow bridge. The bridge has three semi-circular arches, each with three wide ribs, a total span of 114 ft. The width between the parapets measures 24 ft, even though it was widened in the 19c. The gatehouse originally had a single arch and the two outer passages were pierced for the pavements when the bridge was widened. Above the archway is a room measuring 36 × 10 ft which for a long time served as a guard house or gaol. During the Chartist excitement in Monmouthshire, about 1840, rough loopholes for muskets were cut in the walls in order to cover the W approach to the town.

Across the bridge is St Thomas's Church, dedicated to Becket soon after his murder in 1170. The chief architectural feature of the building is the fine Norman arch at the entrance of the chancel, and other original work is the N door and the font. The small font is interesting in that it has a high tapering cover: these formerly stood in the NW corner and in the ceiling can be seen the hole made to accommodate the top of the cover when the timber galleries were added by the Duke of Beaufort in c1833. The church was 'restored' at this time and the elaborate W door and pseudo-Norman porch are of 19c date.

The traffic roundabout stands in St Thomas's Square, and opposite the church stands the Vicarage, older than it looks. Like many other houses in Monmouth the 18c façade has a round-headed window added centrally in the early 19c – one of Monmouth's habits which, along with the porches of the Greco-Roman revival (1790–1820), did much to harm the buildings of the town.

We leave the town by Drybridge Street, wide because it was once a market street, containing many well-proportioned artisans houses, such as those seen on the W side.

This part of the town, called Over Monnow, was protected by its own defensive ditch, called the Clawdd Ddu, the Black Dyke. It is almost certainly Norman and forms a semi-circle as an outer defence to the medieval bridge, and through it a branch of the Monnow was probably diverted. The ditch, broad like the Row Ditches at Hereford, measures 35–40 ft wide, and the bank is 3–6 ft in height. It can be approached by footpath off Drybridge Street or Wonastow Road.

Monmouth to White Castle

Offa's Dyke Path exists as a series of rights of way from Monmouth to Pandy on A465 near Abergavenny and a vast amount of waymarking and stile and footbridge construction has marked out a route, but this length is perhaps the most irksome along the whole way.

Nevertheless the route of Offa's Dyke Path is still inadequately marked in places in Gwent, and even where it is waymarked the route is not necessarily that designated by the Countryside Commission. There are difficulties in finding the correct way off The Kymin, and the path immediately outside Monmouth on the W side has been re-routed through a housing estate. But perhaps the worst stretch, through lack of adequate waymarking, is that through King's Wood, part of Monmouth Forest, 2 mls W of the town. In difficulty it equals only that of Llandegla Moor north of Llangollen.

Through King's Wood parts of the route are almost impossible to find or follow. The RA leaflet suggests an alternative to the official route, but this diversion is not clear to follow either! The key to the way through the wood seems to be Old Bailey Pit Farm, but as its ruinous walls are hidden in the undergrowth it is not easy to find. The stream running in a deep ravine is your guide, for the path goes alongside it. Which side you use doesn't really matter, but the official path follows the S side, as my plan illustrates. This stream is marked on the OS 1 inch maps, but on the 2½ inch edition it appears as though it were a country lane. This error is obviously derived from the 6 inch map, which gives this 'lane' the name of 'Watery Lane.' In no way can the imagination be stretched to see this steep sided gully as even the most rural of paths!

The difficulty of King's Wood is short lived however, for after an ascent of 250 ft for 1 ml almost due W you reach the summit of the track, and the way is then clear for the next few miles. You reach the River Trothy and follow its course upstream in a roundabout sort of way, crossing and recrossing it several times in the course of the next few miles.

Near the Hendre, the Llangattock's family home, you pass right through the site of Grace Dieu Abbey, but not a stone remains to be seen. It was a Cistercian monastery founded by Lord John of Monmouth in 1226, but abandoned at the Dissolution.

A little to the N of the site of the Abbey the official route keeps to the true L bank of the Trothy as far as B4233, but no

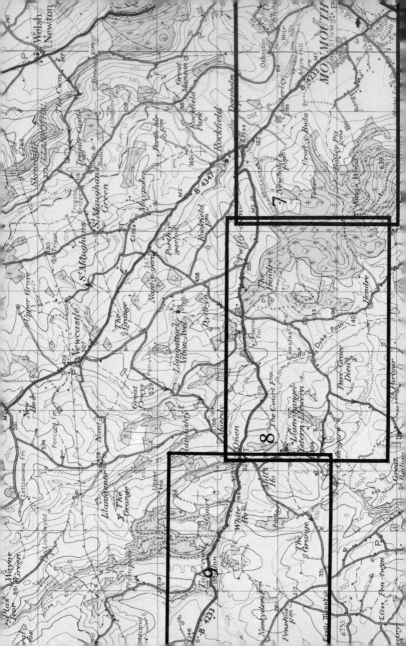

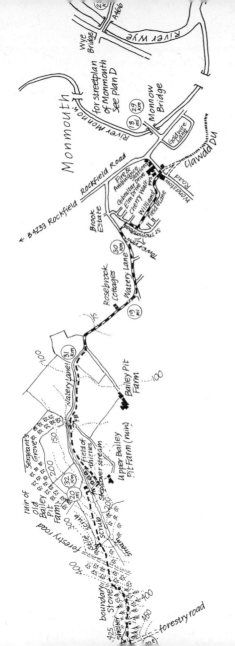

path can be found on the ground, although one is shown on OS maps. The waymarked route follows the R bank of the river by a much more convenient route, leading straight to Llanvihangel-Ystern-Llewern. The RA leaflet describes the official route on the E side of the Trothy, to B4233 at Llymon Bridge, then past Llanvihangel Court Farm to the village.

The name of the village means 'St Michael's of the Fiery Meteor' and the isolated medieval church is said to have been founded where Ynyr, a King of Gwent, set foot on dry land when he emerged from a bog into which he had stumbled.

The next village, that of Llantilio-Crossenny, is perhaps the most interesting place, apart from White Castle, on this short stretch of the journey.

A visit to the remarkable parish church of St Teilo is a must. It is said that a battle with the Saxons took place here and a victory was won, a victory attributed to the prayers of St Teilo, 6c Bishop of Llandaff. The church itself was built in 13c, and the graceful spire on the central tower forms a landmark for miles around.

Four massive posts, each about 60 ft tall, support the bells. Five of the bells are inscribed with prayers for the church and for Queen Anne, and the sixth is dated 1821. Tall Perpendicular arches replace the Early English nave, although the lancet windows survive at the ends of the aisles. Standing in the centre of the W end of the nave, notice that the chancel is out of line with the nave, being deflected to the S.

While the S transept is original the N transept has been replaced by the Cil-llwch chapel, separated from the chancel by three arches. From the chapel the view of the high altar is obtained through one of two squints. A corbel of a kings head in the chapel is said to represent the martyr King Edward II (1307–27).

The chancel is of the Decorated period. Several flat stones in the chancel between the choir stalls are of great interest. Two of the stones show costumes of Stuart days, one of a man who died in 1621 portraying himself, his wife and three sons in the dress of the period. Another is in memory of Vicar Owen Rodger, who died in 1660, and bears three candles, ten angel's faces and a quaint inscription. To the L and R of the E window are very interesting stone corbell heads. The mode of hair-dressing dates these as of the reign of Edward II.

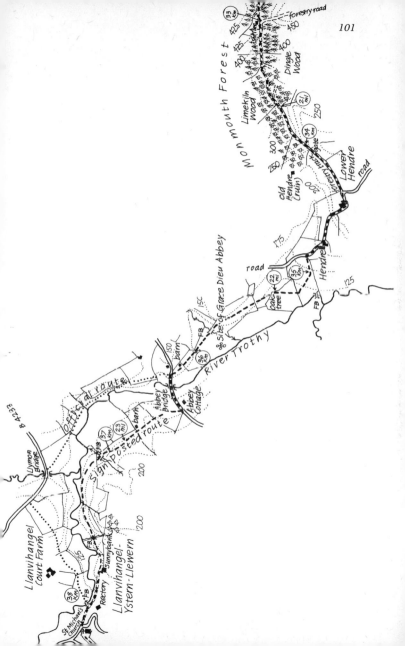

Monmouth Forest

forestry road

Dingle Wood

Limekiln Wood

③③ 425

425

400

④④ 350 Km

250

③④ Km

old Hendre (ruin)

forestry road gate

Lower Hendre road

Hendre

road

②② mi

③⑤ Km

Oak tree

FB

Site of Grace Dieu Abbey

River Trothy

③⑥ Km

barn

FB

Abbey Bridge

Abbey Cottage

Original route

Llymor Bridge

B 4233

③⑦ Km

②③ mi

Sign Posted route

barn

Llanvihangel Court Farm

Rectory

Sunnybank

Llanvihangel-Ystern-Llewern

③⑧ Km

FB

St. Michael's Church

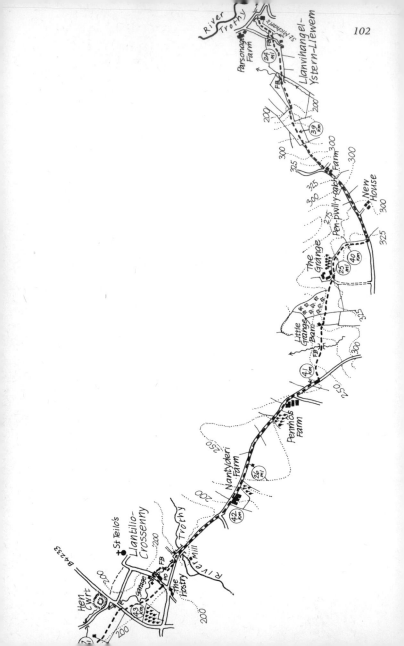

Out of the village on the Abergavenny road is the 18c manor house Great Cil-llwch (meaning 'Dusty Retreat'), now a farmhouse. It was the home of David ap Thomas ap Gwilym, uncle of the Earl of Pembroke, and remained in the family for six generations. In the house is much fine carved oak. The attic is known as the chapel, where mass was held during the

persecution. The house still contains a 16c stained glass window depicting St George and the Dragon.

The Hostry is an ancient inn where the Path leaves the village. There has been an inn bearing this name in the village since 1459, and the present inn was closed in 1859 after a murder and not reopened until 1900. A peculiarity of the building is the octagonal chimney of the hall fireplace which is immediately above the central door and window.

The stretch from The Hostry to Great Treadam is inadequately marked, but then there is a good track up to White Castle. You may prefer to take the road from the village direct to White Castle, in which case you will pass by Hen Cwrt at the road junction with the Monmouth-Abergavenny road B4233.

The moated island of Hen Cwrt (The Old Court) was occupied in 13c and 14c possibly by a manor house belonging to the Bishops of Llandaff, who had held land in Llantilio since early times. The story that Sir David Gam, the Welsh hero who was knighted by King Henry at Agincourt, lived here is probably not true; but in the 15c his son-in-law Sir William ap Thomas, Lord of White Castle, or the latter's son, William Herbert of Raglan, formed a deer park in the parish and the moated site lay in the SW corner of the park. The house must have continued in use until the destruction of Raglan Castle in the Civil War. Only the scant remains of the foundations of a house were uncovered when the site was excavated, and the island now remains as a grassy sward measuring one acre in extent. The site is in the care of the Department of the Environment, and admission is free.
Description of route continues on p 109.

Description of route continues on p 109.

White Castle

White Castle is one of a trio of castles – the other two are Skenfrith and Grosmont, both in the Monnow valley – which formed the defence set up by the Norman Lords Marcher to secure their hold on the Welsh borderland of Gwent. The pressures of the Norman advance beyond the Wye created this triangle of fortresses – the Castles of the Trilateral – as part of a scheme of border defence against Welsh attacks.

The earliest reference to a castle here occurs during the reign of Henry II when it was known as Llantilio Castle, but no remains of early Norman date have been found. The earliest masonry dates from about 1155, and the name White Castle
St Michael's Llanvihangel-Ystern-Llewern (p 103)

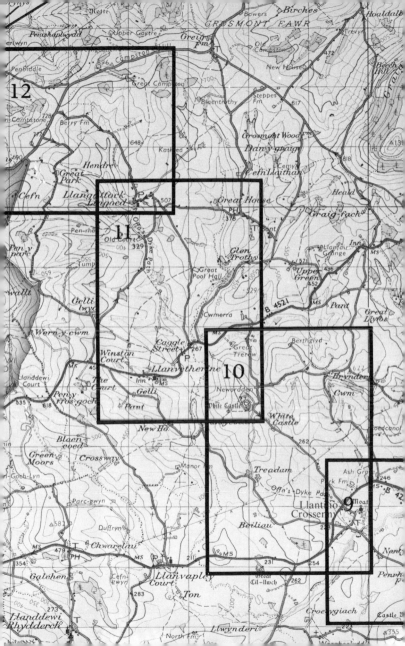

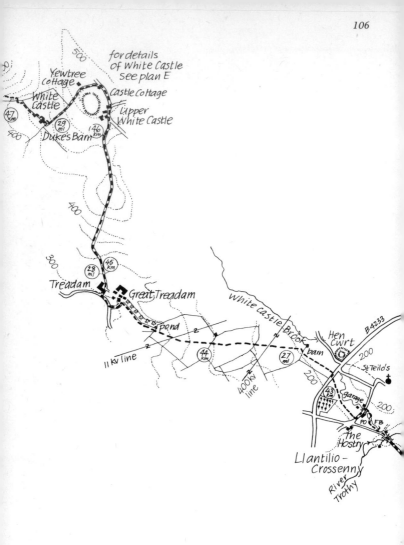

for details
of White Castle
see plan E

Yewtree
Cottage

White
Castle

Castle Cottage

Upper
White Castle

(47 Km)

(29 ml)

(146 Km)

Duke's Barn

500

400

400

300

(28 ml)

(45 Km)

Treadam

Great Treadam

pond

11 kv line

400 kv line

White Castle Brook

(44 Km)

(27 ml)

barn

Hen
Cwrt

B 4233

St Teilo's

200

200

(43 Km)

garage

200

PO FB

the
Hostry

Llantilio-
Crossenny

River
Trothy

must have been given because of the white plaster coating of the masonry, of which little now remains.

The curtain wall of the castle, enclosing an inner ward, was built in the years 1184–6. It is laid out in short straight lengths, joining at obtuse angles, a form commonly in use during the reign of Henry II.

In 1201 King John granted the Castles of the Trilateral to Hubert de Burgh, an officer in the royal service, and in 1205 the castles were transferred to William de Braose, a local magnate. William fell from royal favour and lost his lands in 1207, but his son regained White Castle during the confusion and Civil War at the end of the reign of King John. In 1219 Henry III regranted the Trilateral to Hubert de Burgh, then at the height of his power as Justiciar and Earl of Kent. The powerful Hubert spent a great deal of money on his possessions, but it seems that Skenfrith and Grosmont received a greater apportionment of expenditure than White Castle.

Hubert De Burgh's position depended on his retention of the royal favour, but he fell in 1232 and the Trilateral changed hands. The three castles reverted to the Crown in 1234 and were placed in charge of a royal officer, Waleran. Waleran was still in charge in 1244 when a new hall, buttery, and pantry were added to White Castle. In 1254 the Trilateral were granted to the King's elder son, the Lord Edward, later King Edward I, and in 1267 they were transferred to his younger brother, the Earl of Lancaster.

It was in this period that a serious threat to the western Marches developed. Llywelyn ap Gruffydd, the Welsh ruler, took the offensive during the English Civil War between King Henry III and Earl Simon de Montfort. The Welsh tenants of the border lordships rose in 1262 and several English-held castles were lost, and White Castle was considerably fortified as a matter of urgency. The work may have been done in 1263 or a few years later when the English Civil War was over, for the Welsh threat still remained between 1267–77, the year when Llywelyn was forced to surrender.

Until this time the stone castle consisted of a broad and deep wet moat, with walls enclosing a pear-shaped area measuring about 50 × 40 yds. The curtain wall had no towers, and at one end of the ward stood a square stone keep, with the entrance gateway next to it. This was protected by an extension of the moat to form a hornwork, a crescent-shaped outer line of defence to the S.

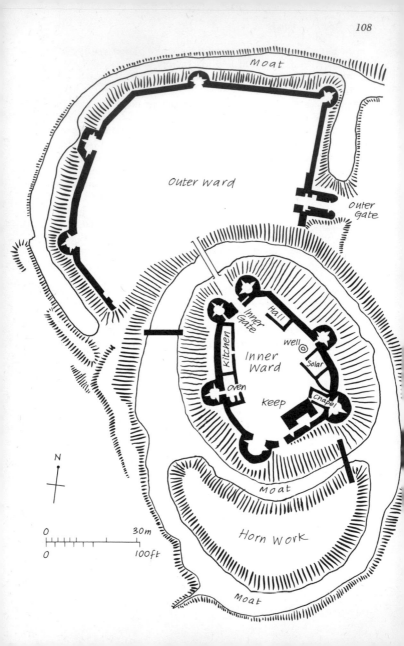

Moat

Outer ward

Outer Gate

Inner Ward

Inner Gate

Hall

Kitchen

well

Solar

oven

keep

Chapel

N

0   30m

0   100ft

Moat

Horn Work

Moat

In the re-fortification the stone keep was demolished, and a huge drum-tower was built at each angle of the six-sided enclosure: the N side is much shorter than the rest so that here there are two towers fairly close together, and this was where the new gatehouse was made. The original gate was replaced with a simple arched opening, serving as a postern gate.

At the same time an outer ward beyond the new gatehouse was enclosed with a stone curtain and flanking towers, and an outer moat and gatehouse completed the modernisation.

White Castle was then a grimly efficient structure, completely lacking in ornamental detail or grace of design. Unlike Grosmont and Skenfrith, White Castle was never intended to be used as a domestic residence: it was essentially military, the garrison being accommodated in simple halls ranged along the inner faces of the curtain wall.

After the Edwardian Conquest of Wales had deprived White Castle of its strategic importance, it still remained an administrative and financial centre. The castle continued in the possession of the Earldom and later Duchy of Lancaster, until this Honour was merged with the Crown on the accession of Henry IV.

A survey in 16c showed the castle to be roofless and derelict. In 1825 it was sold to the Duke of Beaufort, and since 1922 it has been under the guardianship of the Department of the Environment.

Hours of Admission

Open daily throughout the year	*Weekdays*	*Sundays*
March, April and October	*09.30–17.30*	*14.00–17.30*
May to September	*09.30–19.00*	*14.00–19.00*
November to February	*09.30–16.00*	*14.00–16.00*

Small charge for admission

White Castle to Pandy

The castle stands on the summit of a high westward-facing hill overlooking Llanvetherine; the view from this direction, from the vicinity of Duke's Barn, being perhaps the best and most romantic for it illustrates its utter isolation. The walls and towers are seen in a marvellous state of preservation and,

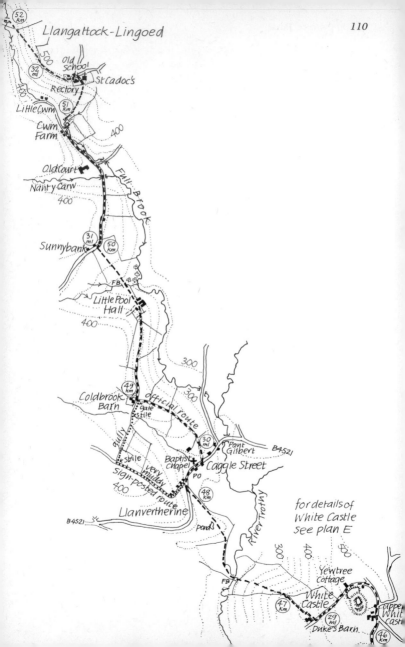

Llangattock-Lingoed

52 km

32 ml

Old school

St Cadoc's

Rectory

51 km

Little Cwm

Cwm Farm

400

Old Court

Nant y Carw

400

Fiddlers Brook

31 ml

50 km

Sunnybank

FB

Little Pool Hall

400

300

300

49 km

Coldbrook Barn

official route

gate stile

30 ml

Pont Gilbert

B4521

gully

stile

very muddy

Baptist chapel

Caggle Street

sign-posted route

P.O.

400

48 km

Llanvetherine

B4521

pond

River Trothy

300

400

500

for details of White Castle see plan E

FB

Yewtree Cottage

47 km

White Castle

29 ml

Duke's Barn

Upper White Castle

46 km

though the towers are roofless, the castle looks pretty much the same as it did over 700 years ago.

It is a short mile to Llanvetherine and Caggle Street and the River Trothy is crossed again at the foot of the hill. The Path is inadequately marked up to B4521, and beyond there appears to be two alternative ways towards Llangattock. A very muddy then overgrown track is shown signposted leading away from the road: it is marked 'Unsuitable for Motor Vehicles' but it really is unsuitable for pedestrians too. The official route takes an easier line on higher ground a little to the NE. Both ways join after $\frac{1}{2}$ ml.

You enter the little village of Llangattock-Lingoed through the churchyard of St Cadoc's, and you leave by passing through the schoolyard. Two more miles in a NW direction brings you down to the Lancaster Arms in the village of Pandy, on the A465 some 6 mls N of Abergavenny.

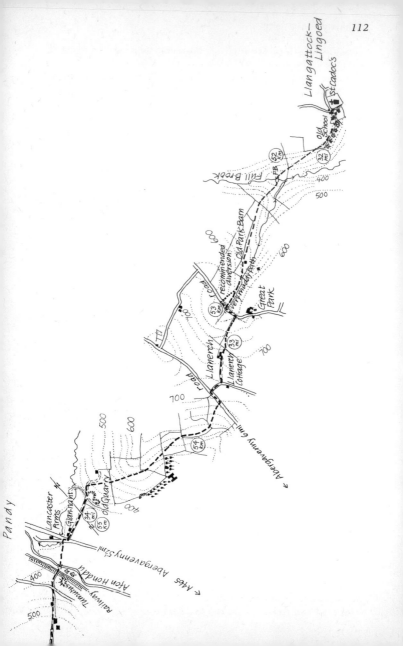

Ahead stretches the highest ground traversed by Offa's Dyke Path, the eastern ridge of the Black Mountains.

This high moorland is formed of hard sandstones known as Brownstones from the upper part of the Old Red Sandstone series, but the hills are properly called black since, from the levels of the Hereford and Monmouth plain, by a trick of light, they stand out in a long dark wall. You will soon notice that the structure of these hills is sandstone if you take any of the paths or tracks on the slopes of the hills, for you will find that trekking-ponies have churned up the surface into a red glutinous mud that is a plague to the walker.

The Hatterall Ridge is the boundary between Gwent and Herefordshire and is the eastern boundary of the Brecon Beacons National Park. The ridge is broad and flat-topped, covered with peat and heather, and raven and pipit, hawk and grouse, sheep and ponies are more plentiful than man. From this ridge views to the west are limited because of the convex slopes of the hills, but to the E is a vast view across several miles of undulating parallel wooded ridges to the Golden Valley hills and beyond, over the wide Herefordshire plain, with the Clees, the Malverns and May Hill in the far distance.

This stretch between Pandy and Hay-on-Wye is a hard 17 miles of walking along the Hatterall Ridge and over the Elfael Hills – the foothills between the Black Mountains and the Wye – but by now you should be fit enough to undertake it in one

day. There is not much accommodation, and what there is tends to be booked up by pony trekkers. It may be better to try to arrange two leisurely days, rather than one hard slog, along the ridge, with a break at Longtown in the Olchon Valley or at Llanthony in the Vale of Ewyas. A descent into this latter valley is desirable, since it will enable visits to be made to Llanthony Priory and Capel-y-ffin. There is a youth hostel and camp site at Capel-y-ffin, and both an inn and hotel at Llanthony.

The Black Mountains

Leave the Abergavenny road at the Lancaster Arms and cross the Afon Honddu and railway, passing a conspicuous little castle mound called 'The Moat.' The start of the ridge begins at the little Iron Age hill-fort of Pen Twyn, where stands a clump of pines. This is the first site of a hill-top fort along the route which stands any comparison with the great forts on the Clywydians further N.

The long Hatterall Ridge stretches ahead. There is a climb of 1000 ft for the first 2 miles, then a long gradual climb of 1200 ft for the 10 miles between Hatterall Hill and Pen-y-Beacon, with only 400 ft of descent in between. Follow a path, sometimes indistinct, across the broad peat ridge. There are few landmarks in mist, and only the occasional post or boundary stone to show the way ahead. The key to the ridge route is the OS survey columns. There are four – the most southerly being at about 1523 ft, the second at 1810 ft above Llanthony, the third at 2010 ft, and the last at 2219 ft on Pen-y-Beacon – and they are indispensable for locating your position for a descent in bad weather. In really bad weather it is best to keep off the ridge altogether, and follow the Vale of Ewyas up to the Gospel Pass (Bwlch-yr-Efengyl).

The easiest descent to Llanthony is by an easy and well-graded 'rhiw' from the col between Hatterall Hill and the Black Daren (i.e. S of the 2nd OS column, near mile 39) and the best way back to the ridge is by a 'rhiw' up the steep Cwm Siapol, E of Loxidge Tump: it is not easy to find the start of this path if you wish to make the descent when travelling S along the ridge.

If you wish to make a separate descent to Capel-y-ffin there is another 'rhiw' leaving the ridge about 1 ml N of the third OS column (i.e. 2010 ft) to The Vision Farm, and the best way back to the ridge is to return the same way. (These 'rhiws' up

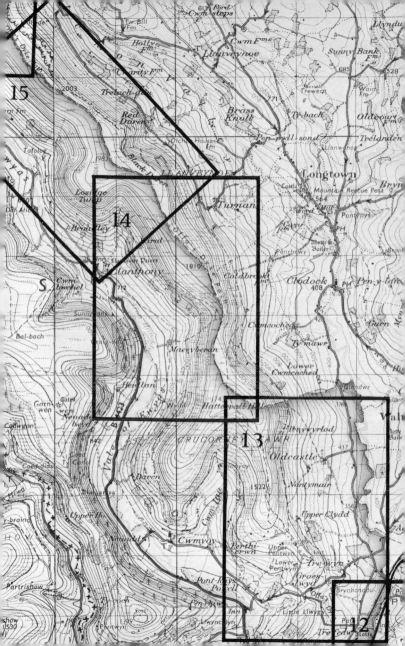

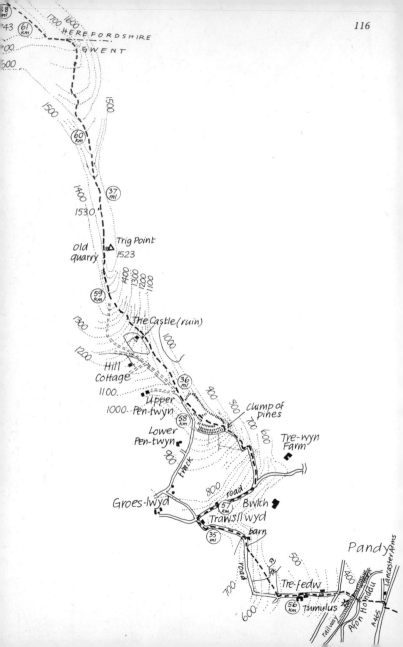

43 (61 km)

HEREFORDSHIRE

GWENT

1700 1600

1500

1500

(60 km)

1400

(37 ml)

153.0

Old quarry

Trig Point
1523

1400 1300 1200 1100

(59 km)

1300

The Castle (ruin)

1200

1000

Hill Cottage

1100

(36 ml)

800

900

Upper Pen-twyn

1000

(58 km)

Clump of Pines

Lower Pen-twyn

700

Tre-wyn Farm

900

600

Track

800

road

Groes-lwyd

(57 km)

Bwlch

Trawsllwyd

(35 ml)

barn

Pandy

road

500

400

Lancaster Arms

700

Tre-fedw

600

(56 km) Tumulus

railway

Afon Honddu

A465

and across the steep rock-strewn slopes must have been man-made, presumably for driving cattle and sheep up to the higher grazing in summer, and they can be found all along the Black Mountain slopes).

If, on the other hand, you have descended to Llanthony and also wish to visit Capel-y-ffin without climbing and descending the ridge again, avoid the narrow and traffic-infested road in the valley and keep to the track on the E side of the river.

Pen-y-Beacon, 2219 ft (or Hay Bluff to Herefordians) is the most northerly point of the Black Mountain range and the highest point reached on Offa's Dyke Path. The top commands extensive and glorious views over broken wooded foothills to the Wye valley around Hay. As the river curves in its great loop from Builth to Whitney it passes through a multi-coloured chequer-work of fields and woods. Beyond lie the Radnorshire hills, and on the blue-grey horizon are the outlines of the long ridges of the Myndd Eppynt and Radnor Forest.

Strictly speaking the official Offa's Dyke Path does not touch the top of Pen-y-Beacon, but takes a gently angled line across the E flank of the hill, along a faint old track that comes up from the Olchon Valley, avoiding a boggy stretch on Llech y Lladron. This N end of the ridge is much more flat-topped than is suggested on the map. The summit ridge path becomes increasingly indistinct and there are some confusing and misleading paths, mostly made by sheep, near 2306 ft. If you are following the official way up from Hay (i.e. from N to S) you have to be careful or you will find yourself on the ridge to Black Hill, too far E.

This is a suitable place to leave a description of the Path, and to describe the places of interest in the Vale of Ewyas. *Description of route continues on p. 127.*

Description of route continues on p. 127.

The Vale of Ewyas

The remote and beautiful Vale of Ewyas, the valley of the Afon Honddu, seems to have attracted men who wished to escape from the evils of the world, for it has several religious sites. The most famous of these is Llanthony Abbey, while higher up the valley at Capel-y-ffin is Llanthony Monastery. Also at Capel-y-ffin are two small and interesting chapels, and we shall have a look at them all.

13 *Pandy to Hatterall Hill (p 116)*
14 *Hatterall Hill Ridge and Llanthony Abbey (page 118)*

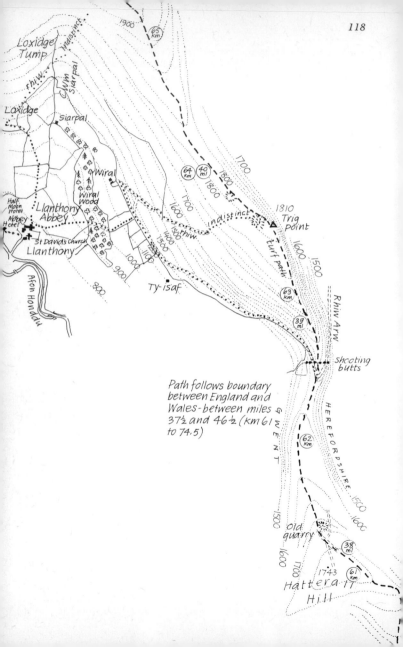

Loxidge
Tump

Loxidge

rhiw

Cwm Siarpal

indistinct

1900

65 km

siarpal

Wiral

Wiral
Wood

Half
Moon
Hotel

Llanthony
Abbey

Abbey
Hotel

St Davids Church

Llanthony

Afon Honddu

rhiw

Ty-isaf

800

900

1000

1100

1200

1300

1400

1500

1600

1700

1800

64
km

40
ml

indistinct

1810
Trig
Point

turf path

1600

1500

63
km

39
ml

shooting
butts

Rhiw Arw

HEREFORDSHIRE

GWENT

Path follows boundary
between England and
Wales - between miles
37½ and 46½ (km 61
to 74.5)

62
km

1500

1600

old
quarry

1500

1600

1700

1743

38
ml

61
km

Hattera H
Hill

Llanthony Abbey

Admission at all reasonable hours without charge.

Llanthony Abbey was the Priory of Augustine Canons, dedicated to St John the Baptist, but before the present structure was built there was a ruined chapel on this site dedicated to St David of Wales, called Llanddewi Nant Honddu.

In Henry I's reign the Norman Marcher Lords were warring with the Welsh and one William de Lacy, Lord of Hereford, found his way into the valley. He suddenly had a deep spiritual transformation and became an Anchorite. He called himself William the Anchorite and decided to spend the rest of his days in seclusion in the valley. William rebuilt the chapel and in 1103 he was joined by Ernisius, chaplain to Henry I, and they created a community of 40 canons under the patronage of Queen Maud. The church they built was consecrated by the Bishop of Llandaff in 1108, and most of the priory was finished by 1115.

Something in the air of the place seems to have had a profound spiritual effect, for soon they were joined by Walter de Gloucester, Earl of Hereford and Constable of England, who ended his days here, and Robert de Bethune, who succeeded Ernisius as prior: under him the present church was built, with extensive domestic ranges.

For a time its influence must have been great and the Priory prospered, with extensive grants of land between 1180–

1200. But the Priory was the target of raiders, and this caused the monks to flee to near Gloucester, where they established a new Llanthony which soon outstripped the old in popularity. The wildness, isolation and grim Welsh neighbours oppressed the spirit of the monks who remained, and gradually caused a decline. Gerald de Barri visited the Abbey in 1188 on his tour of Wales, and he recorded that the Anchorites who first settled there would not clear the woods or till the soil in case the place should lose its solitude and wildness.

By the reign of Stephen most of the monks had left to the house at Gloucester until only a prior and four canons remained, and it had no more than a shadowy existence until the Dissolution under Henry VIII.

Of the great building not much remains, although the ruins are fairly extensive. Though of several building periods there is remarkable unity throughout, in the late Norman style known as Transitional — a well proportioned design, having an austerity in accord with its surroundings, and nearly contemporary with, but far simpler than, the remains of Abbey Dore in the Golden Valley to the E.

The approach from the Hatterall Ridge brings you right into the grass-floored nave of the priory church. The N arcade is the best preserved part of the building, standing to nearly full height. It is one of the earliest examples without capitals and a continuous moulding. On the R are portions of the two W towers, remains of a noble and austere W front: the southern-most of the pair, together with the adjacent priors lodging, have been repaired and extended to form the Llanthony Abbey Hotel. To the E of the nave two sides of the central tower still stand and a fragment of the choir remains. The S transept is the best preserved, with a pair of lancets in its S wall. The E wall of this transept is pierced by an arch that led into a chapel, while to the S is a slype or passage which retains its original quadripartite vaulting.

The two W towers, half of the central tower, and most of the S transept, still stand to nearly full height, magnificent walls with tall and pointed doorways and windows. There are many pillars, all broken and shattered, but some rise up to 60 ft, and those of the choir are still higher.

Llanthony Abbey (p 119)
Parish church, Capel-y-ffin (p 121)
15 *Black Mountains and Llanthony Abbey (p 122)*

Walk across the lawn in front of the hotel and pass through a gateway to a little Norman church, still called St David's, once perhaps the chapel of the monastery infirmary.

You can obtain comfortable and modestly-priced accommodation at the Llanthony Abbey Hotel. More simple, but still comfortable accommodation and good food can also be obtained at the Half Moon Inn, 220 yds up the valley, or at the farm opposite the Abbey entrance drive.

Llanthony Abbey and its whole estate was bought in 1807 for £20,000 by Walter Savage Landor (1775–1864) an eccentric man of letters and a major English classical poet. Landor took up his quarters at the inn and set himself to plant the bare hill-slopes with cedars, beech, sweet chestnut, fir and many other fine forest trees – those which we see today.

On the hillside above the abbey stands a well-built but ruined stable building, sole remnant of a mansion begun by Landor but never completed.

Landor was a friend of Browning and Swinburne, and his most famous work is 'Imaginary Conversations.' His early writings – which included his verses to Rose Aylmer, his first love – were written here. However, Landor's grace of writing was not matched by his temper, and his attempt to play the part of the country squire failed largely because he could not

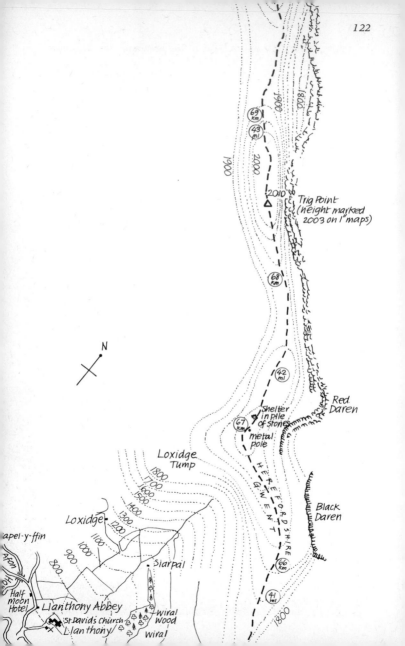

69 km
43 mi

1800
1900
2000

△ 2010 Trig Point
(height marked
2003 on 1" maps)

68 km

N

42 mi

Red
Daren

Shelter
in pile
of stones

67 km

metal
pole

Loxidge
Tump

1800
1700
1600
1500
1400
1300
1200

Loxidge

H
E
R
E
F
O
R
D
S
H
I
R
E

G
W
E
N
T

Black
Daren

apel-y-ffin

1100
1000
900
800

Siarpal

66 km

Afon Ho

Half
moon
Hotel

Llanthony Abbey

1800

41 mi

St David's Church

Wiral
Wood

Llanthony

Wiral

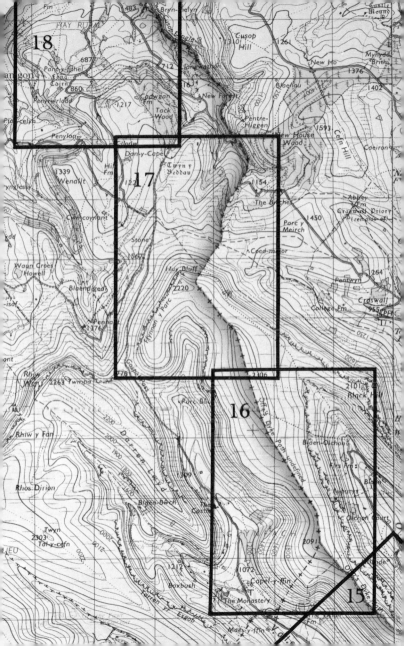

succeed in getting on with his neighbours, who combined to make life there impossible for him. In 1814 his tenants and country society together caused the disenchanted poet to leave to live abroad. The experiment had frittered away a fortune of some £200,000.

Capel-y-ffin

Some $3\frac{1}{2}$ miles up the valley you come to the small village of Capel-y-ffin, whose name means 'Chapel on the Boundary,' for here a projecting finger of Gwent runs out between Herefordshire and Powys, and the three counties meet above the village on the Hatterall Ridge.

There are two little old chapels here in the valley, one Church of England, and the other Baptist, both very similar in age, appearance and size. The Nonconformist Chapel was the meeting house built by the persecuted Baptists in 1762. The Nonconformist chapel, as elsewhere in Wales, can be readily classified: the simple Gothic brick of the Wesleyans, the subdued polychromatic stone of the Presbyterians, and the stone and brick classical façades of the Baptists.

The church may have had some connection with Llanthony Priory. It is a simple, cottage-like building with a wide porch and a short tower, shaded by a circle of great yews.

Capel-y-ffin and the church were noted by the Rev. Francis Kilvert in his Diary 1870–9 as 'the old chapel, short, stout and boxy, with its little bell-turret – the whole building reminded me of an owl – the quiet peaceful chapel yard shaded by seven solemn yews, the chapel house, a farmhouse over the way, and the Great Honddu brook crossing the road, and crossed in turn by the stone footbridge.'

Kilvert had walked over from Clyro to Capel-y-ffin and back – a 25 mile walk over the mountains on an April day – and further on he found monks working in the garden of the monastery, very hot in their black habits, and he reflected how unnatural their life was, since they allowed no women even to do their washing, a fact that was rather perplexing and distasteful to him.

These monks were not at Llanthony Abbey down the valley, but at the Llanthony Monastery close by Capel-y-ffin. This Monastery was built in 1870 by an Anglican clergyman, the Rev Joseph Leycester Lyne, for his own unorthodox foundation of Anglican Benedictines.

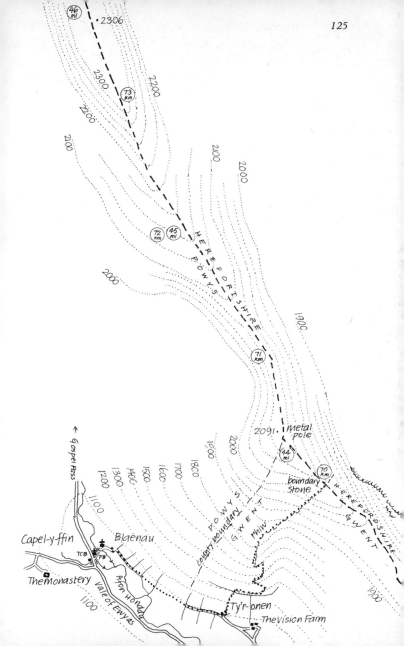

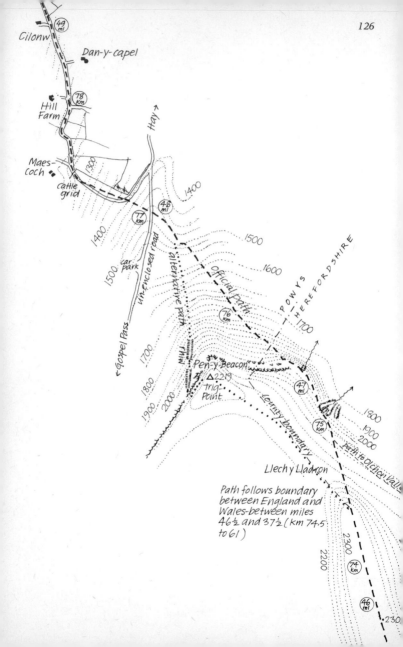

Cilonw

Dan-y-capel

78 km

Hill Farm

Maes-coch

cattle grid

Hay →

1300

1400

49 mi

48 mi

77 km

car park

1400

1500

Gospel Pass

un-enclosed road

alternative path

official path

POWYS

HEREFORDSHIRE

1500

1600

1700

76 km

1700

Pen-y-Beacon

△ 2219
trig point

1800

1900

2000

County boundary

47 mi

75 km

1800

1900

2000

Path to Olchon Vall.

Llech y Lladron

Path follows boundary
between England and
Wales - between miles
46½ and 37½ (km 74.5
to 61)

2200

2300

74 km

46 mi

230

Lyne was born in 1837, a cousin of Dean Stanley, and his bisexual community had its own particular rules and ritual. As Father Ignatius, Lyne ruled his small community for 38 years, preaching at intervals in England and America. His meetings in London caused much stir in late Victorian days, and his magnetism and eloquence produced ample funds for his establishment. Lyne died at Llanthony on 16 October 1908 and the successors of the community made it a dependency of the Anglican Benedictine community on the Isle of Caldy. In 1913, after difficulties with the Anglican authorities, the monks of Caldy sought admission to the Roman Catholic church, and Llanthony Monastery declined.

The great church, which had never been completed, became ruinous and dangerous and by the early 1920's the vaulting of the chapel had collapsed. In 1924 the property was acquired by Eric Gill the sculptor, who used it as a house and workshop. He created a small chapel of Our Lady and St David in part of the cloister buildings and decorated it with his own lettering in Latin words on the rafters. In 1935 the buildings were converted to a girl's school, then it became a Roman Catholic guest house, and in the 1950's it was a youth hostel. It is now privately occupied. The ruins of the Monastery and the Gill Chapel can be visited at any reasonable time without charge.

Capel-y-ffin to Hay-on-Wye

To regain the Offa's Dyke Path you may either ascend the Hatterall Ridge by the 'rhiw' near The Vision Farm, or continue beyond Capel-y-ffin and the youth hostel by the narrow and tree-lined lane ascending by the side of the Honddu to reach the Gospel Pass, 1778 ft (Bwlch-yr-Efengyl). If you go this way an alternative to the road, which can be notoriously busy in summer, is to take the track which contours at about 1250 ft on the W side of the valley and which joins the road where it opens out on to the unenclosed moorland.

The Gospel Pass is a wide and open height, covered with snows or parked cars according to season, giving a sight of Radnor Forest and the hills that follow the Wye. Its name may come from that preaching and fund-raising itinerary for the Third Crusade, which Gerald de Barri, Archdeacon of Brecon, undertook with Archbishop Baldwin in 1188. That laborious undertaking, which summoned crowds all over Wales to hear and take up the Cross, has left its mark in many

17 *Pen-y-Beacon*

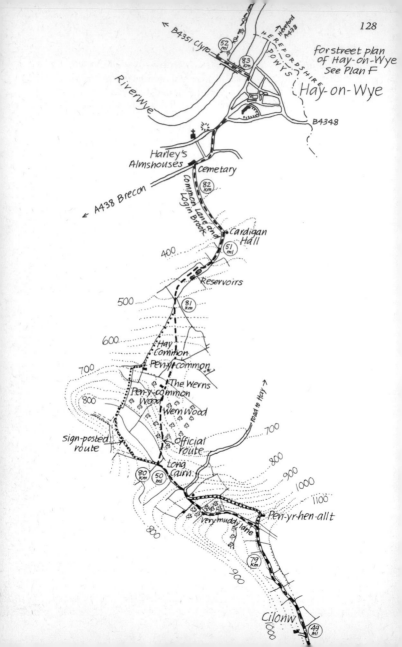

128

for street plan
of Hay-on-Wye
See Plan F

Hay-on-Wye

← B4351 Clyro

52 ml
83 km

HEREFORDSHIRE
POWYS

← Hereford A438

B4348

River Wye

Harley's
Almshouses

Cemetery

← A438 Brecon

Common Lane and
Login Brook

82 km

Cardigan
Hall

51 ml

400

Reservoirs

500

81 km

600

Hay
Common

700

Pen-y-common

The Werns

Pen-y-common
Wood

Wem Wood

800

road to Hay →

Official
route

sign-posted
route

700

800

900

1000

1100

Long
Cairn

80 km 50 ml

Pen-yr-hen-allt

Very muddy lane

800

79 km

900

Cilonw

1000

49 ml

place-names in the area.

If you have climbed to the top of Pen-y-Beacon there is a steep but easy 700 ft descent from the OS column at 2219 ft, or alternatively there is an easy shelf-path or 'rhiw' cutting diagonally across the scarp slope, beginning about 125 m SW along the Ffynnon-y-Parc ridge.

A descent of 1000 ft in a mile takes you across the open common and the Hay-Gospel Pass-Llanthony road, and from a cattle grid you follow metalled lanes towards Hay. Between Pen-y-Beacon and Hay is one of the worst stretches through lack of signposting. The farmer at Pen-yr-hen-allt farm does not admit the official path – a very muddy lane, becoming overgrown – to be a right of way, and it is preferable to follow the road. Some confusion may also occur on the way through Wern Wood because the path which is signposted is not the official path. However, if you keep N you will cross Hay Common and follow a pretty little path beside a stream to emerge on the western outskirts of Hay-on-Wye at the Brecon Road, A438. Immediately opposite are Harley's Almshouses, built 1836. Turn R and enter Hay-on-Wye.

Description of route continues on p 135

Hay is set on a hill at the edge of the Elfael Hills below the
Black Mountains overlooking the pastoral country of the Wye.
Its site was cleverly chosen because the approaches from E
and W are fairly steep ascents and to the N is a steep drop
down to the Wye.

There is a very large Roman fort on the Powys bank of the
Wye but there are no indications of any settlement on the
height which stands above the river earlier than about 1090.

'Hay' comes from the Norman French *La Haie* – an enclosed
place or hedged enclosure – and Welsh references to it as
Y Gelli Gandryll – the clipped hedge – seem to confirm that this
described an early defensive enclosure. The obvious location
for this would be the area later enclosed by the town walls,
but St Mary's Church lies outside these defences.

St Mary's Church was founded in Henry I's reign about
1120 by William Revell and lies well to the W of the town,
separated from it by a steep dingle. On the town side of the
dingle stands a large motte which may have been the site of
Revell's castle. Together they mark the site of the original
Norman settlement. The church was rebuilt in the 19c, except
for its fortress-like tower, in an appalling variety of the
'churchwarden' style. The strangest feature is a quasi-Moorish
arcade separating the nave from the chancel.

The walled town and castle was built in the 1150's by
Roger, Earl of Hereford and Lord of Brecon, to try to block
the 'royal progress' of Henry II (whose 'Fair Rosamund' lived
in the neighbouring castle at Clifford) whose intention it was
to restore royal control over the border barons. (As it happened
Roger withdrew from his planned rebellion and left his ally,
Mortimer of Wigmore, to stand the King's onslaught).

From then on Hay found itself too much in the path of
the English Kings. Hay passed to William de Braose of Abergavenny and his wife Maude in 1175 – a Marcher lord and his
wife whose names were bywords for ruthlessness and treachery
– and after King John had turned against them in 1208 it
became a key point in the alliances of their son Giles, Bishop
of Hereford, with Llywelyn, in the struggle for Magna Carta.
The town was burnt by John in his last campaign in 1216;
destroyed by Llywelyn in 1231, and was sieged between
1263–5 when it was the centre of struggles between the

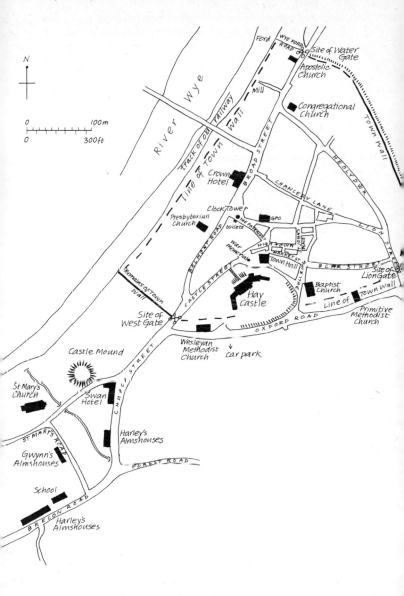

alliance of Simon de Montfort and Llywelyn the Last against
Mortimer and Prince Edward. Simon occupied Hereford, with
Henry III as his prisoner, and Hay was one of Simon's last
struggles for he escaped from there only to be overthrown by
Edward at Evesham in 1265.

Despite these many incidents in the 13c this compact little fortress town prospered. Hay was granted a market in 1233, and in 1237 there was a grant for the building or repair of the town walls which overlook steep slopes to the Dulas Brook on the E and the Wye on the NW. The castle defended the weakest side, the SW. A compact little town grew up in a haphazard maze of streets within the shelter of its triangular shaped walls. The walls vanished without trace after the town was sacked by Glyndwr about 1400, but the tight street plan of this medieval town still bears witness to its role as a frontier outpost of Norman England.

Hay is crowned by the castle which is now an impressive house of early 17c Jacobean style – complete with tall chimneys, gables and finials and a walled garden – attached to the remnants of the Norman castle, represented by a gateway and a tower.

The fragmentary castle that survives was set up by William de Braose or, according to tradition, by his wife Maude de Valerie who, as *Maude Walbee* was credited with superhuman powers. Local legend has it that she built the castle single-handed, but there can be no doubt that she was strong-minded. She alone among the Norman aristocracy had the courage to accuse King John to his face of murdering his nephew, the young Prince Arthur, whom Shakespeare paints so movingly in his *King John*. For this tactlessness she was imprisoned in Corfe Castle and was starved to death. William feared for his life and fled to France. Although Maude was held in affection William was a real villain – cunning, greedy, treacherous and cowardly – and Hay was well rid of him.

Hay Castle is now the headquarters of a firm which claims to be the largest second-hand booksellers in the world. Richard Booth, Booksellers, supply books to all parts of the world and an exploration of this literary labyrinth is a time-absorbing experience. Not only does the Castle hold books, but there are other shops scattered throughout the town, each of them dealing with different subjects.

In the castle itself are rare books and complete editions. In Castle Street are British topography and field sports; in the Castle Drive is a large building which houses all the novels; a former cinema holds books devoted to general subjects, literature, art, military, house and garden, and theology. There is also a former warehouse dealing with books on natural

Hay-on-Wye. The Clock Tower

history, science, physics and medicine, while in Lion Street are illustrated books and fine bindings.

Outside the Castle is a public car park so large that one suspects at once that in this quiet town more must happen than just the selling of books. Hay is the centre for a large agricultural region, and on the Tuesday market days and the regular pony sales days the town is packed out. On such days the streets are full of life and you can get plenty of local colour by visiting the bar of The Crown or The Swan.

10 Hay to Kington

The River Wye is broad and shallow at Hay and we can
reflect upon the changing scene from fine woods and romantic
gorges near Tintern to these pastoral landscapes here, and
recall those words of Wordsworth:

How oft in spirit have I turned to thee
O sylvan Wye! Thou wanderer through the woods
How often has my spirit turned to thee!

13 July 1798

Regretfully we have to turn away from the Wye when we
leave Hay.

Clyro

The river is crossed by a lofty bridge that carries the road
into Powys to Clyro (Cleirwy), only a mile away. On the
approach to this pleasant little village is a tree-clad knoll
concealing a motte-and-bailey – all that remains of the Norman
castle There is a good modern pottery in the village, but
Clyro is best known as the home of the Rev Francis Kilvert,
who was curate here from 1865–72.

Kilvert lived at 'Ashbrook House' opposite the Baskerville
Arms (called the Swan Inn in his day) and here began to write
his well-known Diaries, nine full volumes between 1870–9,
vividly portraying the simple country life in this area of the
Welsh Border in mid-Victorian days. The names of the farms in
this large parish which stretched over Clyro Hill, and Kilvert's
encounters with the peasants who lived in them, are familiar to
his readers. He was such a keen observer of the scenery and
atmosphere of the local countryside that this district is full of
romance for the Kilvert addict.

Hay to Gladestry

The Offa's Dyke Path does not visit Clyro but passes it to the
E, following the banks of the river for 2 miles, past a huge 25
acre Roman fort called Gaer.

You leave the Wye at a bend in the river and cross the
Hereford road, and enter a region of moorland hills and valleys
almost wholly unknown. Many twisting lanes lead up into the
hills, the 'stony narrow green-arched lanes' with their 'vista
to the blue mountains' which Kilvert so often describes.

On your way north to Newchurch you pass St Michael's Chapel
at Bettws Clyro, now isolated in a field with views across the

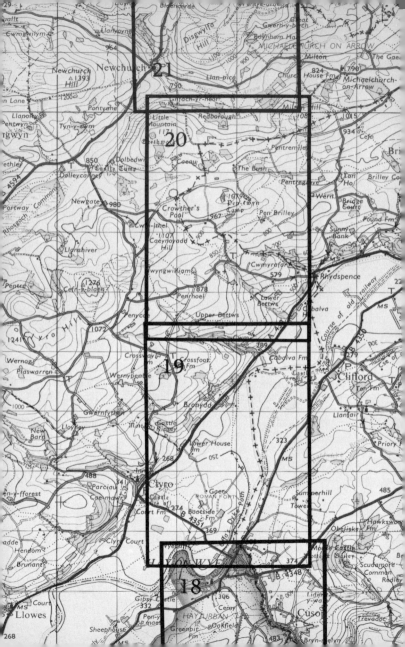

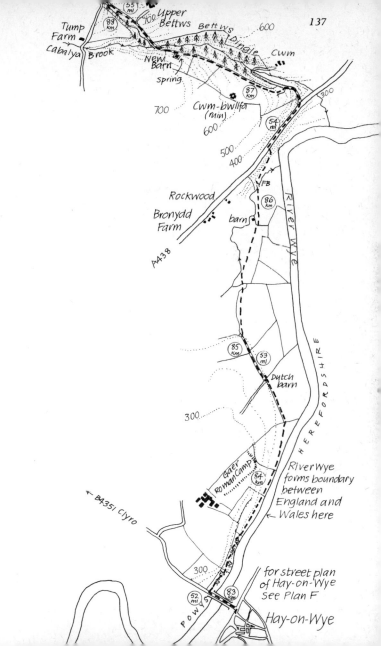

Tump Farm

Cabalva Brook

Upper Bettws

Bettws Dingle

Cwm

New Barn

spring

Cwm-bwllfa (ruin)

700

600

500

400

300

Rockwood

Bronydd Farm

barn

FB

A438

River Wye

Dutch barn

300

Gaer Roman Camp

← B4351 Clyro

River Wye forms boundary between England and Wales here ←

300

HEREFORDSHIRE

for street plan of Hay-on-Wye see Plan F

Hay-on-Wye

POWYS

55 ml · *89 km* · *87 km* · *54 ml* · *86 km* · *85 km* · *53 ml* · *84 km* · *83 km* · *52 ml*

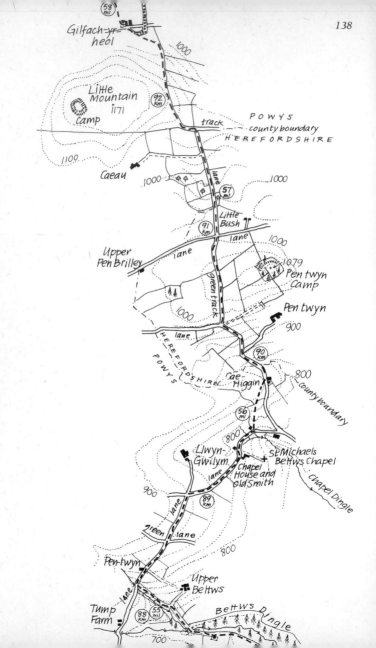

Wye. Francis Kilvert took services here when curate of Clyro:
the key may be obtained from Llwyn-Gwilym Farm.

For a short distance you are back in Herefordshire and pass
Pen-Twyn Camp, then you return to Powys for the gentle
climb up to Little Mountain. There is a strange little earthwork
to the W of the summit, and from here there are satisfying
views of the Black Mountains escarpment and Mynydd Troed,
with the richly timbered Wye valley in the foreground. To
the SW is a view over Rhos-goch bog to Painscastle where
Henry III built a castle in 1231.

A short descent brings you into the small hamlet of
Newchurch in the valley of the River Arrow, where Kilvert
saw the gorse that 'flamed fiery gold' and the lapwings
'squirling and wailing' as he went to visit his parishioners,
and then there is a climb up to Disgwylfa Hill, a pleasant
stretch of hill-common, grazing ground for moorland ponies.

The Path continues northwards towards Gladestry, but just
to the E on the country boundary lies the village of Huntington.
Description of route continues on p 141.

Huntington
Huntington was a medieval borough whose history and
fortune was closely related to that of Kington, 3 miles away,
and we shall take a closer look at this relationship when we
consider the history of this latter town.

Huntington Castle was built about 1230 and its remains
suggest a round keep on a motte 40 yds in diameter and 30 ft
high, and a curtain wall, in one place 20 ft high, with round
towers enclosing an oval inner bailey. There is a crescent-shaped
outer bailey further to the NE.

The Church is dedicated to St Thomas of Canterbury and is
probably of 13c date. It stands 4 miles S of the castle, outside
the likely defences of the 'town'. The town was ravaged by
Mortimer and Prince Edward in 1264 because of the adherence
of the Lord – Humphrey de Bohun – to Simon de Montfort.

Gladestry
Gladestry lies on the Path, a large scattered village occupying
both banks of its brook, and a meeting place of several roads.

You come off the hill beside Stone House Farm – where the
route of the Path is confusing – a Georgian house with seven

sash windows all in a row.

Gladestry Court in the village is a rebuilt farmhouse on the site of the former Manor, and it contains an elegant late 17c oak staircase and panelling. Not to be confused is the similarly named The Court of Gladestry, a farmhouse on the NW side of the village. It was the home of Sir Gelli Meyrick who owned Radnor Forest; he was executed in 1600 for participating in Essex's rebellion.

There is a shop in the village with Gothic-revival ogee-headed stone windows, where the Baptists held services in the earliest days of Victoria's reign. The Church of St Mary has a fine light chancel with pairs of late Perpendicular windows on either side.

Gladestry to Kington

There is one hill between Gladestry and Kington and it is the highlight of this day's walk. The Hergest Ridge is 3 miles long and leads you right into Kington. (Hergest is pronounced Hargest, the 'g' hard.) Although it rises only 1400 ft high it gives wide views of the hills behind Kington and away to Radnor Forest. It is a glorious ridgeway on short cropped turf between bracken and gorse, fine open grazing land, and although the traverse may only take you a little over the hour it pays to linger to savour the landscape stretching out in front of you.

Away to the NW stretches Radnor Forest, an area of rounded green hills on the edge of the Elenith of Central Wales. Black Mixen, one of the highest hills at 2135 ft is topped by a TV mast, and the Forestry Commission seems to have taken the name of the area literally for they have blanketed the slopes with conifer plantations, with Bache Hill and the Whimble standing clear of the swelling green tide.

The Forest remains an island at the edge of the central peat moors of Wales, a spur of Powys thrusting itself eastward towards the Dyke in defiance of Offa, a country where sheep and horses still outnumber man.

The Hergest Ridge and Bradnor, Rushock and Herrock Hills are the outliers of the Forest and between them is the expanse of Radnor Vale, prey to invaders from England in any age. Remains of the years of struggle lie everywhere: small earthworks near New Radnor may date from Harold's invasion of 1064; mottes of the Normans stand at New Radnor and Burfa

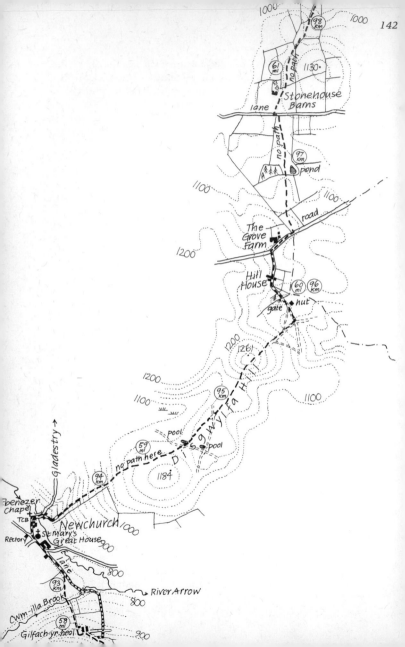

and elsewhere, and stories of Harold and Owen Glyndwr are
still told.
Description of route continues on p 153.

New Radnor/Maesyfed

New Radnor lies on the edge of the Vale at the foot of the hills.
It seems to have succeeded Old Radnor about the year 1250,
and it remained the county town until it itself was supplanted
by Presteigne.

Old Radnor/Pencraig

Old Radnor was a place of importance long before the rise of
New Radnor, but today there is only a cluster of houses near
the splendid parish church – claimed to be the finest in Wales.
The Church of St Stephen the Martyr is a landmark on the
edge of the Vale, standing on a hill-spur of volcanic rock at
840 ft a.s.l. Its fine Perpendicular tower – a rarity in Wales –
looks out over the plain. The church is large and is built in the
Late Decorated style, although it has some Norman details. The
interior is of unusual interest and has often been described in
superlatives. Indeed it merits some, in spite of the 19c restorers
who picked the painted figures off the screen and removed the
three-decked pulpit and the box pews.

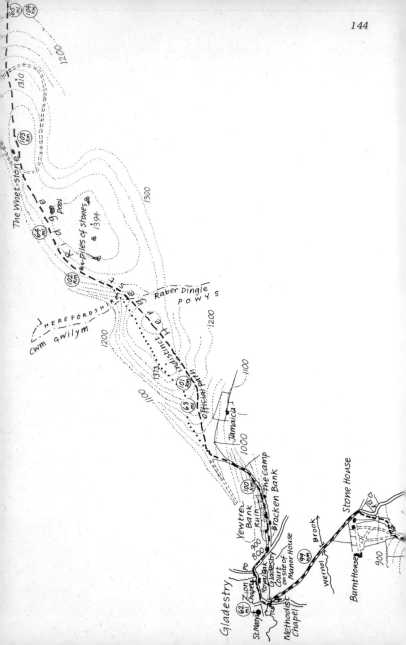

144

There is good late 15c carving in the roof, and an exceptionally beautiful Perpendicular screen of delicate craftsmanship
which extends across the breadth of the church. It is said to
have been made by a Gloucestershire school of carvers, and
has been compared with the screen at Cirencester. A quality of
lightness and balance is given by the matching aisles which are
continued to form chancel chapels. In the N chapel, now used
as a vestry, is a window, St Catherine in late medieval glass,
and 18c paintings of Moses and Aaron. In the S chapel is a
large monument by W Tyler, 1777, to accommodate which the
E window here was removed. The church contains a unique
Tudor organ-case – the oldest in the British Isles – about
1500, with several panels of 'linen-fold' carving, but with 19c
pipes and mechanism. Other items of interest are a crudely
fashioned pre-Norman font, medieval choir stalls, and six bells
of 1724 by Rudhall of Gloucester.

Kington is a small and ancient market town, set in pleasant hill country with the River Arrow flowing through. It remains important for its weekly sheep and cattle markets, and big autumn sales of Clun Forest and Kerry Hill sheep are held in the border town. (ECD Wednesday.)

Kington is said to derive its name from the time of Edward the Confessor who sent his forces into the area to avenge the sacking of Hereford on 14 October 1055 by the Welsh under Griffith ap Llewelyn, Prince of North Wales. The Welsh fled back across the Marches pursued by Harold, Earl of the West Saxons. As the people of Kington had probably joined in the raid on Hereford Harold claimed the land and town for himself and his King called it 'Kingtown'.

Kington and the adjoining manor of Huntington were granted by Henry I to Adam de Port in 1108. In 1173 Roger de Port rebelled against Henry II and some of his lands were granted to William de Braose. Kington was absorbed into the new Marcher Lordship of Huntington and Kington Castle was abandoned some time before 1230. The outlines of a new borough were sketched out at Huntington between the castle and the church, but Huntington failed to make any progress; one suspects that its growth was inhibited by the thriving settlement at Kington.

Kington was extended in about 1267 and referred to as 'Kington in the fields'. This is the compact little town with its long line of shops ranged along the High Street in one of the open fields outside the old town.

The large grey stone church of St Mary on a hill at the western end of the town indicates your arrival in Kington. You can take a short cut through the churchyard, avoiding part of the A44, and pay a visit.

The Norman S tower was built about 1200 and was once detached from the church. It now stands outside the S aisle, not quite on the axis, with its doorway inside the church. (The two truncated pyramids and the broach spire were rebuilt in 1794). The chancel is good Early English, with a group of 3 stepped, widely spaced lancet windows to the E and 6 evenly spaced smaller lancets to the N.

The nave was then rebuilt and given aisles – arcades of 5 bays with octagonal piers, each with different capitals. In the Victorian era unfortunate alterations were made by the addition of an outer N aisle and at the same time, 1874, the old N aisle was widened into what amounts to a N nave.

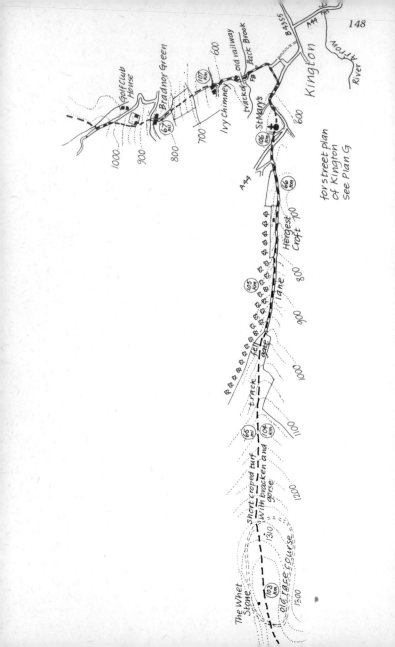

148

Kington

River Arrow

for street plan
of Kington
see Plan G

Golf Club House

Bradnor Green

Back Brook
600
old railway
Ivy Chimney
track
FB
St Mary's

700
800
900
1000

B4355
A44

A44

600

700
Hergest Croft
800
900

Lane
fell
track
gate

1000
1100
1100

1200
The Whet Stone
1300
1310
short cropped turf with bracken and gorse
1300
old race course

67 mi
107 Km
106 Km
66 Km
105 Km

65 mi
64 Km

103 Km

The south chancel chapel is of the Decorated period, and has a fine tomb with the alabaster figures of Thomas Vaughan and his wife Ellen. Vaughan fought on the Yorkist side and was killed at the Battle of Banbury in 1469. His vengeful wife was given the nickname Gethin ('Terrible'). While still in her teens she attended a fashionable archery tournament, and when her turn came she turned away from the target and shot her arrow through the heart of her brother's murderer. Their home was Hergest Court, between Kington and Huntington, and is reputed to be haunted by a black bloodhound. Perhaps the ghost of this hound still roams the hills: the tale was used by Conan Doyle for his Sherlock Holmes adventure *The Hound of the Baskervilles*. The Baskerville family was related to the Vaughans according to a tablet in the Vaughan Chapel.

Opposite the church is the Lady Margaret Hawkins Grammar School, founded in 1632 by one of Queen Elizabeth's ladies and wife of the Admiral. Church Road runs into Church Street and from here into the centre of the town there is little of interest, except for a widening of a side road called The Square. The Terrace here is an early 19c composition of 7 bays and 2½ storeys with a pretty central doorway of Tuscan columns and broken pediment – the entrance to the Tourist Board Information Office.

At the corner of Church Street and Mill Street is the ugly Market Hall of 1885 (by Kempson, replacing one of 1654 by John Abel the same designer of the Lady Hawkins' School in 1632) of red brick, with a Victorian Jubilee tower of 1897. Opposite, in Mill Street, is the Burton Hotel, red brick of 1851, with two porches across the pavement, and an added Assembly Room of 1856, still curiously Georgian in its simplicity.

High Street is narrow and often crowded and on market and cattle-auction days it is colourful and lively. It is lined with old houses, although many interesting buildings were either swept away or restored out of all recognition in the mid-Victorian period. Many have been re-fronted, like those in Monmouth, but some good Georgian houses escaped. In the High Street nos. 51–53 were formerly the 18c Chained Swan Inn, and the inn sign still exists on the 3rd-storey elevation. At the main junction in the town centre (Bridge Street forms a T with

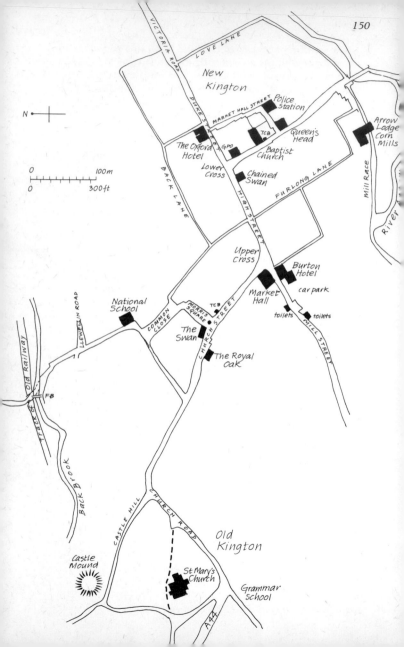

High Street) is the Town Hall, built in 1845 and now the Midland Bank. It has a five-bay centre, Corinthian pilasters and cornice looking down Bridge Street. Opposite stands a modest Georgian building, formerly the Albion House Hotel.

You can leave Kington either by retracing your steps to The Square and Common Close or by taking a narrow entry off High Street that leads to Back Lane and Common Close, ready to cross the Back Brook at Crooked Well.

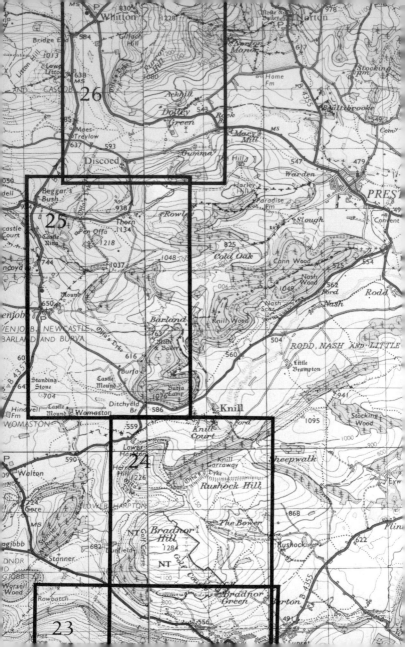

North of Kington to Montgomery the Dyke crosses a well-defined mountain mass isolated on the W from the Cambrian Mountains by the upper valleys of the Wye and Severn. This mass is structurally a high plateau, dissected by rivers which run from W to E, so the Dyke, cutting across the grain of the country, tends to present a switchback course. The earthwork shows no material breaks in continuity for more than 20 miles from Rushock Hill to the Kerry Hill ridgeway. The Dyke is built on the grand scale so often seen on moorland plateaux, and apart from a modern cross-track or two is undamaged. It is in a good state of preservation, being dug and built of Upper Silurian shales, but where it crosses narrow belts of alluvium in the valleys of the Lugg and Teme it has largely vanished, or was never built.

Just outside Kington you rejoin Offa's Dyke and you follow it for 30 miles over a considerable stretch of upland. Although there are traces of the Dyke at Lyonshall and beside the River Arrow to the E of Kington we do not meet the Dyke until we have climbed to the top of Rushock Hill, nearly 3 miles N of the town.

River Arrow to Hindwell Brook
In Kington retrace your steps along Church Street as far as The Square, then turn L into Common Close, R, then L again

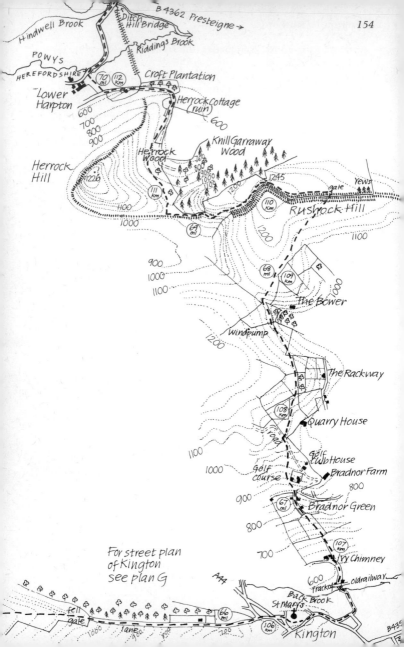

Hindwell Brook

B 4362 Presteigne →

Ditch Hill Bridge

Riddings Brook

POWYS
HEREFORDSHIRE

70 ml   112 km

Croft Plantation

Lower Harpton

Herrock Cottage (ruin)

600

600
700
800
900

Knill Garraway Wood

Herrock Wood

Herrock Hill

1226

111 km

69 ml

1100

1000

Yews

gate

1245

110 km

Rushock Hill

1200

1100

900

1000

1100

68 ml   109 km

The Bower

Windpump

1200

The Rackway

108 km

Quarry House

road

Golf Club House

Bradnor Farm

Golf course

1100

1000

800

900

67 ml

Bradnor Green

800

700

107 km

Ivy Chimney

For street plan
of Kington
see plan G

600   old railway
track

A44

Back Brook

St Mary's

fell
gate

lane

1000

66 ml

106 km

Kington

B43

at the Old National School to cross the River Arrow at Crooked
Well. Pass between the abutments of an old railway embankment
bridge and follow paths steeply up to a cluster of cottages at
Bradnor Green on the slopes of Bradnor Hill, National Trust
property and a splendid viewpoint. From the golf course are
views across to the Black Mountains, Radnor Forest and the
Malvern Hills.

A sunken path crosses the fairway and leads you round the
E side of Bradnor Hill, across the head of the Bower Dingle, and
makes for three yew trees on the skyline ahead. These three
yews, called The Three Sisters, crown the bank of the Dyke and
are reckoned as a landmark of great antiquity: they are visible
from great distances and provide a meeting point for parish
boundaries. They were planted in 18c for three Garbett sisters
of Knill Court, below to the N, but they are also known as
The Three Shepherds from a local legend that has them as a
memorial to three men who died in a sudden winter snowstorm
whilst tending their flocks. Yews are frequently seen on ancient
earthworks in S England and they are found elsewhere on the
Dyke and in the Wye valley area.

Here on Rushock Hill the Dyke is seen again. The Dyke comes
in from the E beyond the yews, where the hill has a definite
ridge, but here it widens into a flat and featureless plateau. The
alignment on the plateau is irregular and suggests a forest
cover, but it is direct, running almost due E-W. Though this
course is unusual – a NW course from Lyonshall up the Bower
Dingle to the col between Rushock and Herrock Hills would
have, it seems, provided a more direct route from the plain –
the layout is normal, and it maintains visual control of ground
to the S and W. The Dyke takes in the summit of Rushock Hill,
1245 ft, by an odd right-angled bend, and Fox held that this
summit was a point agreed between Offa and the opposing
Welsh Prince.

From the summit of Rushock Hill the Dyke returns to its
direct E-W alignment by first reaching for the head of a small
re-entrant of the Hollywell valley which separates Bradnor Hill
from Herrock Hill. On the shoulder of the hill there is a
definite lower ditch and upper spoil trench. Further down the
slope the Dyke is a considerable bank, apparently with an upper
ditch only, now occupied by a trackway.

On Bradnor Hill, looking N (p 153)
24 *Kington to Herrock Hill (p 154)*
Herrock Hill from Rushock Hill (pp 156, 157)

We leave the Dyke for a moment when we reach the saddle between Rushock and Herrock Hills. The Path does not visit the summit of Herrock Hill, 1226 ft, and the spectacular views from the steep gorsey slopes of this hill bastion are therefore normally missed. It is well worth the effort, however, to leave your pack at the col and to trace the Dyke to the summit of the hill, or take the path through bracken, to obtain the superb view.

The sweeping panorama over the Vale of Radnor to Radnor Forest is magnificent. Looking to N and W the Dyke can be seen on the S slope of Llanvair Hill, 12 miles away, and the Welsh mountains form the skyline. The hill also provides the best bird's-eye view of the Dyke itself to be seen anywhere – that over the Hindwell Brook, past Burfa to Evenjobb and beyond.

Offa's Dyke

Offa's Dyke Path

The course of the earthwork on Herrock Hill is remarkable: it is as though the builder of the Dyke, after turning his back on the Hereford Plain and before turning to the mountains, selected the most commanding position in the March as the angle of his frontier line, and kept high on it as a gesture of defiance. The Dyke occupies the best tactical position, following the hill-face round at between 1100 ft and 1200 ft, nearly to the crest, then passes down the NE ridge, descending the exceptionally steep slope directly, a most unusual method.

The Path gradually descends the eastern flank of Herrock Hill to the level of the Hindwell Valley. (If travelling from N to S be careful to take the correct path after the ruin of Herrock Cottage.) The line of the Dyke across the valley floor is very well defined, a fine work, broad and high, and forming the boundary between fields.

Hergest Ridge   Hanter Hill   Worsell Wood   Stanner Rocks

Offa's Dyke

Offa's Dyke Path

The Black Mountains   The Hergest Ridge

The objective of the Dyke after leaving Herrock Hill is a spur of Newcastle Hill, $2\frac{1}{2}$ miles away NNW, but it cannot take a direct route because two main obstacles intervene – Burfa Bank immediately opposite and the Evenjobb ravine – and these are the determining factors governing its layout. The entire traverse from the Hindwell Brook to the River Lugg is erratic on plan, but in actual fact the best that could be devised, having regard to the essential conditions which any alignment satisfactory to the engineer had to fulfil. It consistently maintained an ample view to the W and it avoided the crossing of ravines; the gradients are reasonably easy and it was possible to lay out the Dyke in straight stretches.

Hindwell Brook to River Lugg

The course of the Dyke across the alluvial flat of the Hindwell Brook is direct and avoids Burfa Bank ahead by taking a wide curve round the foot of this steep and isolated hill, gradually rising from valley level.

Ditch Hill Bridge spans both the Knobley and Hindwell Brooks, but no trace of the Dyke can be found between the streams and the quarry near Burfa Farm. It is uncertain whether the Dyke followed the line to the trackway or whether it contoured at a higher level before dipping steeply to the stream. Beyond the quarry the Dyke is seen as a small ridge with an upper ditch, persisting in dense scrub up a steepening slope, diagonally, to Burfa Farm, where it presents as a well defined berm running along the slope at the 700 ft level.

Old Burfa Farm is a medieval farmhouse and has been restored, and here the Dyke makes a change in alignment as it leaves the steep and wooded slopes of the hill behind.

Burfa Camp, high above the trees, is a characteristic work of a class associated with the Celts of the Early Iron Age, and in such a situation, on the edge of the lowlands, was almost certainly constructed before the Roman conquest of Wales. There is certainly nothing to suggest that to the designer of the Dyke this contour hill-fort, or the plateau ring-work of Castle Ring on Newcastle Hill, had any significance: it was just that the hill tops on which they stand form in themselves suitable trig. stations.

View from Herrock Hill, looking SW (p 158 top)
View from Herrock Hill, looking S (p 158 below)
View from Herrock Hill, looking NNW (p 159 top)
View from Herrock Hill, looking N (p 159 below)

The new alignment is taken from the highest point of Burfa Bank, 1062 ft, to the southern flank of the Evenjobb ravine – the obstacle in the direct line between Burfa Camp and Castle Ring. This alignment involves a gradual ascent from the 600 ft level to the 1000 ft contour. Between the ancient and modern Burfa Farms the Dyke is present, in a damaged condition, but

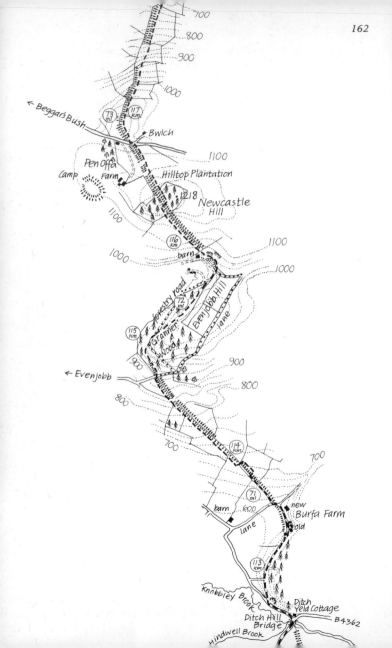

700

800

900

1000

← Beggar's Bush

73 mi

117 km

Bwlch

1100

Pen Offa
Camp
Farm

Hilltop Plantation

1100

1218

Newcastle
Hill

116 km

1100

1000

barn

1000

forestry road

72 mi

Granner
Wood

Evenjobb Hill

lane

115 km

← Evenjobb

900

900

800

800

700

114 km

700

71 mi

barn

600

new
Burfa Farm

lane

old

113 km

Knobbley Brook

Ditch
Yeld Cottage

Ditch Hill
Bridge

B4362

Hindwell Brook

traceable as a work once massive. Near the Burfa trackway junction the ditch has become over-deepened as a result of traffic on the lane. As the Dyke makes the long easy climb it has a high narrow-crested bank with W ditch: it is on a massive scale, the largest to be seen since leaving Tintern.

At about 900 ft the Dyke meets the Evenjobb – Discoed lane and here it is very well marked, a high bank with an unusually broad ditch and a massive counter scarp. The hill-road or ridgeway from Evenjobb to Discoed and Presteigne is crossed, here a holloway. This holloway certainly represents an ancient route from the upland to the Vale of Radnor, a haunt of men from the Early Bronze Age onwards, and the counterscarp bank here may be unrelated to the Dyke.

Once across the metalled lane the Dyke leaves the open country behind and enters Granner Wood on the flank of Evenjobb Hill and imperceptibly swings round the nose of the hill, taking a level line at about 1000 ft contour along the whole length of the steep NW face of the Evenjobb ravine. This green woodland way is on a berm with slight traces of a bank, and grows 7 ft high bracken and brambles in summer. The whole of this stretch is then so overgrown that it is better to take the lane running to the E over the top of Evenjobb Hill, rejoining the Dyke and Path at the head of Evenjobb Dingle.

You emerge from Granner Wood at the head of the Evenjobb Dingle, a broad berm leading you out into the open. There is a tangle of quarry roads, mounds and holes, because the former head of the ravine has been quarried away, and the Dyke is missing.

From the head of the ravine a N W course was taken, the line passing over Newcastle Hill to its northern spur just across the Beggar's Bush road. The immediate objective, the top of the hill, is visible from the ravine, and although the slope is steep in the rough near the quarries the line is corrected as the Dyke gains the hilltop. The Dyke is in open moorland pasture on both sides of the hilltop, but in the plantation it is of moderate size.

The view from the hilltop plantation is of a landscape which even in this superb countryside is exceptional. Behind you a falling sweep of downland ends abruptly at Granner Wood – a dark green wall, above and beyond which are Burfa, Herrock, Rushock, Bradnor and Hergest Hills. Slightly to the right Colva forms the background to a broad lowland patched with

colour and light, from which emerge the wooded slopes of lesser hills – Stanner, Old Radnor and Hanter. Further round to the W is the misty green of the Vale of Radnor, backed by the heights of Radnor Forest.

The Dyke is low and insignificant near Pen Offa, a mere hedge bank as it drops down the Beggar's Bush road at Bwlch, just avoiding a narrow but deep valley opening to the E. The Beggar's Bush road is the old ridgeway from Radnor Forest down to Presteigne and here it was deflected through a narrow opening which must have been intended as a 'frontier control point' for authorised traffic between Offa's kingdom and Wales.

The Dyke changes direction beyond the road on the spur of Newcastle Hill, and as the slope of the hill becomes steeper the Dyke grows in size, so that at 900 ft it is a massive bank of striking dimensions, continuing all the way down to Yew Tree Farm at Discoed.

Fox was in no doubt that the transition from the minor to the major scale, associated with a change from an irregular

line to a straight one, had a physiographical origin: the hill
top was forest and the slope was open cultivated country. The
course of the Dyke on the hillside was chosen with great skill.
It is bordered on the W by a dingle down which a brook runs
from Beggar's Bush, and the Dyke has a good field of view nearly
all the way along, that to the W being magnificent.
Description of route continues below.

Presteigne

Presteigne is an old world spot on the River Lugg, one of
the largest feeders of the Wye. Its houses are of a fairly uniform
Georgian style and the place is called Llanandras in Welsh,
although no Welsh is spoken in it.

The Church of St Andrew is a handsome building, Norman in
origin, but remodelled in the Decorated period of 15c. It
comprises nave with N and S aisles – part of the N wall and
two pillars in N aisle are Norman – chancel, Lady Chapel and
tower. In the tower is a fine peal of 8 bells (tenor weighs
14 cwt) on which the curfew is still rung. The curfew has been
rung in Presteigne for nearly 400 yrs, and it is one of the few
towns where the practice still continues.

The 'Radnorshire Arms' is a picturesque hotel in High Street,
and bears the date 1616 over its porch. It is said to have been
for a time the residence of Sir Charles Hatton, who had been
Queen Elizabeth I's secretary. It was first opened as an inn in
1792, and here the coaches used to stop on their way to and
from Aberystwyth.

River Lugg to River Teme

Between the valleys of the Lugg and the Teme, a distance of
5 miles, is a series of hills running N-S and forming a stretch
of upland from 1000–1300 ft in height. Furrow, Hawthorn and
Cwm-Whitton are isolated from the mountain mass to the W
by the Lugg Valley and a brook in a deep cwm flowing S to
join the Lugg at Whitton village. The hill flanking the Teme
valley, called Ffridd, is similarly isolated by a valley through
which runs the A488 and the Gwernaffel Brook, a tributary of
the Teme. The Dyke passes over the flattened crests of these
hills, taking a course which is fairly straight and level, and
which avoids the deeply serrated western scarps. The traverse
View from Evenjobb Hill, looking SE (p 164 top)
Offa's Dyke at Pen Offa, on Newcastle Hill, looking SE (p 164)
Offa's Dyke at Pen Offa, on Newcastle Hill, looking S (p 165)

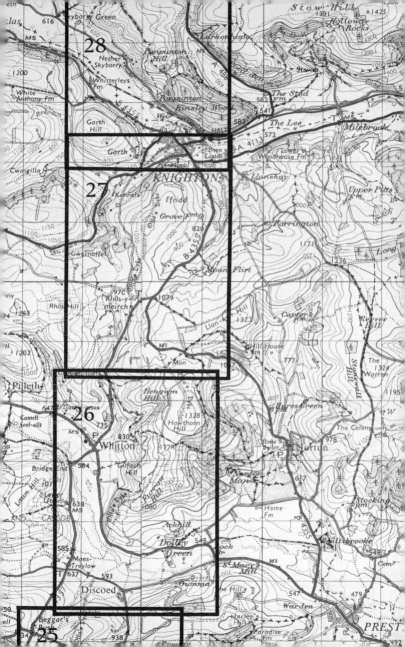

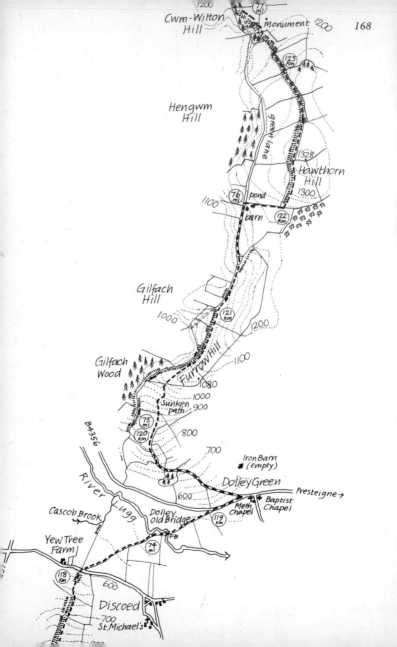

Cwm-Wilton Hill

Monument 1200

1200

(77 ml)

(123 km)

Hengwm Hill

green lane

1328

Hawthorn Hill

1300

1100

(76 ml) Pond

barn (122 km)

Gilfach Hill

1000

(121 km)

1200

Furrow Hill

1100

Gilfach Wood

1080

1000

Sunken Path 900

800

(75 ml)
(120 km)

700

Iron Barn (empty)

Dolley Green

Presteigne →

B4356

600

River Lugg

Meth. Chapel

Baptist Chapel

Cascob Brook

Dolley Old Bridge

(119 km)

Yew Tree Farm

FB

(74 ml)

(118 km)

600

Discoed

700

St. Michaels

is typical of the Offan engineer in this broken country.

There is no trace of the Dyke, nor could such be expected, on the narrow marshy flat of the Lugg valley. A hedge bank and the Cascob Brook indicate the alignment from Yew Tree Farm to the river, and a small section, showing a large Dyke, is visible on the steep slope between the Lugg and B4356 opposite the Cascob Brook. There is little doubt that the parish boundary marks the approximate or actual line of the Dyke on the steep hillside above the road, but definite traces are hard to find until you reach the 800 ft contour.

The Path follows meadow paths from Yew Tree Farm across the River Lugg by Dolley Old Bridge to Dolley Green on B4356, then doubles back to climb the hillside diagonally to Furrow Hill. Though small and faint the Dyke is traceable, the boundary fence approximately, but not actually, on the line of the Dyke. The weak Dyke faces up the Lugg valley towards Pilleth where Owain Glyndwr's forces won their bloodiest battle in 1402 – making the 'news from Wales' which sets the plot for Shakespeare's 'Henry IV, Part I'. The view further W is the familiar gaunt and bare hill country, but that to the E – as you climb higher to Hawthorn Hill – is of a well-watered and wooded land, dominated by an outlier of the mountain zone – Wapley Hill beyond Presteigne, steep scarped and crowned with a magnificent countour fort of Early Iron Age type.

From the top of Hawthorn Hill, 1328 ft, the views are magnificent – Kerry Hill and Radnor Forest to the W, to the S Newcastle, Herrock and many other hills, backed by the Black Mountains. Looking back you can see the line of the Dyke ascending the slope to Newcastle Hill, following the same alignment as the ascent from Furrow Hill to Hawthorn Hill. This shows that these two hills are key points in the layout. That the Dyke shows marked deflections from this alignment does not weaken the conclusion: the direct line having been chosen was adhered to as closely as the ground permitted, and when of necessity it departed from it (as in the Gilfach re-entrant and on the Furrow Hill spur) the line was regained as soon as possible.

On the crest of Hawthorn Hill the Dyke is on an ample scale and in alignment, but it is oddly constructed and poses an interesting problem. The ditch is on the Mercian, or wrong, side of the Dyke, and the line wavers about across the hill as though its builders had to guess their way through thick woodland.

From Hawthorn Hill the Dyke swings to cross the western end of the Llan-wen Hill ridge which links Ffridd to the higher plateau: the alignment across the slope of Cwm-Whitton Hill is direct and very cleverly chosen. The view of the W is ample save for a short stretch south of the Presteigne road where the Dyke passes behind Cwm-Whitton Hill.

The Dyke is indistinct as you cross the open moorland on the descent of the hill, but then it becomes a considerable work, with a broad shallow spoil trench on E and a narrower well defined ditch on W, as it passes between the Cwm-Whitton re-entrant and the head of Bach Dingle. The Monument on the hillside commemorates a railway-promoting landowner, Sir Richard Green Price MP, first Baronet of Radnor, 1803–87. It was largely through his efforts that the railway was constructed between Knighton and Llandrindod, as well as to Presteigne and New Radnor.

The Dyke passes through a belt of gorse and a clump of beech trees to cross the Presteigne road B4355 at its highest point. The Dyke was almost levelled in the early 19c when the road was made. In 19c a small stone was laid to identify the

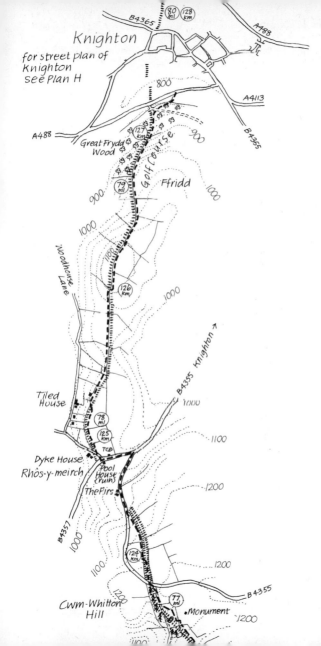

B4365
80 ml
128 km

Knighton

for street plan of
Knighton
see Plan H

A488

A4113

B4365

800

127 km

Great Frydd
Wood

900

Golf Course

900

79 ml

Ffridd

1000

1000

1000

Woodhouse Lane

126 km

1000

B4355 knighton →

Tiled
House

1000

78 ml

125 km

TCB

1100

Dyke House
Rhôs-y-meirch

Pool
House
(ruin)

The Firs

1200

B4357

1000

1100

124 km

1200

B4355

1200

Cwm-Whitton
Hill

1200

77 ml

Monument

1200

1000

feature to passers-by although it gives the Dyke the unlikely date of 757, the first year of Offa's reign.

You follow a short stretch of Dyke then come to the road again at 'The Firs'. You have to follow B4355 and turn L along B4357 to Rhos-y-meirch: between The Firs and Pool House the ploughed-down ridge is just visible in the fields.

From Rhos-y-Meirch there is the long gradual ascent to the summit of Ffridd, the last hill before Knighton. The southern end of this hill is a broad plateau, but above Jenkin Allis Farm this narrows and there is a narrow gap in the Dyke. This opening, just over 8 ft wide, is original, and the Dyke adjacent to the gap on either side is on an unusually massive scale. The transition is as striking as that noted in Caswell Wood near Tintern. No signs of the ancient trackway which may have passed through it are apparent – the natural crossing point of an ancient and almost certainly pre-Offa traffic line is a short distance to the S.

Both bank and ditch are on a grand scale until the crestline is crossed at about 1100 ft, and at this point, marked by pine trees, the Dyke changes again. It becomes an ordinary looking hedge bank and this character is maintained as the slope steepens, even when it leaves the open fields to enter Great Ffrydd Wood, traversing diagonally across the W face of Ffridd Hill and down into Knighton.

Description of route continues on p 181.

As you emerge from Great Ffrydd Wood Knighton reveals itself
as a huddle of dark grey stone houses with blue Welsh-slated
roofs clambering up and down steep and narrow streets in a
trough-like valley. (ECD Wednesday. Market – Thursday – pubs
open all day 1030 – 2230.)

Knighton is situated at the junction of the River Teme –
here the boundary between Powys and Shropshire – and
the Wilcome Brook, surrounded by high hills clad with wood
and pasture. A dominant mass, Garth Hill, 1130 ft, divides the
one valley from the other, and at its foot is a knoll, a moraine

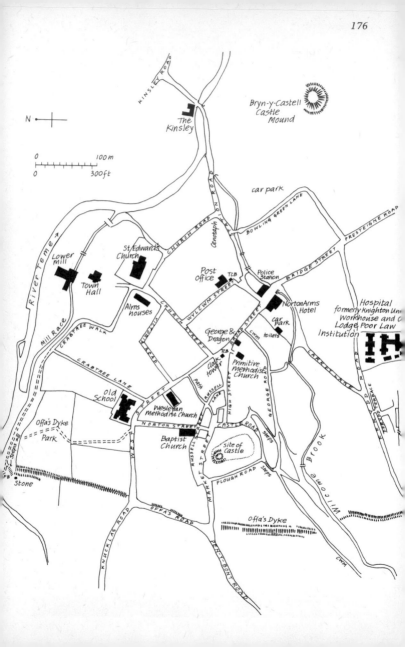

N

0 ____ 100 m
0 ____ 300ft

The Kinsley

Bryn-y-Castell Castle Mound

car park

Kinsley Road

Cenotaph Road

Church Road

Bowling Green Lane

Presteigne Road

River Teme

Lower Mill

St Edwards Church

Town Hall

Post Office

TCB

Police Station

Bridge Street

Norton Arms Hotel

Hospital formerly Knighton Union Workhouse and Cwm Lodge Poor Law Institution

Mill Race

Alms houses

Crabtree Walk

Wylcwm Street

George & Dragon

car park

toilets

cwm

Crabtree Lane

Church Road

Clock tower

Primitive Methodist Church

George Road

Larkey Lane

Ludlow Terrace

Old School

Russell Lane

High Street

Wylcwm Street

Path

Offa's Dyke Park

Wesleyan Methodist Church

Norton Street

Castle Road

Steps

Site of Castle

Wilcombe Brook

FB Steps

Stone

Baptist Church

Russell Street

Market Street

Plough Road

Steps

cwm

Knucklas Road

Offa's Road

Penybont Road

Offa's Dyke

hillock, the crest of which is 80 ft above the streams. Along the westward face of this knoll, fronting Garth Hill, Offa's Dyke is straightly aligned. The old town occupies the eastern face of the knoll, the medieval castle being situated at the highest point, between town and dyke. The Dyke, constructed on a noble scale, creates in the triangle of ground between the streams a very strong promontory fort, and it is not surprising that a Saxon town – which the Welsh called Tref-y-Clawdd – meaning 'Town on the Dyke' – should have sprung up within these natural and artificial defences.

The Normans may have established their first castle on the mound called Bryn-y-castell to the E of the town, but the place was deserted for over 30 years after the Welsh ravages of 1052–5. It is possible that these defences were later re-occupied, but in 1182 a new castle was built, of which there are now but the scantiest traces on Castle Bank. The church was built about the same time for its dedication to 'St Edward, King and Martyr' must be associated, not with Edward's martyrdom in 978, but with the presentation of that saint's relics to Leominster Priory when Henry I re-founded it.

King John disposed of the manor, first to Llywelyn the Great then to de Erdinton, who disposed of it to the Mortimers of Wigmore. They scored heavily over the county town of Presteigne, 7 miles away, when in 1230 they obtained a charter for an autumn fair, which is today one of the largest in Wales. In 1260 a grant of tolls for walling the town came too late to save it from being burnt by the Welsh. There is no trace of a wall built with the next grant in 1272, although the townsfolk are said to have defended their 'strong wall' against Owen Glyndwr's men in 1402. The Mortimers seem to have abandoned the castle about 1304 in favour of Knucklas, $2\frac{1}{2}$ miles up the valley, where they also tried to establish a borough.

It appears that most of the town was grouped on the hillock around the outer bailey of the castle, and Market Street and High Street occupy this area of the town. At the bottom of High Street is one of those dreadful municipal clock-towers, similar to that we saw in Hay. Many Welsh border towns possess a specimen – Rhayader, Machynlleth, Clun and Ruthin are a few – all of which are made to similar repulsive patterns.

Church Street leads off High Street towards St Edwards, standing on the edge of the town near the banks of the Teme. It is double-naved and has a Norman tower, its timbered belfry

H *Knighton*

typical of those found in Herefordshire. The lower portion of
the church dates from mid-12c, but the upper portion has been
restored from time to time, the present nave and chancel being
built between 1876–97.

The Dyke in Knighton

A stretch of A488, called Offa's Road, is on the line of the
ditch, and it turns away at the road junction with Market
Street. This is the highest point of the Dyke on the knoll, and
it can be seen dropping down to the Wilcome Brook and up the
other side.

The knoll is steep-sided where it borders the Teme: on the
edge of this the Dyke appears as a high narrow ridge with W
ditch, the line chosen through Offa's Dyke Park being a very
favourable one since the ground falls sharply to the W. Rising
to a higher level the W ditch is in the gardens of a row of
houses and the bank forms their boundary with the meadow.

The crossing point of the Teme is similar in geographical
character to the crossing points of the Edenhope and Mainstone
brooks further north. It is more advantageous in that the line

chosen avoids the weaknesses present in the others – the passage across the foot of an eastward facing spur: it is less advantageous in that two streams have to be crossed instead of one.

Knighton is nearly mid-way on the Offa's Dyke Path and the Offa's Dyke Park was the site of the official opening ceremony on 10 July 1971, commemorated by a stone monolith. This park was created in 1970 by the Tref-y-Clawdd Society because it was threatened by factory extensions. The new society took their name from the old Welsh name for Knighton – Tref-y-Clawdd. The Youth Hostels Association have bought the old village primary school adjoining the Park which now houses the Offa's Dyke Association's office and Mid-Wales Tourism Council Information Centre. A youth hostel is likely to be created in the old school by 1976.

River Teme to River Clun

The Dyke does not appear on the Shropshire side of the
Teme until well up on Panpunton Hill, some 400 ft higher.
However, a parish boundary follows the line of the Dyke from
the river steeply up through Kinsley Wood, and although no
trace of the Dyke has been found in the wood it seems that this
could have been a likely route of the earthwork. Another
possible course follows the W margin of the wood from
Panpunton on A488, but again traces of a bank in the required
direction between river and road are absent.

You leave Knighton therefore by taking a riverside path
restored by the Tref-y-Clawdd Society, crossing the river by
footbridge then across the railway to B4355, which used to be
the main road from Gloucester to Montgomery. Go up the steep
hillside opposite keeping the edge of Kinsley Wood on your
R, and at about 1100 ft you pick up faint traces of the Dyke on
its diagonal ascent across Panpunton Hill. A cairn – unusual for
this countryside – gives a good birds-eye view of Knighton. It
was erected by local people at the time of the opening of the
Path and stands at the farthest point of the Dyke visible from
the Park.

On Panpunton Hill the constructional features of the Dyke
suggest that the earthwork was in the mind of its builders a
boundary bank. The E ditch is irregular, more a succession of
spoil holes than an element of the structure, and all that was
necessary was that the bank should be sufficiently defined to
mark the frontier through what was doubtless forest. Where the
Dyke crossed open, probably arable, land as on Skyborry Spur,
material was taken from both sides to ensure clear definition.

The Dyke follows along the crest-edge of the plateau, once
more taking a sinuous course, forming field boundaries
between arable (plateau) and downland (slope) across the
Skyborry Spur. Across the neck of the spur and along the
edge of a pine wood, then the Dyke crosses a track before
going over an open pasture field and another belt of fir trees
to the head of the tremendous gorge of Cwm-Sanaham, whose
stream lies 450 ft below. The Dyke is traceable with difficulty
round the head of the cwm to a scarp on the N side, defined
by a belt of larch woodland. It then climbs sharply up a rocky
slope then follows another steep scarp to the top of Cwm
Sanaham Hill.

The views from the top to the W are superb. You can
look down on to the winding Teme, with the railway sweeping

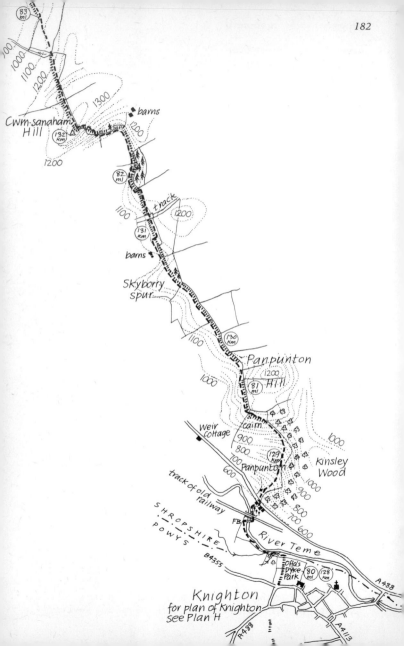

83 m¹

700
1000
1100
1200
1300

barns

1200

Cwm-sanaham
Hill

132 Km

1200

82 mi

1100

track

1200

131 Km

barns

Skyborry
spur

1100

130 Km

Panpunton

1200

81 mi Hill

1000

cairn

Weir
Cottage

900
800
700
600

129 Km

Panpunton

1000

Kinsley
Wood

1000

track of old railway

800

700 600

FB

S H R O P S H I R E

P O W Y S

B4355

River Teme

Offa's
Dyke
Park

80 mi 128 Km

A 488

Knighton
for plan of Knighton
see Plan H

B4 4 8

A4113

along to the viaduct below Knucklas' Castle Hill and into the hills.

There is a tradition that the long vanished castle of Knucklas was Caer Gogyrfan, from which Guinevere married King Arthur. In the 15c Llanstephen manuscript, in which the marriage is described, it says her father was a local giant known as Gogyrfan or Cogfran Gawr. The camp is set on a lofty, isolated hill, with an almost sheer drop of 300 ft on either side. The little village below was once one of the group of 'Radnor Boroughs' entitled to send a Member to Parliament, and this practice lasted between 1542 and 1880.

A little further up the Teme Valley is the village of Llanfair Waterdine, its church and inn squarely facing each other on opposite sides of the road.

The church suffered the usual fate at the hand of the 'restorers' but fortunately a wealth of good woodwork was preserved. There is a magnificent portion of the original rood screen, dating from about 1500, which has survived without being mutilated. It is finely carved with foliage, bunches of grapes, figures of men and women and a collection of animals — pigs, rabbits, dogs and even a lion and a dragon. It now does

Panpunton Hill

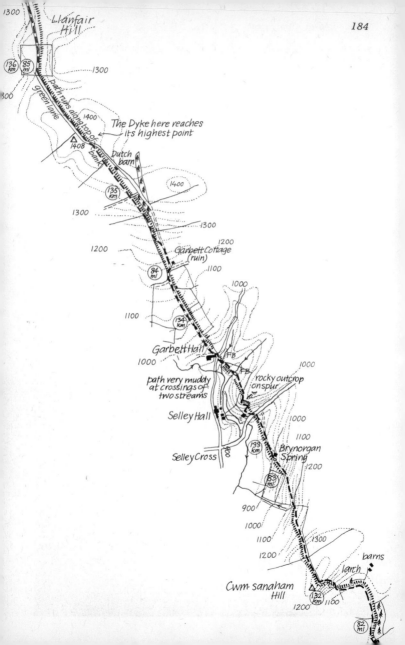

Llanfair Hill

1300

136 km   85 ml

300

Path runs along top of green lane

1300

1400

The Dyke here reaches its highest point

△ 1408

Dutch barn

135 Km

1300

1300

1200

Garbett Cottage (ruin)

1200

1100

84 ml

1100

1100

134 km

1000

Garbett Hall   FB

1000   FB

path very muddy at crossings of two streams   rocky outcrop on spur

1000

Selley Hall

1000

1100

Selley Cross   133 km   Brynorgan Spring

900   1200

83 ml

900

1000

1100   1300

1200

barns

larch

Cwm sanaham Hill   △ 132 km   1100

1200   82 ml

duty as an altar rail, and bears a cryptic inscription which has caused a good deal of learned controversy:

SYR MADE AMURAC PICHGAR COL UNW AGOSOD ODDEC PUND CYRUFUDD

English, Welsh, Latin and Hebrew scholars have all had a go at translating it without being sure of success. The generally accepted English version is 'Sir Mathew and Meyrick Pichgar of Clun set it up for ten pounds together'.

Other interesting woodwork in the church are the pew ends, having the names of all the farms in the parish painted on them.

On the summit of Cwm Sanaham Hill, 1343 ft, the Dyke makes a remarkable alignment — it turns a right-angle, and the bank contains a small enclosure, like a watchman's post. As this site does not command the valley Fox thought it to be a post-Offan work, perhaps for use when a beacon was lit on the top.

The alignment from Cwm Sanaham to Llanfair Hill is well chosen: the eastern facing slopes behind Selly Hall were avoided and the line is direct, convenient, and straightness has not been sacrificed. On the Cwm Sanaham plateau the Dyke is faint, likewise another stretch on the downhill slope. Notice how skilfully the Dyke is built across the head of a small ravine

carrying a stream, thus giving the easiest descent, diagonally, across a very steep slope to Brynorgan. There are magnificent views from this hillside and you can see the whole alignment to Llanfair Hill.

Beyond Brynorgan the Dyke is of modest scale, gradually descending through pasture fields, forming hedge boundaries, and sinking gently to the floor of a side valley to a spring at the Selly Cross road. There are some awkward crossings of little spurs with deeply dissected side valleys in this locality – now provided with footbridges and stiles, although approaches are muddy and overgrown – and the Dyke's course and construction is most interesting. The Dyke crosses the road and climbs direct over a rocky scarp, swings round the tip of a spur on a tongue of high ground. The Selley Brook is divided into two branches, and between them the Dyke is on a fine scale, cutting across the nose of the dividing spur. Beyond the second branch of the brook the Dyke is seen as a rounded hump merging into the steep scarp, and you emerge on a trackway at Garbett Hall.

There is a long gradual climb in front of you and you follow a farm track alongside the Dyke, through an ill-drained field then through a field to where it is constructed on the grand scale. Beyond the ruins of Garbett Cottage the great bank climbs up through a larch wood to reach the level of the Llanfair moorland.

When the level upland (1350–1400 ft) of Llanfair Hill is reached the Dyke is less massive, but it is a fine structure and singularly perfect: one of the most magnificent stretches of its course. The Path follows the Dyke, and sometimes you are on one side of the lane which runs parallel, and sometimes on the other. In places the Dyke is 10 ft high with a deep ditch on the Welsh side; although no legal right of way exists upon it you can follow its crest, for stiles have been provided. From this open upland a wide stretch of country can be seen opening out. The Dyke can be seen climbing the dark and forbidding mass of Cwm Sanaham Hill and beyond the Teme valley all the great hills which the frontier has crossed – Ffridd, Hawthorn and Herrock – can be seen on a clear day. There is not a building in sight, except a hideous modern barn in the foreground.

The Dyke crosses the moorland track at 1408 ft – the highest point reached in the whole of its course – and goes straight over

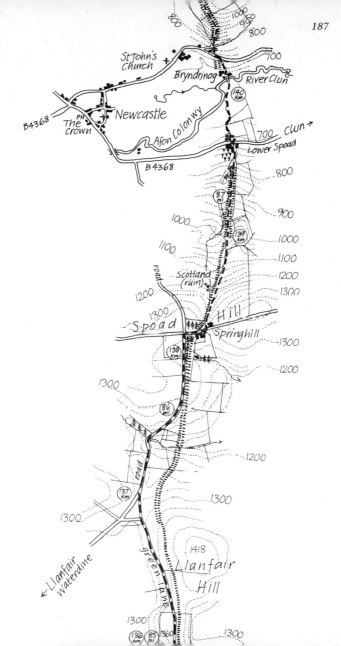

a narrow watershed. The Dyke turns away from the green lane at 1360 ft and as there is no right of way upon it we have to follow the lane, and when this reaches the road coming up from Llanfair Waterdine we have to follow it all the way to Springhill on Spoad Hill. This is most unfortunate, because the Llanfair-Springhill section is perhaps the most magnificent of all.

On the slope of Llanfair Hill the Dyke is massive, and for 700 yds it has a bank on the counterscarp. A little valley divides the moorland of Llanfair Hill from the cultivated fields of Spoad Hill: the gap at the brook, through which passes a parish boundary, is as narrow as possible. A straight stretch of Dyke then follows, 370 yds long, to a marshy hollow, the source of a rivulet, and the Dyke curves to avoid this and crosses the Spoad Hill road at Springhill.

Springhill stands on a road which follows the line of an ancient ridgeway all the way to Kerry Hill and the rolling upland of Clun Forest. There is no evidence of the original traffic-gap for this trackway, but the modern road may occupy the site.

Spoad Hill is a level plateau and the Dyke crosses it as a massive and finely preserved bank and ditch, especially in the pine wood opposite Springhill Farm. From the crest of Spoad Hill to the floor of the Clun valley the Dyke is a magnificent work and is throughout ditched on the W. A rivulet rises near Scotland and has carved a ravine, and in masterly fashion the earthwork takes advantage of the western-facing slope on the side of this little valley as it approaches Lower Spoad. The Dyke disappears in the orchard near the old quarry behind the farm.

Lower Spoad is one of the most interesting farmhouses along the Path, with some remarkable timber-work in the great cruck-built barn and a carved hunting scene in the farmhouse dining room. This carving is on a beam over the fireplace, and although it looks like a Norman lintel it dates from the Elizabethan age. The imaginative scene shows in the middle a doe and a stag facing each other. L and R of these are two hounds, one above the other, and L of R of these are three more hounds, again on top of each other. The technique resembles the plan-view rabbits and other lively creatures seen on the rood-screen remains in Llanfair Waterdine church, over the hill.

Brynorgan and Cwm Sanaham Hill (p 189 top)
On Llanfair Hill, looking N to Springhill, Spoad Hill (p 189 below)

Newcastle village lies ½ mile up the valley below the steep heights on which stand a prehistoric camp. It stands on B4368 which leads in 3 miles to Clun.

Description of path continues on p 195.

Clun

The town is spread over the banks of the river which gives its name not only to the town, the castle and the forest, but also to a group of four villages and hamlets:

Clunton, Clunbury, Clungerford and Clun
Are the quietest places under the sun

A E Houseman *A Shropshire Lad*

The small town was not always quiet and peaceful, and evidence of its stormy history is all around. Caractacus, the Ancient British chief, resisted the Romans hereabouts, and it was around Clun that Edric the Wild, the English earl, harried the Normans. The complex manor of Clun, composed of several separate units, suggests that it formed a tribal core in a Celtic society long before the settlement of this borderland by the Saxon state of Mercia. It may have been an important religious centre when the Celtic church was flourishing.

The large manor, of which Clun was the centre, was worth 25 lbs of silver a year to 'Wild Edric' but reduced to 3 lbs when he finally lost it to the Normans in about 1074. The land was awarded not by the Conqueror but by Earl Roger de Montgomery to Picot de Say, one of his chief followers. Picot de Say and his successors as Lords of Clun built their castle high on the bend.

Clun was never a base for any main operation against the Welsh, so it is somewhat surprising to find the de Says settling to work in early 12c to build a huge and expensive fortress for the 'capital' of their semi-independent Marcher Lordship. They built a great stone keep against the castle mound and the Norman nave pillars in the church. They probably were also responsible for the laying out of the streets by the castle, with a market place in the outer bailey. A chapel of St Thomas, established for the burgesses, gave its name to one of the town gates.

Fate decreed, with its usual irony, that the male line of the de Says should fail in the middle of 12c – (but they are

From Springhill, looking N (p 190 top)
Spoad Hill, Newcastle, from Graig Hill (p 190 below)

commemorated in the name of Stokesay Castle, 9 miles E, near
Craven Arms) – and the Lordship passed by marriage to William
Fitz Allan of Oswestry, a trusted follower of Henry II.

In 1204 his son obtained a royal charter from King John for
its Martinmas fair. From 1210–15 it was held by one of King
John's favourites, then having been taken by John Fitz Allan
it was attacked and burnt by King John in his campaign in
1216. Clun suffered again at the hands of Llewelyn in 1233. In
the later part of the 13c the Fitz Allans became Earls of
Arundel. Clun Castle ceased to be maintained as a baronial
residence and nobody was later sufficiently interested in it to
do any more than keep it in repair.

Clun had evolved into a borough by 1272 – the older of the
pair of boroughs – Clun and Bishops Castle – and it had a
Saturday market and fairs at Martinmas and Whitsun. Its
privileges were recognised in a Charter of Edmund, Earl of
Arundel, in 1325, after it had suffered in disputes with the
Mortimers, Lords of Wigmore, but the borough never had a
royal Charter.

For centuries Clun had been disputed between the English
and the Welsh: four times between 1195 and 1400 the Welsh
attacked the Castle and burned the town.

When the Marcher Lordships were abolished in 1536–42,
Clun was first placed in the new county of Montgomery, then
rejoined to Shropshire in 1546, to include it in the English
shire system.

St George's Church stands on the S side of the river, isolated
from the rest of the town and surrounded by a deep ditch.
There is no direct evidence of a parish church before the
Norman Conquest, but the position of the manor gave it the
mother church of a large number of medieval chapels that are
themselves separate parishes today, and suggests that there
was a church here in pre-Conquest times. The church has a
massive squat W tower worthy of a castle fortress. It was
occupied by Parliamentary forces during the Civil War and
partly burnt in a battle with the Royalists. After the Restoration
Charles II ordered a national collection to be made to pay for
repairs to the damage: the great west door dates from this
time and was consequently given the name of the Royal Door.
There is more Norman work in the church, but this and work of
later centuries was restored by G E Street in 1877. The Jacobean
pulpit has a horizontal sounding board and the altar a handsome

I *Clun*

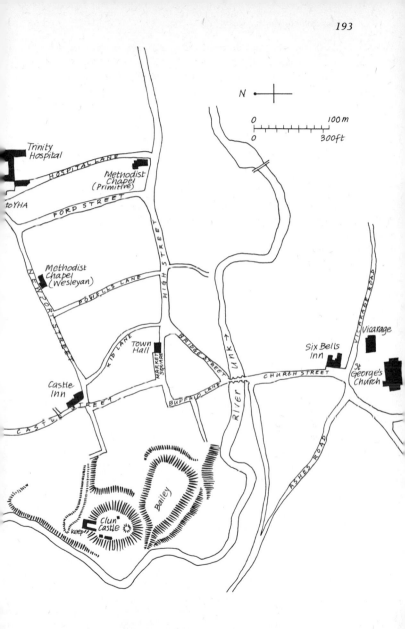

N

0   100m
0   300ft

Trinity Hospital

HOSPITAL LANE

Methodist Chapel (Primitive)

FORD STREET

to YHA

Methodist Chapel (Wesleyan)

POWELL'S LANE

NEWTOR STREET

HIGH STREET

KID LANE

Town Hall

BRIDGE STREET

RIVER UNK

Vicarage

Six Bells Inn

St George's Church

VICARAGE ROAD

CHURCH STREET

MARKET SQUARE

BUFFALO LANE

Castle Inn

CASTLE STREET

ASHES ROAD

Bailey

Clun Castle

keep

wood canopy. Outside the church is a copy of the original 17c lychgate.

The river is crossed by an ancient and picturesque saddle-backed bridge with five low arches separated by projecting angled piers which provide convenient recesses for pedestrians to take refuge from the traffic.

Clun Castle deserves preservation. The fortifications that remain consist of an impressive ruined Norman keep and some formidable earthworks. The keep is a rectangular tower built on the edge of a great mound: about 80 ft high and with walls 11 ft thick it has three storeys, and each floor had a fireplace and 5 windows. The entrance door was on the S side and a mural staircase led to three floors. The fortress was defended by the horse-shoe bends of the river, but on the landward side there was a ditch and defensive outworks of three platforms separated by moats.

On the eastern edge of the town are almshouses founded by Henry Howard, Earl of Northampton, in 1614. They are known as the Hospital of the Holy and Undivided Trinity.

Clun Forest

The River Clun traverses a vast area which consists not so much of a range of hills but a succession of rounded heights

split by valleys then merging into the wild undulating moorland
of Clun Forest. These hills rise as high as 1600 ft, culminating in
Kerry Hill, across the border. The Forest is noted for its
prehistoric relics – camps, stone circles, earthworks – and for
the famous breeds of mountain sheep, the Clun and the Kerry.
The Clun is related to the Radnor breed, short-limbed and low-
set, with speckled face and legs. The Kerry Hill have white
faces, black markings on nose and around the eyes.

River Clun to River Caebitra

N of the river the Dyke follows a switchback course across
a series of small steep valleys. Across the road just N of
Lower Spoad as a broad bank levelled to form a trackway, and
a very broad W ditch, it leads towards the River Clun, but after
a short while it runs out. There is no trace of the earthwork
visible across the alluvial flat of the Clun valley, but the Path
follows its approximate line. Bryndrinog farm stands on the N
bank of the river and the remains of the bank are visible on the
river's edge. Behind the farm the Dyke is seen as a magnificent
rampart, tree clad, with W ditch, and after a road is crossed it
continues through a field as a well-wooded green ridge with a
deep W ditch. It then crosses a track and passes upwards on to
the open downland of Graig Hill, crossing a steep dip to the
1100 ft contour on the edge of the hill crest. Here the Dyke is a
broad rounded bank, passing through a grove of pines and
between ploughed fields, and is very massive in one pasture
field. In one field the ground is wet, and a narrow gap in the
Dyke, probably original, permits the drainage from a boggy
patch to ooze through. The Dyke flanks the side of the hill
and is clearly visible across the rough moorland and scrub to
Bridge Farm, on an alignment which gives consistently wide
views to the W. Where a farm track crosses the Dyke the
earthwork is obliterated, but in the home-field of Bridge Farm
it is present as a high rounded ridge with a W ditch. As it
passes diagonally down the slope it is very straight and much
ploughed down though still clearly visible until it reaches
a stream.

At this point the valley we have been following meets
another at an acute angle, also with its little stream; the two

streams join, flowing eastward. The Dyke, coming round from
the low saddle across the flank of Graig Hill swings round the
end of the spur (Mount Bank) which divides these two streams
and ascends the flank of the second valley at right angles to its
previous course.

There is no trace of the earthwork on the narrow marshy flat
between the southern stream and the road. The present junction
of the streams is 100 yds above the original waters-meet. The
Dyke is carried across the foot of the Mount Bank spur as a
high ridge. Its construction blocked the natural course of the
northern stream (the pre-Offan channel of which is still
apparent), deflecting its waters into the ditch, which is
consequently very deep and steep sided.

Beyond a cottage the Path follows a farm track for a short
way and passes a quarry and house ruins. Above the 900 ft
contour the slope steepens and you cross a scrubby waste,
then you see the Dyke again in a commanding position across
the slope. The Dyke descends to cross a small lateral re-entrant
then climbs steeply and directly to turn abruptly round the
spur of Hergan Hill. Follow the crest of the great bank where it
runs as a terrace across the slope of the hill, heading for the

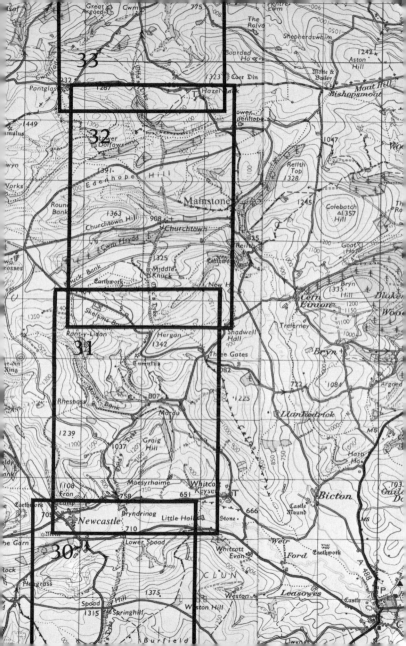

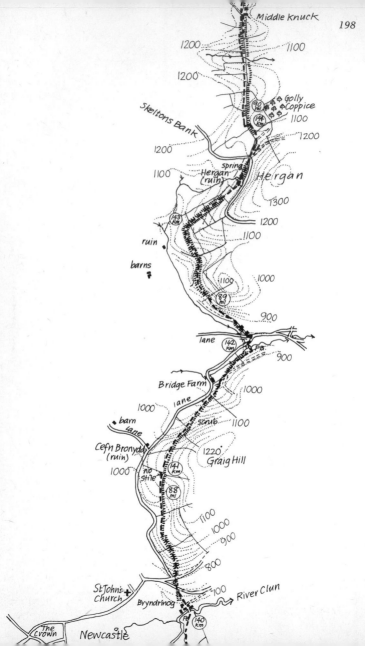

Middle Knuck

1200   1100

1200

Golly
Coppice

Skeltons Bank

1200   1100

1200

spring
Hergan
(ruin)

Hergan

1300

1200

1100

ruin

barns

1100   1000

900

lane

P.B.

900

Bridge Farm

1000

1000   lane

barn
lane

scrub

1100

Cefn Bronydd
(ruin)

1220
Graig Hill

1000   no
stile

1100

1000   900

800

St John's
Church

100   River Clun

Bryndrinog

P.B.

The
Crown   Newcastle

col at 1186 ft, between Hergan Hill and Skelton Bank in a nearly straight line. The Dyke is much damaged near the ruined cottage of Hergan, the ditch forming the trackway to it. Here there is a piped spring of cold clear water called Ffynnon-y-saint welling out of the bank, a delightful place to stop to admire the massive earthwork: here it has double dykes.

At the col where the Dyke crosses the ridgeway there is a stretch where a massive terrace bank comes up from one direction and a differently constructed stretch comes up from the other and the two ends of the Dyke are joined at a right-angle by a weak bank. Here we can study the two different constructional techniques.

This junction is awkward and incomplete and it presented Fox with a complicated problem. He rejected the idea that the Hergan Hill section was an earlier work, such as a short dyke across the Skelton Bank ridgeway, for, although situated partly on a col it is not carried far enough on the N side towards the ravine to obtain the protected flank which all cross-ridge dykes – such as those on the Kerry Hill ridgeway – require.

Fox takes the more acceptable explanation that there were two gangs at work between Hergan and Middle Knuck. The gang which carried out the Hergan section finished on the

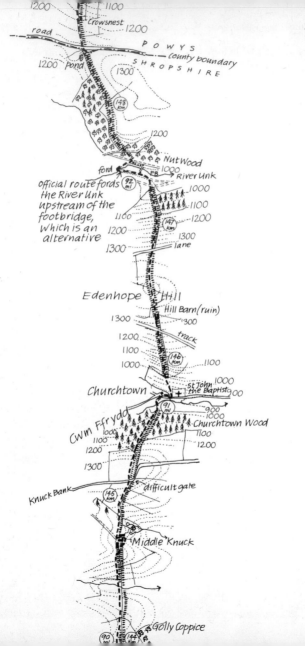

1200   1100
Crowsnest   1200
road
1200   Pond

P O W Y S
county boundary
S H R O P S H I R E
1300

148 Km

1200

Nut Wood
1000
ford   FB   River Unk
92 m

official route fords
the River Unk
upstream of the
footbridge,
which is an
alternative

1000
1100
1100   1200
147 Km
1200   1300
1300   lane

Edenhope   Hill
Hill Barn (ruin)
1300   1300
1200   track
1100
1000   146 Km   1100

1000
Churchtown   St John
the Baptist   900
91 m   900
1000
Cwm Ffrydd   Churchtown Wood
1000   1100
1100   1200
1200
1300

Knuck Bank   145 Km   difficult gate

Middle Knuck

Golly Coppice
90 m   144

col as instructed and left the gang to the north to join up
when they got there. Fox had no doubt the Hergan section
was finished first, and the builder of the northern portion was
forced to diverge from what he naturally regarded as the
ideal line, in order to link up. Priority was probably given to
the Hergan gang as it was a more important portion in the
mountain zone. The Dyke here appears to embody the principles
of Mercian defensive works and was probably constructed by
the same gangs who built the defensive outer works on the
Kerry Hill ridgeway. The portion coming from Middle Knuck
on the other hand is less carefully constructed and is just
sufficient to define the line of the boundary.

From the River Clun to Hergan, a stretch of over 2 miles, the
engineer of the Dyke had found convenient western facing slopes
around Graig Hill and Hergan Hill, but this advantageous route
involved the difficulties of crossing of eastward facing valleys
between Skelton Bank and Knuck Bank, so an alignment was
made passing though Middle Knuck to avoid these steep slopes.

The two stretches of Dyke follow straight alignments, but
the short link between them forms the odd right-angle. This
short link shows three gaps of which the middle one (that on
the parish boundary) may be original, and it swings round the
head of the wooded ravine to join the main alignment. The
Dyke then ascends a gentle slope, across a patch of moorland

where it presents a high narrow ridge, fairly well preserved.
It descends sharply, on a moderate scale, to a small hollow
down which a rivulet flows. The gap at the stream is only
23 ft wide. Beyond, the Dyke ascends another steep slope to
reach Middle Knuck Farm, where it is damaged and gapped.
Note how all the older farm buildings are to the E of the Dyke.

Cross the farm track and keep to the crest of the Dyke as it
crosses a spring in a small dingle, then climb steeply to the lane
on the Knuck Bank ridge. The Dyke then descends a very steep
hillside into Cwm Ffrydd, the narrow valley of the Mainstone
Brook, through a break in the wood, and is seen beyond rising
to Edenhope Hill. Throughout this portion the Dyke is carried
out on a grand scale, and is complete save on the valley floor.
The Mainstone valley is 300 ft below the shoulders of the hills
which flank it. The hamlet of Churchtown is at the point
where two steep ravines, separated by the high whale-backed
ridge of Churchtown Hill meet, and the Dyke is aligned on this
point, thus avoiding the switchback which a straight alignment
between Hergan and the Kerry Hill ridgeway would have
involved. This gives a diagonal descent and ascent which are
almost always chosen on hillsides.

The 'ford' of the stream was the point of passage of the Dyke.
In the valley bottom you have to negotiate a field of junk to
reach Churchtown which consists of two cottages and a church
with fine woodwork. This church of St John the Baptist
belongs to the village of Mainstone, a good mile away. It is a
simple, aisleless building, and resting on the floor beside the
pulpit is the smooth granite boulder from which the village is
supposed to acquire its name. Another interesting possession
is an old clarinet and bassoon which were bought in 1828 and
for 50 years were used every Sunday to lead the singing.

The very steep climb out of the Mainstone valley leads to a
green lane running up from Mainstone to Edenhope Hill and
reaches the top of Edenhope Hill a little way beyond. The Dyke
follows a straight course up a gentle slope, on the full scale
characteristic of plateau country. Just before the green lane is
crossed there is a gap, possibly original, which almost certainly
permitted the passage of an ancient ridgeway. From the top of
the hill are superb views over Clun Forest and to the E are
views over to the Long Mynd and Stipperstones.

Cross the next road and go down the steep northern flank of Edenhope Hill towards the River Unk. The Dyke presents a striking appearance, a high narrow bank and well-marked W ditch on the steep slope. It is less sharply defined alongside a wood and is gapped by a track, 11 yds wide, although it is still well marked. Traces of the Dyke are difficult to find in the valley floor, which is probably swept by floods, but immediately beyond the Dyke runs nearly to the stream, the eroding action of which has destroyed a few yards of it.

The ascent through Nut Wood is steep and rough: fences, bracken, brambles and undergrowth may make it difficult to follow up to the Kerry Hill ridgeway. As it rises through the wood it crosses the steep slope diagonally, is first gapped by the shallow trackway to Upper Edenhope, then it presents a small berm on the lower (W) side of the bank and a well-marked ditch on the upper side. It is a fine stretch above the wood,

the W ditch and bank are well defined and of moderate size.
The Dyke follows a sinuous course, determined by the
contours, along the W face of the hill, to reach the Kerry Hill
ridgeway. Just before you reach the road and leave the open
moorland there is a gap in the Dyke, through which the
county boundary runs and across the hedge in an arable field

the Dyke is visible as a ploughed-down bank.

The Kerry Hill ridgeway must always have been one of the most important routes from Wales into England, leading as it does from the heart of the central mountain system of Wales into Shropshire without leaving the high plateau country and without negotiating a single stream. It forms the northern limit of the upland country stretching up from Radnor Forest, and the steep northern face of Kerry Hill presents a wall-like formation overlooking the valleys of the 'Vale' of Powys. The ridgeway passes through the Dyke by a gap obviously modern; but a few yards to the S of the point of passage, close to an ancient hedgerow, the high ridge of the Dyke abruptly terminates, presenting one flank of an original and very narrow opening – the original opening left for the passage of the ancient highway. The boundary between the counties (and England and Wales) confirm this view, as it is for miles coincident with the existing trackway, and it is sharply deflected from it near the Dyke, passing through the gap.

There is a group of earthworks in the Kerry Hill area which, though situated at a considerable distance from the Dyke – the nearest is over 2 miles away – merit attention. The chief of these are the cross-ridge dykes which span the Kerry ridgeway, shown on the ordnance maps as the Upper and Lower Short Ditches.

The Lower Short Ditch appears to be an earthwork skilfully sited by lowland folk as an outlying barrier against dwellers in the mountain zone, who used the ridgeway as a line of approach to their territory. A little further to the W, in Long Plantation is Wantyn Dyke, and further W again the Upper Short Ditch.

Cross-ridge dykes were not the only means employed by the lowlanders for dealing with the menace of attack from the Kerry Hill area. In the early Middle Ages the Bishops of Hereford had a castle at the lowland terminal of the ridgeway – Bishop's Castle – and they had previously constructed a motte and bailey – Bishop's Motte – on the ridge 2 miles E of the Dyke. At an earlier date a small ring-fort, known as Caer Din, was built only 1 mile E of the Dyke.

Fox thought it possible that the Kerry Hill ridges and the Caer Din Hill fort were of the same period and related to Offa's Dyke. It is a notable fact that Offa's Dyke is at no pains to cross the ridgeway at a favourable 'tactical' point, where the

Knuck Bank from Edenhope Hill, looking S

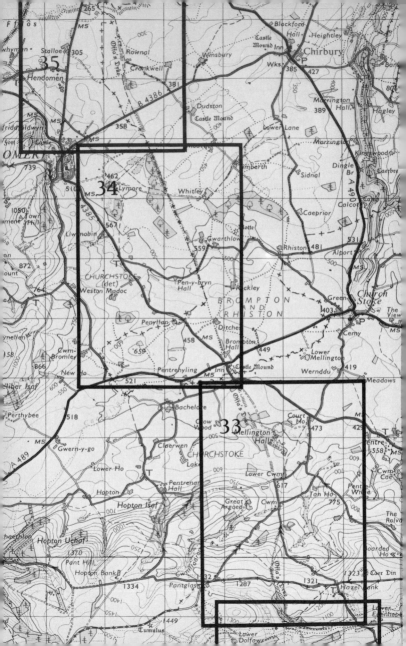

ridge is narrow, such as that chosen for the Lower Short Ditch.

It was the opinion and conclusion of Fox that these earth-works represent the military outpost works of the Mercians – in their defensive aspect – in the pre-Offan period when the tide of English conquest ebbed and flowed on the frontier; and that when the lowlanders had realised the limits of their advance and consolidated (and the military minded will wonder how they were held and maintained in a country which lent itself to the old tactics of the Welsh) Offa's Dyke formed an agreed boundary, and not a defensive barrier, across the debatable land.

The ridgeway is called Yr Hen Ffordd – the old road – and passes through a modern opening. From the ridgeway to Crowsnest we are in upland pasture: the Dyke is a high bank, the ditch being used as the farm access road. The Dyke begins a long descent to valley of the Caebitra – a drop of 700 ft in one mile – and the policy governing the layout of the Dyke is here strikingly illustrated. It follows a course sensitive to the bold relief of the country, keeping clear of the eastern facing re-entrant S of Drewin and giving magnificent views to the W.

The Dyke has been damaged by cultivation in the neighbourhood of Crowsnest, but its remains are present W

Kerry Hill   Ridgeway

Nut Wood

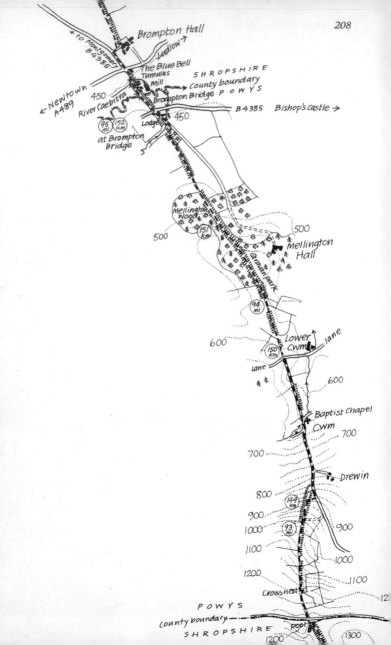

← to Montgomery

Brompton Hall

Ludlow →

B 4385

← Newtown
A 489

The Blue Bell
Tumulus
mill

SHROPSHIRE

County boundary
Brompton Bridge P O W Y S

450

River Caebitra

B 4385   Bishop's castle →

450

95 ml   152 km

Lodge

at Brompton
Bridge

Mellington
Wood

500

500

151 km

500

Mellington
Hall

Glandulas park

94 ml

600

Lower
Cwm

lane

150 km

lane

600

Baptist chapel

Cwm

700

700

700

Drewin

800

149 km

900

900

93 ml

1000

900

1100

1000

1200

1100

Crowsnest

12

P O W Y S

county boundary

SHROPSHIRE

pool

1200

1300

of the house. The field of view is limited at first, but as the Cwm-y-Lladron – the robbers ravine – opens out to the W so does the view, although the Dyke is on a well-marked reverse slope. It is a grassy ridge descending a steep slope and gives wide views over the Plain of Montgomery to Long Mountain and the Vale of Severn.

The Dyke reaches a lane which comes down from the Kerry Hill ridgeway and for several hundred yards, through the hamlet of Cwm, the road runs along the line of the Dyke. For a distance of over ½ mile through Cwm to the park of Mellington Hall the course of the Dyke is practically a straight line, and it may be assumed that it was laid out by an observer standing on the slope of the hill near Drewin farm. Apart from one small stretch the Dyke continues on its normal scale, and the earthwork is accompanied by the lane on a switch-back course.

At first both bank and ditch are seen in a wooded belt bordering the road, and a cottage near the Baptist Chapel stands on the ridge of the Dyke. By the Chapel the bank is very prominent and presents a massive fragment fronting the road.

Near Lower Cwm a by-way is crossed and deeply eroded, but later than the Dyke as its deflection at the crossing-point shows.

The stretch of Dyke through Mellington Park is very over-grown and in high summer it is better to leave the earthwork and pass through the caravan park, past the hotel and country club, and down the driveway, although you miss a fine stretch of Dyke.

The Dyke follows a sinuous but direct course by Mellington Park, a well-marked bank forming the W boundary of the Park for over 1 mile. It runs on a well-drained slope, entering Mellington Wood as a high undamaged ridge with a deep W ditch, a finely preserved stretch. At a typical point the overall breadth of the work is 54 ft and the scarp measures 20 ft on the slope. This character and condition is maintained until you leave the wood, and then it deteriorates. In parts the bank is poorly preserved, but this is due to its course over an ill-drained flat. The ditch forms a drainage channel and is over-deepened. When a stream comes in from the SW you leave the Dyke and walk along the Mellington Hall driveway and out of the park through the lodge gateway to join B4385 Bishops Castle – Montgomery road.

Between the lodge gateway and the River Caebitra is a stretch of Dyke at its full height, but beyond the river it has been entirely destroyed, doubtless when the adjacent motte and bailey castle was constructed (marked tumulus on OS maps, standing behind a white cottage). A mutilated fragment is then present just before a watercourse, and a deflection of this stream by the bridge preserves the alignment of the ditch. The Dyke is seen in the garden and orchard of the Bluebell Inn at Brompton and disappears at the crossroads with A489.

Montgomery can be visited by following B4385 for 3 miles from this junction at the Bluebell Inn. We may if we wish also travel B4385 in the opposite direction to Bishop's Castle.

It is convenient for the purpose of this Guide to describe Bishop's Castle and Montgomery here, although in practice it may be better to follow the Dyke for another $2\frac{1}{2}$ miles to the B4386 Chirbury – Montgomery road just E of the county town.

Description of the route follows on p 223

The Kerry Hill Ridgeway and Nut Wood from Edenhope Hill, looking N (p 207)

33 *Kerry Hill Ridgeway to Brompton (p 208)*

Nut Wood and the River Unk from Edenhope Hill, looking N
Edenhope Hill from Nut Wood, looking S (p 211)

Bishop's Castle

Bishop's Castle is half-town, half-village where black and white timber buildings mingle with Georgian brick. (MD Friday.) It clings to a steep little hillside, yet it is overtopped by the hills which surround it, the outlying hills of Clun Forest.

The town was originally known as Lydbury Castle and arose on the ecclesiastical estate of the Bishop of Hereford. The story of its growth is this:

King Ethelbert of East Anglia fell in love with Alfreda, the daughter of the Mercian King Offa, who built our Dyke. Offa approved of the match but his queen was jealous and determined

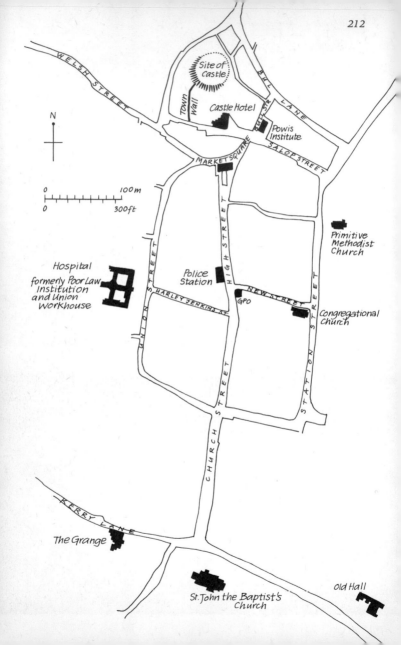

Site of Castle

WELSH STREET

Town Wall

Castle Hotel

Powis Institute

MARKET SQUARE

SALOP STREET

BAL LANE

N

0   100m
0   300ft

UNION STREET

HIGH STREET

Primitive Methodist Church

Hospital
formerly Poor Law Institution and Union Workhouse

Police Station

GPO

HARLEY JENKINS ST.

NEW STREET

Congregational Church

STATION STREET

CHURCH STREET

KERRY LANE

The Grange

St. John the Baptist's Church

Old Hall

to kill her daughter's suitor. She offered her prospective son-in-law some advice and invited him to her room where a seat had been specially prepared for him over a trapdoor. When Ethelbert fell helplessly into the pit below her guards stabbed him to death. The murdered King was buried in Hereford Cathedral and canonized as a saint, and his shrine became a resort for pilgrims seeking a cure for various kinds of diseases.

Among those restored to health at the shrine was Egwin Shakehead, whose ailment was indicated by his name. He was the Saxon lord of Lydbury North and in gratitude of being cured of his palsy he presented his manor of 18,000 acres to the Bishops of Hereford, about the year 792. It proved to be a most useful acquisition, for it was a natural market centre as well as a stronghold. The manor was protected by the Bishop's Motte, 2 miles to W on the Kerry Hill ridgeway, and by another fortress called Lea Castle, 2 miles to the E as well as its own castle.

Probably in Early Norman times Lea Castle was a residence and Bishop's Motte a frontier post, but when the new castle was built in 1120 the amenities of life and the necessity of defence were established here. The place was called Lydbury Castle and it was not until the late 13c that the name Bishop's Castle was established.

In the Anarchy it was held by Hugh Mortimer, who was compelled to retore it when Henry II suppressed his rebellion in 1155.

In 1249 Charters for market and fairs in his manor of Lydbury were granted to Bishop Peter de Aquablanca, one of the Savoyard favourites of Henry III. In 1263 he was ordered to

defend the castle against the Welsh, but in July it was stormed
by Richard of Arundel, Baron of Clun, then allied with Simon
de Montfort, who killed the Constable and plundered the
Grange and the whole manor and burnt the houses of the town.

The first reference to a borough and to the name of Bishop's
Castle come in a survey of 1285. It had little land and little to
show in trade or crafts; so dependent was it on outside trade
that when the Bishop was in residence there in 1290 he had to
send to Ludlow market for supplies.

There are few references to Bishop's Castle in the later
Middle Ages. In 1539 Leland found the castle 'well maintained,
set on a strong rock, but not very high', and that the town had
'a very celebrated market.' The castle still had 'thirteen rooms
covered with lead' (presumably in the keep, as well as a stable
tower and a prison tower.) In 1573 Queen Elizabeth I granted a
Charter of Incorporation, under which they sent MPs to
Westminster until 1832 and managed to survive as the smallest
municipal corporation in England until 1967.

The Church of St John was at first only a chapel of Lydbury
Manor, but it has a Norman tower and a fine early 13c doorway.
Very little original work remains for the church was fired and
ruined during the Civil War when the town was loyal to the
King.

The church stands at the lower end of the town, more than
600 yds S of the castle, separated by plots retaining the shapes
of curved open-field strips. These branch off from Church Street
and run parallel to the ancient Kerry Lane, which passes the
church. To the E of the church is the fine Tudor house, The
Old Hall, believed to be the birthplace of Edward Plowden,
builder of Plowden Hall, 4 miles SE.

As Church Street rises it becomes High Street and at the top
stands the 18c Town Hall forcing the road to bend past it. The
Town Hall is one of the smallest in England and has an
interesting prim façade, with the clock-tower above and
an old stone lock-up in its basement. Included in the town's
insignia are two fine silver maces, hallmarked 1697.

Beside the Town Hall is a narrow cobbled passage, straddled
by the aptly-named House on Crutches, another Tudor house
with its upper storey supported on two wooden posts. Another
Tudor house in the town is the Old Porch House and there are

several Georgian houses. The oldest inn in the town is probably the Three Tuns, whose history has been traced back to 1642 but may well go beyond. The inn is distinguished today by being one of the few left where the landlord still brews his own ale. The brewhouse stands beside the inn.

The Castle had been largely demolished before the Civil War broke out in 1642 and very little now remains apart from a few fragments of wall behind the shops at the head of High Street. The semi-circular street around the yard of the Castle Hotel must have been determined by the outline of the Motte.

Montgomery is the smallest county-town in Britain and quietly
drowses below the ruins of a castle built by Henry III as one of
the key points in attempts to conquer Wales.

From the long line of the Kerry Hills which form the northern
boundary of the high mass of Radnor and Clun Forests a spur
projects into the Severn valley, and terminates in an outcrop of
igneous rock forming a natural defensive position. To the NW
is the Severn Valley, to the SE is the wide Camlad corridor to
Bishop's Castle and to the NE the broad valley plain occupied
by the Rea Brook points towards Shrewsbury.

The terminal hill is occupied by a great Celtic 'Iron Age'
fort called Ffridd Faldwyn. The huge ramparts of the camp and
the elaborate SW entrance cannot fail to impress, and excavations carried out in 1928 and 1937–9 have shown that it was
in occupation for some considerable time before the Romans
arrived. The view embraces Cader Idris in the NW and Clee
Hill in the SE, and from here one can also see the remains of
Montgomery's other fortifications.

When the Romans came they built their camp on the bank of
the Severn, but nothing can be seen above ground except the
faint outline of the earth ramparts. The camp, known in later
times as Caer or Caer Fflos or Forden Caer, stands close by the
ancient ford of the River Severn at Rhyd Whyman which was
for ages the traditional meeting place for Welsh and English
battles and the scene of treaties and truces.

The first Norman settlement and stronghold was planted
close to the Roman camp in the years immediately after the
Conquest of England. Roger de Montgomery, one of William's
principal advisers and most resolute leaders in the Battle of
Hastings, was made Earl of Shrewsbury. He founded a castle
at Shrewsbury and made it his HQ, and in his attempts to
conquer the Welsh he pushed out along the Roman road
towards the Severn and built his motte-and-bailey earthwork
at Hen Domen, some time before 1086.

This Norman timber castle looked down on the site of the
Roman camp and has been accepted as the original site of
Montgomery. The Welsh captured it in 1095 from Roger's
brother Hugh. After suppressing the Earldom on 1102,
Henry I granted Montgomery Castle and barony to Baldwin de
Bollers, whose descendants held it until the death of Baldwin II
in 1207. The Welsh name 'Trefaldwyn' suggests that it may be
one of these Baldwins who established a borough here, but

Bishop's Castle. The House on Crutches

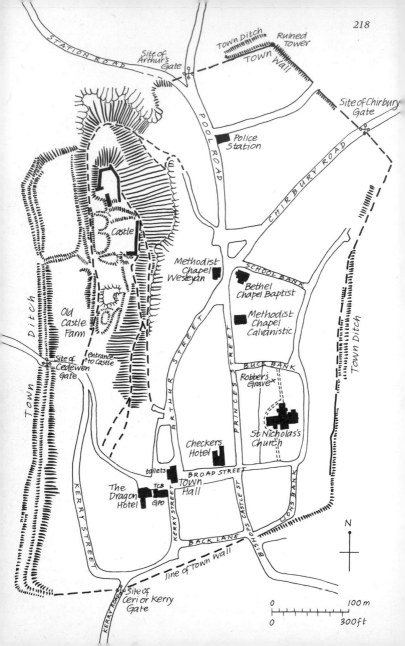

STATION ROAD

Town Ditch

Ruined Tower

Site of Arthur's Gate

TOWN WALL

POOL ROAD

Site of Chirbury Gate

Police Station

CHIRBURY ROAD

Castle

SCHOOL BANK

Methodist Chapel Wesleyan

Bethel Chapel Baptist

Methodist Chapel Calvanistic

TOWN DITCH

Old Castle Farm

Town Ditch

Site of Cedewen Gate

Entrance to Castle

BUCK BANK

Robber's Grave

ARTHUR STREET

PRINCES STREET

St Nicholas's Church

Checkers Hotel

toilets

BROAD STREET

Town Hall

The Dragon Hotel

TCB

GPO

KERRY STREET

BACK LANE

BISHOPS CASTLE ST

LIONS BANK

Line of Town Wall

KERRY STREET

Site of Ceri or Kerry Gate

N

0   100 m

0   300 ft

earlier excavations only showed evidence of wooden buildings suggesting a guard post rather than a baronial castle. Minor excavations have been going on at this site since 1960 in the hope of further discoveries.

Hen Domen was abandoned in 1220's when Henry III began the building of a new castle and the planting of a new town scarcely a mile to the S of the old settlements. It is not clear what motivated the rebuilding of Montgomery, but it was probably due to the resurgence of power in Wales in the early 13c under Llewelyn the Great. The forces of Llewelyn besieged Builth in 1223 and in the same year Henry III decided upon the building of a new castle in a much stronger position. The castle was completed in 1225, but was never captured by the Welsh, although the town suffered in subsequent raids.

A Borough Charter was promised in 1223 but was not formally granted by Henry III until 1227, and it was extended by Hubert de Burgh in 1229. The town was burnt by the Welsh in 1231, again in 1245, and yet again in 1257. It was also involved in the fighting between Simon de Montfort's followers and the Marcher Barons in 1264. The town's first defences were a ditch and a palisade, and this latter was removed and replaced by a stone wall in 1279. The town wall probably had towers at the corners and along the SW stretch, which was

difficult to defend. Almost all the stonework has disappeared, although traces were found in excavations in 1938 and 1939.

The castle is perched high on the precipitous crag above the town, but only a few fragments remain. The castle and the town lie directly in the way of the road from Shrewsbury and whoever lay in possession of them was master of the only effective road to Mid-Wales and the Coast.

The castle became the home of the Herberts. The end of 15c saw the rise of this powerful family, one of whom was made Steward of Montgomery, and his descendant, the Earl of Powis, is the present Lord of the Manor. George Herbert, the poet and divine, was born in the castle in 1593. His brother, Lord Herbert of Chirbury, was a distinguished diplomat who wrote poems in Latin and English and an amusing autobiography. Lord Herbert attempted to keep a philosophic neutrality during the Civil War and he surrendered the castle to the Parliament-arians in 1644 when Sir Thomas Myddleton was trying to recapture it, but it was not lost to the King until 1649. It was so badly damaged that it was no longer comfortable for the Herberts to live in it, and it was then abandoned and subsequently demolished.

The town nestles against the wooded bluff below the castle, now a remote and quiet backwater far removed from the main lines of communications and trade along the Severn valley. The structure of the medieval-planned town can be clearly traced between the castle and the parish church on the edge of the 'town ditch'. Apart from the castle and the church the town possesses no buildings earlier than 15c. There are many excellent little buildings, a few black and white cottages, Tudor, Elizabethan, Jacobean and Queen Anne, but most of the houses are un-spoilt Georgian. Broad Street, which is like a market square, is shut off at the W end by the fine late-Georgian Town Hall, and all about are Georgian features such as bow windows, dentil eaves, cornices, shop fronts, Venetian windows, 'Gothic' casements and cobbled pavement.

The interesting parish church of St Nicholas is worth inspecting for its rood-screen, its timber-framed barrel roofs and the Herbert monuments.

The church has a magnificence that seems out of proportion to the size of the town. The original building may be dated *c*1225 with transepts added at the end of the century. Most of the church dates from middle 14c but the tower was added in 1816 on the N side and the whole 'restored' by Street in

1875 – the tiled pavement and the rather crude glass, making the church dark, are trademarks of this period.

The western portion of the nave roof has hammer beams with arched principals and quatre-foil braces, while the eastern portion is a semi-circular waggon or barrel roof with oak ribs and coloured bosses which is very striking.

There is a fine 15c rood screen with richly decorated loft and carved Elizabethan gates. It was brought here by the Herberts from the abbey church at Chirbury, demolished at the Reformation.

In the S transept is the magnificent canopied tomb of the parents of George Herbert. He is in armour and she in an embroidered dress. Behind them kneel the figures of 8 children and underneath is a shrouded cadaver. Besides this, on the floor of the transept, are two medieval effigies. The earlier one is the smaller and shows the arms of the Mortimers on the jupon over the coat of mail. It is thought to be the effigy of Shakespeare's 'Revolted Mortimer', son-in-law of Owain Glyndwr. The other effigy is probably Sir Richard Herbert, great grandfather of George Herbert. Both figures have been restored and are covered with a reddish paint to give uniformity.

In the churchyard is a well-known spot where one John Newton Davies was buried, convicted of a robbery in 1821 but always protesting his innocence. As proof he swore that no grass would grow on the grave of a man wrongly condemned; and for a long time no grass grew on his own. Details of the story of the Robber's Grave are given in a pamphlet issued in the church.

K *Montgomery (p 218 and 219)*

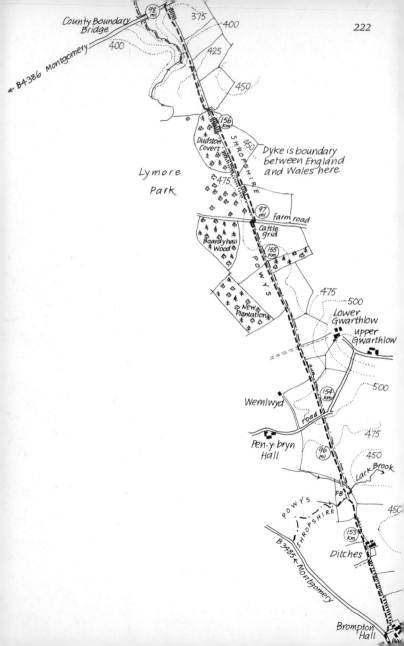

County Boundary
Bridge

← B4386 Montgomery

222

98 ml

375
400
425
450
400

156 Km

Dudston
Covert

450

SHROPSHIRE

Dyke is boundary
between England
and Wales here

Lymore
Park

475

97 ml

farm road

Cattle
grid

Boardyhall
Wood

155 Km

POWYS

475
500

New
Plantation

Lower
Gwarthlow

upper
Gwarthlow

154 Km

500

Wernlwyd

road

Pen-y-bryn
Hall

96 ml

475

450

Lack Brook

FB

POWYS

SHROPSHIRE

450

153 Km

B4385 ← Montgomery

Ditches

Brompton
Hall

River Caebitra to River Camlad

The Dyke crosses the Plain of Montgomery with brutal military
directness but without the deliberate impressiveness of parts of
the upland Dyke. Between A489 at Brompton and B4386 the
Dyke traverses a long stretch of plateau-like country, climbing
a hardly perceptible gradient of 60 ft in $1\frac{1}{4}$ miles then descending
140 ft in the next $1\frac{1}{4}$ miles.

Any traces of the Dyke have been eliminated in the
neighbourhood of Brompton Hall. The Dyke is well-marked
in a narrow strip of woodland, and the Path runs alongside in
the field as far as the track to Ditches farm. The bank of the
Dyke runs alongside the track, and passing the farm the work
is levelled. Ditches farm is a name that is a reminder of the
ancient name of Offa's Dyke – Offa's Ditch or Offediche
as it was recorded in 13c.

Leaving Ditches farm the Dyke is a high ridge and, approach-
ing the Lack Brook, it is as a low, flat, broad bank, well wooded.
The Lack Brook and an adjacent tributary stream here were
both doubtless canalized by the Dyke builder to pass at one
point, through a gap about 12 yds wide, but the tributary has
found another gap nearby.

At this point the boundary of England and Wales comes in
from the W, and the boundary follows the Dyke for 2 miles.
You continue along the line of the Dyke, alternately in Wales
and England, and sometimes right on the boundary.

Leaving the level of the Lack Brook, where the bank is much
spread, the Dyke forms a narrow belt of rough woodland but
as it rises to the lane both bank and W ditch are very well
defined. This contrast indicates how the underlying rock
dictates the condition of the Dyke. On the N flank of the small
valley Ordovician shales form the subsoil, giving an
exceptionally fine and clear-cut Dyke, but on the floor these
shales are overlaid by stony clays and the Dyke is only a foot
or two above ground level – a mere shapeless hummock.

From the lane near Pen-y-bryn Hall to the field track to
Lower Gwarthlow the whole work is well-preserved, forming a
belt of scrub between fields. On the approach to Lymore Park
the Dyke forms the boundary between pasture fields, being
much lowered by cultivation. Lymore Hall, now tragically
demolished, was one of the most superbly beautiful half-
timbered mansions in the whole Border.

The half-timbered mansion was built in 1675 and was part of

34 *Brompton to Montgomery*

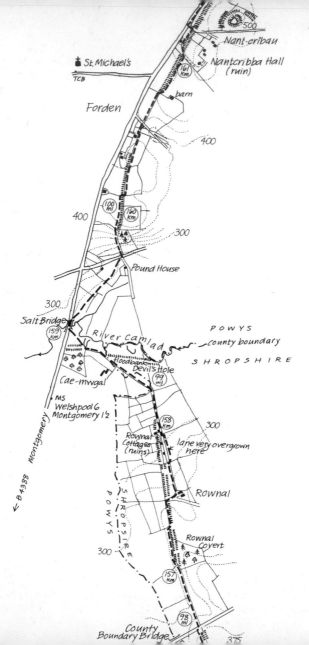

500

Nant-cribau

161 Km

Nantcribba Hall
(ruin)

⚓ St. Michael's

TCB

Forden

barn

400

400

100 ml

160 Km

300

Pound House

300

Salt Bridge

159 Km

River Camlad

POWYS

county boundary

SHROPSHIRE

floodbank

Devil's Hole

99 ml

Cae-mwgal

MS
Welshpool 6
Montgomery 1½

158 Km

300

Rownal
Cottages
(ruins)

lane very overgrown
here

POWYS

SHROPSHIRE

Rownal

← B4388 Montgomery

Rownal
Covert

300

157 Km

POWYS

98 ml

County
Boundary Bridge

375

the property of the Earl of Powis. In spite of protests it was
demolished in the 1930's and the great Jacobean staircase sold
to America. However, it has now been returned to this country
and re-erected in Aldborough Hall, Yorkshire.

The Dyke forms the eastern boundary of Lymore Park – a
well-preserved and, for the area, unusually massive portion –
with ancient oaks and thorns growing on the bank. On the
boundary of Dudston Covert the Dyke is a high bank and when
you leave the wood behind you can see the deep W ditch. The
county boundary bears away from the Dyke to join and follow
a stream and you reach the Chirbury-Montgomery road B4386
just E of County Boundary Bridge. At the point where the road
crosses the Dyke the earthwork is no larger than an ordinary
hedge-bank, which seems to suggest that it was levelled in
order to provide road ballast. Just before you reach the road
a narrow gap marks the original crossing point of the highway,

which has been straightened in modern times.

The B4386 is a straight road linking Chirbury with
Montgomery. Chirbury to the E was a fortified borough with
its monastery, but those with time for a historic detour will
usually turn W towards Montgomery, whose castle ruins and
war memorial stand silhouetted at the end of the road, one
mile away.

Just N of the road the Dyke is at first just a hedge bank,
but after two fields it is a fine earthwork in Rownal Covert –
the scale here being definitely larger than that at Lymore.
There is a traffic-gap in the wood on the crest of the knoll –
it is narrow, and its terminals are neither thickened or recurved.
That it may be original is suggested by its position on the crest
of a knoll where the Dyke changes alignment. From this
prominent knoll the Dyke changes direction through 10 degrees,
and its line is exactly aligned with Hem Hill on the other side
of the Camlad valley.

The path runs outside the wood parallel to the Dyke in
Rownal Covert, then along the earthwork to Rownal farm.
Near the derelict Rownal Cottages the farm track is so overgrown
that the Path has to take to the field, but it soon rejoins the
green lane as it approaches the valley. The floor of the Camlad
valley is over $\frac{1}{2}$ mile wide and the change from the gradual
slope is marked by the decreasing size of the Dyke. The
constructional difficulties across the valley drainage system
must have been considerable, but the Dyke provides another
example of the determination of the builders to leave no
portion of the boundary in doubt. The course of the Dyke is
for a short distance obscured by watercourses and drainage
trenches, a pond called The Devil's Hole, and by the floodbank
of the River Camlad – the only river the Path crosses which
rises in England to flow into Wales. The line is marked by two
ancient oaks. On the far side of the river after a few yards the
Dyke reappears as a hedge bank 3 ft high running up to Pound
House.

The Path leaves the Dyke at the marshy Devil's Hole and
runs behind Cae-mwgal farm across meadows to Salt Bridge
carrying the B4388 over the Camlad. This road, like B4386, is
remarkably straight: it is not Roman but probably an 18c
turnpike, directly aligned on Montgomery Castle.

River Camlad to Leighton Park

From Salt Bridge the Path goes diagonally across a field to rejoin the Dyke at Pound House, then N of Pound House it traces a wide curve over the flattened crest of the hill, forming the hedge boundaries of large fields. The Dyke has suffered at the hands of the farmers, having been much ploughed down, and the short steep climb up the hillside opposite Pound House has recently been planted with conifers, so that the Path is likely to be lost.

The Dyke and B4388 run parallel for nearly 2 miles and at Forden near Nant Cribau farm you have to join the road because part of the Dyke has been ploughed out.

In the clump of trees at Nant Cribau is the mound of a long-destroyed castle of the Corbets of Cause. The farmhouse fronting the Montgomery-Welshpool road is built right on the bank of the Dyke. Forden church dates from 1805 and in the

Powis Castle

Leighton Hall

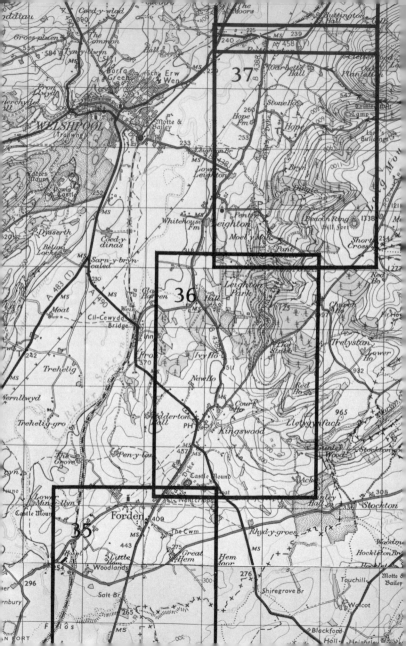

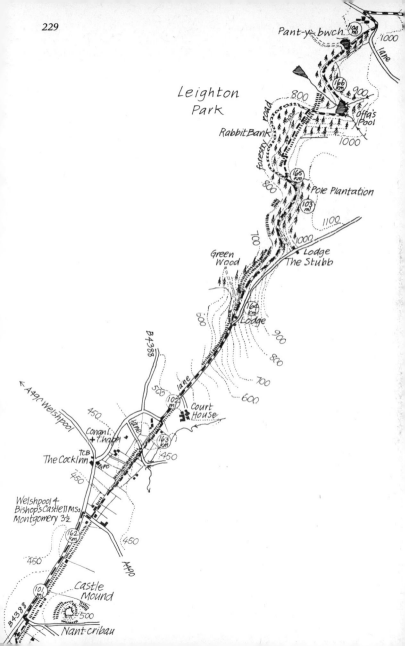

churchyard, under a yew tree, is an epitaph of 1827 to John Roberts:

> *Beneath this tree lies singers three*
> *One tenor and two bases*
> *Now they are gone, its ten to one*
> *If three such takes their places.*

Just E of the Montgomery-Welshpool-Chirbury road junction the Path rejoins the Dyke and follows it for ½ mile through a rich countryside broken up into small pasture fields. At about the 500 ft contour a lane comes in from the L from the Forden-Leighton road B4388, and the Path follows this lane up the rising slope. At first the lane occupies the ditch of the Dyke, then as the slope becomes steeper it swings across the bank – here about 4–5 ft high – to occupy a holloway which flanks the Dyke on the E. The lane running up the slope eventually becomes the road crossing Long Mountain.

The large, isolated hill mass of Long Mountain is bounded on the N and W sides by the River Severn and on the S and E sides by the Camlad and the Rea Brook. The ridgeway which follows its crest has long been a convenient alternative to the valleys and it has been assumed, possibly wrongly, that this ridgeway is a Roman road.

The Romans had a camp at Viroconium (on the banks of the Severn near Wroxeter, between Shrewsbury and Wellington) and the more westerly of the two Roman roads from this place down into South Wales led to Caer near Montgomery, via Westbury at the northern end of the Long Mountain axis. It had been assumed that the valley of the Rea Brook was forest and swamp and that the Romans must have chosen the devious route over the hill crest to avoid these obstacles. It seems more likely that their road followed along the southern foot of Long Mountain above the Rea Brook, the route now followed by B4386 through Worthen and Marton.

It was also suggested that the remarkable straightness of Offa's Dyke on the S side of Long Mountain was due to it being thrown up on top of a straight stretch of Roman road. A sunken track burrows deep behind the reverse slope of the Dyke following its line up from the lowlands. Fox excavated the Dyke at one point and found the ridgeway track to be younger than the Dyke and there were no indications of any earlier or Roman tracks below the foundations of the Dyke.

36 *Forden to Leighton Park (p 229)*
View from Offa's Dyke in Leighton Park, looking N (p 231)

The popular theory was not proved by the excavation: as no traces of a Roman road could be found it is probable that it followed the Rea Brook valley. The gentle rise and slightly undulating character of the country favours the straight alignment of the Dyke as it leaves the pastoral and agricultural country for the steep, wooded slopes of Long Mountain. You will wonder why did Offa not run the Dyke straight along the river between Forden and Buttington, as he did between Buttington and Llanymynech, saving 4 miles of digging on steep slopes, or else keep to a lower contour through Leighton, say along the route of B4388, which would still have given a reasonable line? Fox thought that the Princes of Powys (whose successors built the red castle crowning the ridge S of Welshpool on the far side of the Severn) had established their claim to the Leighton meadows. A military critic saw the Dyke here as a fall-back line for Mercians who might have been driven back

from the river by Welsh attacks, but as in other stretches – the
Wye valley for example – Offa's dominant aim seems to have
been to see and be seen.

Through Leighton Park the Dyke cleverly maintains visual
control over the Vale of Powys. For nearly 2 miles it follows a
devious course closely related to the relief of the country
(which is very hilly and deeply dissected by lateral valleys).
Dense woodland and undergrowth and much afforestation in the
1870's make the course of the Dyke difficult to follow, and the
Path therefore follows forestry roads or rides. The route may be
badly overgrown in parts, but there is always an alternative.

The Dyke leaves the line of the Long Mountain ridgeway and
you enter the S end of the Park beside a lodge at a gate marked
Royal Forestry Society and Private. (These notices are to
restrict access to the great redwood groves: take no notice of
them if you are following the Path). A trackway used for log-
hauling occupies the site of the Dyke at first and you follow
this as it makes a steep ascent, and when another trackway
comes in from the Long Mountain road the forest roads contour
round the side of the hill, giving magnificent views embracing
the Vale of Powys and the mountains beyond, while below can
be seen occasional glimpses of the church and high-towered
mansion of Leighton Hall.

Description of route continues on p 234.

Leighton Hall

The Hall and park was the estate of a Victorian banker from
Liverpool, John Naylor, whose baronial mansion and woodlands
were laid out as a challenge, perhaps, to the Herberts and Clive
of India wealth across the river at Powis Castle.

Naylor bought the estate in 1849 and engaged a well-known
architect, W H Gee, to build the great house in the 'Gothic
revival' style. Built in the year of the Great Exhibition (1851)
it has a carillon in the tower. The internal decorations of the
mansion were by Grace, who painted the murals in Barry's
Houses of Parliament. The parish church is a perfectly preserved
specimen on the nouveau riche élan of the 1850's. There is an
octagonal mausoleum of the Naylor family, having an angel
pointing upwards and lined with uniform marble tablets
commemorating the family. The tall church spire can be seen
from the woods on the side of Long Mountain, and the nave
of the roof is so steep that the walls have to be supported by
buttresses.

In the park and on the hill slopes below the Dyke Naylor had planted Wellingtonias, 'monkey puzzle' trees, and the great Redwood grove – all fashionable new trees of the period, now tended by the Royal Forestry Society. It is said that he had bison and kangeroos in the park. All these things however, pale in comparison with the remains of his agricultural engineering enterprises.

The farms on the estate were provided with elaborate new buildings – those on the home farm were all lit by gas from Naylor's own gasworks. The gas also lit the Hall and the Church, and Naylor used pitch-fibre gas pipes – 50 years ahead of their general use.

Even more impressive was the water engineering. Small streams were dammed near their sources above the house – Offa's Pool and another are passed on the Path – and they were channelled to drive a turbine at the farm which powered milling, chaff-cutting and sheep-shearing equipment. There was not enough water from these sources for all his schemes, so a by-pass channel was cut from the River Severn to drive a hydraulic ram which pumped the river water up to the great buildings 600 ft above river-level on the knoll called Moel-y-Nab. The Severn by-pass channel was crossed by a bridge (Leighton Bridge) bearing the family coat of arms and the date 1872 but this was removed to make way for the new road bridge.

The main feature of the buildings on Moel-y-Nab was a great tank in which the water was added to guano and bone-meal to make liquid manure. All these supplies were brought up to the tank by a funicular railway, the bone meal being ground down in the 'bone mill'. Remains of these buildings still survive. The liquid manure was piped back down to taps in the upper part of each field and they could be turned on to provide irrigation and fertilisation for all the arable and meadow land. The system is said to have been taken up and the scrap used for the World War I effort, and all Naylor's engineering works are now derelict and ruinous.

After that the estate was divided up and sold. Over 500 acres of the farmland were bought in 1931 by the County Council for small-holdings. Part of the Hall was demolished, but it remained a substantial residence and was bought by Major C P Ackers, managing director of a forestry products firm, who presented the great Redwood grove to the Royal Forestry Society in 1958. The Hall was later owned by Senator Rupert

Davies, a Canadian newspaper owner, who had left his native Montgomery as a young man. On his death the Hall was bought by an American firm with a factory in Welshpool, for business conferences and executive recreation.

Leighton Park to Buttington

The Path curves round a coombe, up the very steep slope of which the Dyke climbs to the shoulder of the plateau. A forestry track follows the Dyke, but if you miss it you can continue on the track you have been following, bearing R at each junction, and you will rejoin the Path after 500 metres. The Path crosses the Dyke and runs alongside it and rejoins the main track which contours round the hillside. The Dyke goes steeply down the slope of the coombe, but the Path continues along the forest track round the head of the coombe where is situated Offa's Pool, one of Naylor's constructions.

The Dyke changes direction here and the Path turns away. The Dyke descends diagonally across the western slopes of Long Mountain. From an elevation of nearly 1000 ft it drops directly below Moel-y-Nab to the river plain, at one point having a gradient of 1 in 2 on a slope of 70 yds.

The Path keeps to the forestry road which contours round the hillside as far as the second pool, then climbs up a path on the inside edge of a wood to reach the Welshpool-Trelystan road. From Pant-y-bwch the Path follows a lane, becoming a track, on the edge of Phillip's Grove plantation, and from the far corner follows field hedgerows and fences up the gentle slope to Beacon Ring.

The earthwork of Beacon Ring hill fort (Cefn Digoll) stands on the summit of Long Mountain, 1338 ft. It features frequently in Welsh history and legend and commands the great circuit of hills and valleys to the W and the wide Shropshire plains to the NE. The plantation of beech and pine inside the circle was planted in December 1953 as a memorial to Helen Solveig Ackers, formerly of Leighton Hall.

The Path passes through a plantation of re-planted forestry and contours round the head of Cwm Dingle. From the edge of the plateau at 1200 ft the path follows a cart track on the spur between Cwm Dingle and Salvagog Dingle, across a lane and down to Stone House and the Leighton road B4388 near Buttington, emerging at the road where traces of the Dyke are picked up again. You can see a raised ridge beyond the drains

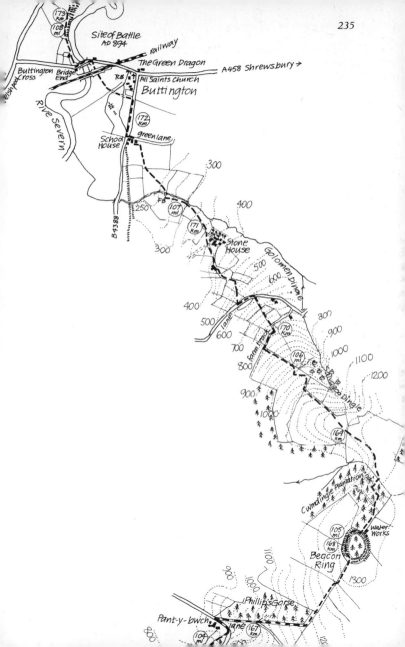

and channels leading away from the road, pointing directly to the river. 1200 years ago the Severn may have followed a course nearer to the high ground, and Fox was justified in assuming that the construction of the Dyke finished here. He had seen that the direct alignment of the Dyke on to the Severn at Llanymynech and its presence on the very bank of the river would indicate its continuation on the opposite bank.

The selection of Buttington as a point to cross the River Severn is interesting and deserves attention. Ancient roads and tracks lead towards Buttington Bridge (or the ford which preceded it) from either side of the river. The Dyke was then so placed as to give access from Mercian territory to an important crossing of the Severn. It was at Buttington that the English overtook the Danes in AD 894. This circumstance strengthens the probability that it was a nodal point on the traffic lines of the border.

Buttington is a small place, the church a medieval building, restored in 1786, standing at the road junction. The font in the church is formed from a capital of a pillar from the ruins of Strata Marcella Abbey.

Description of route continues on p 243.

The gap between the Long Mountain and the Berwyn foothills made by the Severn gives Welshpool its claim to be the Gateway of Wales. Lloyd George called it the Gates of Paradise; for him Wales was the Garden of Eden.

Once concentrating like other neighbouring towns on the flannel industry, Welshpool has widened its interests and its prosperity now rests primarily on its position as an agricultural centre in the rich alluvial land of the Severn valley. It is strategically placed on road, railway and canal and thus has been able to benefit to the disadvantage of Montgomery and Bishop's Castle. For over 7 centuries there has been a market here on Mondays, and the livestock section is the largest in Wales. (MD Monday. ECD Wednesday.)

Welshpool is a handsome Georgian town, built along a wide main street, with a few old houses mostly built in brick in the 18c and 19c. Brick is the distinctive character of the town: neither the slate of the western part of the country nor the stone of the north is found here in the Severn valley.

The large parish church of St Mary of the Salutation was built about 1240 on a commanding site and yes, you've guessed it, restored (by G E Street in 1866, with new sandstone arcades). The fine oak roof came from Strata Marcella Abbey at the Dissolution. The church contains monuments to the town's connection with the Earls of Powys and there is a Stuart Royal Arms over the W arch. The glass is Victorian, but there is an early 16c Flemish triptych, interesting monuments and the colours of former County Regiments.

Adjacent to the church in Salop Road is a buff brick museum to which a visit should certainly be made. The Powysland Museum was founded in 1874 to illustrate the archaeology, history and literature of the area. There are fossils, shells, Roman antiquities and an Iron Age shield amongst relics of the Kingdom of Powys.

Hours of Admission

Monday, Tuesday, Saturdays	*14.00–16.30*	
Thursday and Fridays	*11.00–13.00*	*1400–1630*
and during April–September also	*18.00–19.00*	

High Street has several good houses. Anderson's antique shop, just above the Town Hall and on the opposite side of the road, contains a Jacobean staircase with tall 'jewelled' newel posts and a little higher up the street are one or two good old

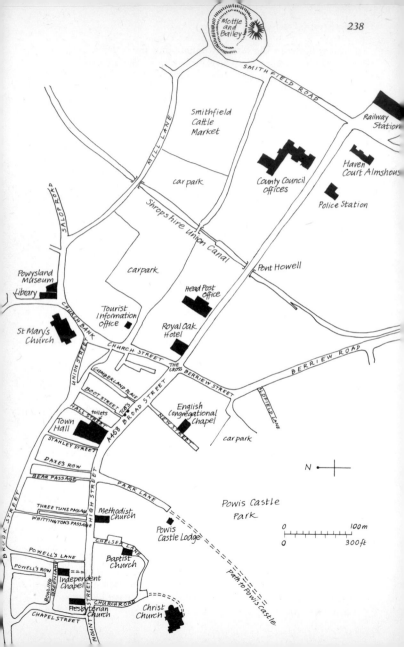

Mottle and Bailey

SMITHFIELD ROAD

MILL LANE

Smithfield Cattle Market

car park

Shropshire Union Canal

Railway Station

County Council offices

Haven Court Almshous

Police Station

SALOP ROAD

Carpark

Pont Howell

Powysland Museum

Library

Head Post Office

Tourist Information office

Royal Oak Hotel

CHURCH BANK

St Mary's Church

CHURCH STREET

THE CROSS

BERRIEW STREET

BERRIEW ROAD

UNION STREET

CUMBERLAND PLACE

BROAD STREET

RADFIELD LANE

BOOT STREET

TOC's

New Street

English Congregational Chapel

car park

HALL STREET

toilets

A458

Town Hall

STANLEY STREET

DAXE'S ROW

BEAR PASSAGE

PARK LANE

Powis Castle Park

HIGH STREET

THREE TUNS PASSAGE

Methodist Church

WHITTINGTON'S PASSAGE

Powis Castle Lodge

N

BROOK STREET

POWELL'S LANE

CHELSEA LANE

100m

POWELL'S ROW

Baptist Church

0

300ft

BOWLING GREEN

Independent Chapel

CHURCH ROAD

MOUNT STREET

Presbyterian Church

Christ Church

Path to Powis Castle

CHAPEL STREET

'Black and White' timber-framed buildings. At the back of High Street stands Christ Church, a pseudo-Norman structure in a charming situation on the edge of the Park and with some good stained glass.

At the opposite end of the town, beyond the Cross, in Severn Road are the County Council offices in neo-Georgian style, as are the Evans Almshouses built in 1940 opposite the Railway Station. Although Welshpool is a pleasant town, the most impressive building is Powis Castle, in a wooded park just S of the town and access for pedestrians can be obtained from High Street.

Powis Castle/Castell Goch
Owned by The National Trust
Hours of Admission
Gardens 1 May – 30 September
Castle   1 June – 30 September
Daily except Mondays and Tuesdays 14.00–18.00, but also open Spring Bank Holiday Monday (Gardens only) and Late Summer Bank Holiday Monday (both Gardens and Castle) from 10.30– 17.30.
Separate admissions for castle and gardens.
Teas and light refreshments available.

Throughout its long history the interests of the town have been connected with those of Powis Castle, the fortress home of the ancient princes and medieval lords of Powys.

The Welsh princes of Powys (roughly speaking Montgomery-shire and north Radnorshire) were often hostile to the princes of North Wales, but they were also sitters on the fence, taking the Welsh or the English side as their interest dictated. In the 12c they allied themselves to the English cause of Henry III and Edward I against Llywelyn the Great and Llywelyn the Last, and they preferred to reside in this Castle, founded in 1250 by Owain ap Gruffydd, so near the English border rather than in a remoter stronghold. The princes were restored to their lands when Edward I finally succeeded in conquering Wales in his campaigns of 1277 and 1282.

In 1587, Sir Edward Herbert bought the castle and added the Long Gallery and its fine plaster ceiling made in 1592. In 1644 the castle was captured for the Parliamentarians by Sir Thomas Myddleton, though it was spared from demolition by the

L *Welshpool*

orders of Cromwell himself. In 1667 the castle was repaired and there is much work of this period including the entrance to the outer courtyard, the east portal and staircase, the state bedroom and the grand staircase.

The Powis family had been Jacobites but were re-instated in 1722. In 1784 the daughter of the last Earl of Powis (of the Herbert family) married Edward Clive, Governor of Madras, the

victor of Plassey, who was the son of the famous Robert Clive.
Edward Clive changed his name to Herbert and recreated the
Earldom of Powis when he became Earl in 1804.

The fourth Earl of Powis (of the new creation) gave the
castle and its grounds (except the deer park) to the National
Trust in 1952, and the fifth Earl still retains residence, thus
making the castle inhabited without interruption for over
700 years.

The path rises up to the impressive red sandstone building,
set in the centre of 55 acres of beautiful parkland. The gardens
claim the tallest tree in Britain – a Douglas Fir over 150 ft high,
but the most distinctive part of the scene are the oaks, planted
by 'Capability' Brown who founded the tradition of the British
landscape garden in the early 19c. Even when the Castle and
Gardens are not open Lord Powis kindly allows the public to
walk through the Park along the main drives.

The restoration of the Castle in the time of Charles II
affected the gardens in 1722 to the extent that part of them
were splendidly terraced in the style the exiled Stuarts had
learned to appreciate at Saint Germain in France. These early
18c formal gardens are famous, and the surrounding area
contains numerous fine trees and shrubs, well-planted and
maintained.

Unlike most of the other great Welsh castles Powis has been
continuously lived in and it has never ceased to develop
architecturally as each generation adapted it to their needs. The
oldest part of the castle was built in Edward I's time and since
then it has been heavily modernised and restored. The most
prominent features are the huge embattled drum-towers, which
rather dwarf the later Tudor mansion.

The castle is shown and there can be seen fine late Stuart
interiors: work by Grinling Gibbons, late 16c plasterwork and
panelling, a fine late 17c staircase and murals by Lanscroon.
The principal contents – which include many fine paintings
and tapestries, early Georgian furniture, and objects connected
with Clive of India – were accepted by the Treasury in lieu of
estate duty and transferred to the National Trust in 1965.

Powis Castle

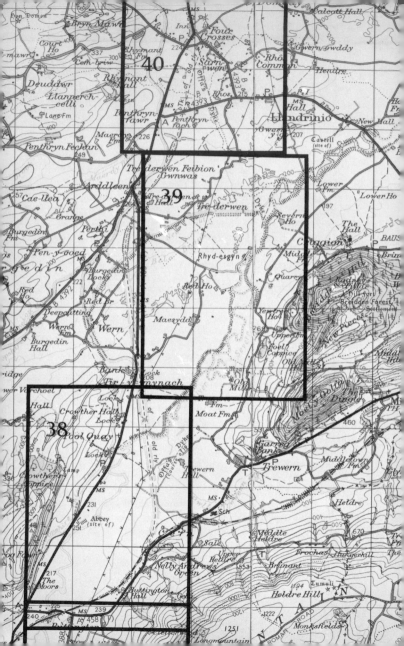

18 Welshpool to Llanymynech

Between Buttington and Llanymynech the Dyke is only present through the water meadows on the alluvial flats between the Severn and the Vrynwy, some 5 miles north of Buttington. Some writers have assumed that the Dyke was originally present on the R or E bank of the Severn throughout this stretch: the OS map indeed, marks a stretch over a mile long near Trewern Hall, opposite Pool Quay, as the 'site of' Offa's Dyke. These and other possible alignments were examined by Fox and were found to be flood or hedge banks and the obvious explanation was that the Severn formed the boundary, just as did the Wye through the Herefordshire plain.

This stretch of the Path is tedious going; 8 miles on the flat, along overgrown stretches of the Shropshire Union Canal and Severn floodbanks, and two long stretches of busy highways without footpaths. You can't see much of the river or the canal, and what you do see does not tempt you to swim. The only points of interest are the three peaks of the Breidden Hills, which dominate this flat and monotonous landscape. These steep hills would give you better walking if you can afford to add an extra day to your intinerary, but unfortunately the official route keeps to the floor of the valley.

Buttington to Pool Quay

The Path begins at Buttington where the bridge carries A458 over the Severn. Pass in front of Tal-y-Bont cottage and along the bank of the river, and then along the flood bank to join A483 where the river comes close to the road. There is a short stretch of main road to follow and soon the Shropshire Union Canal runs immediately alongside the road and we are able to leave the traffic behind for a while. Between the road and the river at this point is the site of the great Cistercian abbey of Strata Marcella (Abaty Ystrad Marchell). It was founded by the Prince of Powis in 1170, who retired there in 1195 to end his days. The abbey was demolished when all the monasteries were dissolved by Henry VIII and a shallow depression in the meadow is all that can now be seen. Like Grace Dieu near Monmouth its demolition was absolute and its foundations are almost unrecognisable.

The stretch along the towpath of the Montgomery Canal, a

38 *Buttington to Pool Quay (p 244)*
The River Severn at Buttington, looking SE (p 245)

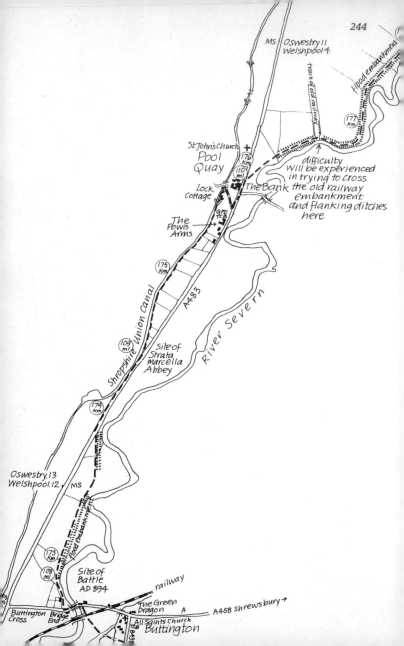

MS Oswestry 11
Welshpool 4

track of old railway

flood embankment

177 km

St John's Church
Pool Quay

176 km

110 mi

difficulty
will be experienced
in trying to cross
The Bank the old railway
embankment
and flanking ditches
here

Lock
Cottage

The
Powis
Arms

175 km

A483

River Severn

Shropshire Union Canal

109 mi

Site of
Strata
Marcella
Abbey

174 km

Oswestry 13
Welshpool 12

MS

flood embankment

173 km

108 mi

Site of
Battle
AD 894

railway

The Green
Dragon

A458 Shrewsbury →

Buttington Bridge
Cross Bridge
End

All Saints Church

Buttington

disused branch of the Shropshire Union Canal, can be very overgrown and difficult. Even though the jungle-bordered bog was cleaned in 1971 it is easier to continue along the main road as far as Pool Quay. The choice is difficult. Would you rather risk being run over by a lorry on this fast, straight road without footpaths, or drown by inadvertently stepping into the canal when you thought you were walking on the towpath?

Although overgrown the canal is in good condition, with water throughout most of the section between Welshpool and Llanymynech. The Earl of Powis is President of the Shropshire Union Canal Society, which campaigns for the restoration of the Montgomery Canal. They have recently greatly improved the stretch through Welshpool: a converted boat, operated by the Society, carries passengers along the restored section on Sundays, or by prior arrangement at other times. British Waterways propose to continue the work further N to Pool Quay and beyond, under the auspices of the Prince of Wales Committee and financed by the Variety Club of GB to the tune of £¼ million. A ride on a narrow boat to Pool Quay or to Ardleen, Four Crosses and even to Llanymynech would be more than welcome.

The plans for the Ellesmere Canal were published in 1791 and

Salvagog Dingle

Garbett's Hall

School House

Buttington

Stone House Farm

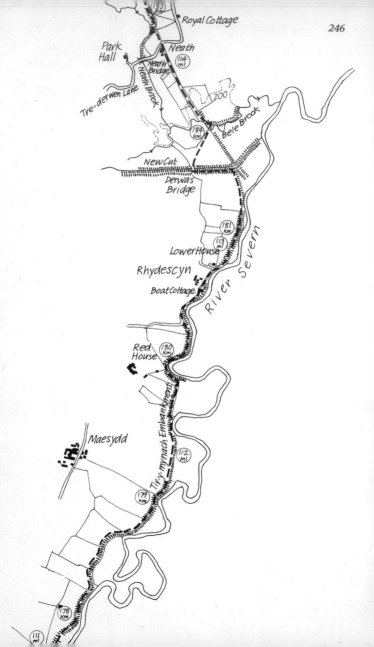

Royal Cottage

Park Hall

Neath

Neath Bridge

Tre-derwen Lane

Neath Brook

Bele Brook

New Cut

Derwas Bridge

Lower House

Rhydescyn

Boat Cottage

River Severn

Red House

Maesydd

Tir-y-mynach Embankment

114 ml

183 Km

184 Km

181 Km

113 ml

180 Km

112 ml

179 Km

178 Km

111 ml

intended to serve the iron and coal fields around Ruabon and connect the Mersey to the Severn. A branch to the limestone quarries at Llanymynech was opened in 1796 and this inspired a separate company to plan a canal from Llanymynech to Newtown, a distance of 35 miles. The canal was authorised in 1793 and by 1797 the line was open all the way except the last five miles to Newtown. The traffic on the canal was mainly agricultural and, apart from the limestone, it existed to serve the farms and villages through which it passed. The canal was never really able to make a profit and the lack of capital and income greatly delayed its completion. The canal became known as the Montgomery Canal and the extension to Newtown was not finally opened until 1821, having been financed by a separate company: in fact, the canal was built by three companies over a period of 30 years.

The Ellesmere Canal Company failed to make the vital connections with the Dee and the Severn. The Montgomery Canal was the southern-most extension and the line northwards to Chester stopped at Pontcysyllte, with a navigable feeder to Llangollen.

Beside the Severn

The Path leaves the Montgomery Canal at Pool Quay and follows the Severn flood embankment for two miles. There is a very overgrown stretch near the disused railway line, but otherwise

Rodney's Pillar
Breidden

Moel-y-Golfa

the Tir-y-mynach Embankment is passable throughout its
length. The walking is easy where the adjoining pastures are
grazed, but rough in other places. The rather battered stiles
along the floodbank are all waymarked, even through the
back garden of a cottage at Rhydescyn.
Description of the route continues on p 250.

The Breidden Hills
The Path along the floodbanks enables you to get a close look
at the Breidden Hills which rise abruptly out of the chequer-
board landscape of the valley. The group is called locally merely
the Breidden, the double 'd' pronounced as a thick 'th'.

The prominence of these hills is due to volcanic lava heaved
up and cooled beneath the crust of the Ordovician world. The
sharp peak of Moel-y-Golfa, 1324 ft, is an andesite, and the
adjacent Middleton Hill, 1195 ft is a conglomerate. Breidden Hill
proper, 1200 ft high, is a dolerite, a hard, heavy, greenish
rock so good for road metal and ballast that the hill is being
gradually quarried away. Their hard, resilient rocks weather
slowly so that the soil cover is thin and even absent on the
steepest slopes. The hills have been upfolded to form a feature
known as laccolite and they consist of two parallel ridges
separated by an intervening valley – rounded Breidden on one
side, with the sharply-peaked Moel-y-Golfa on the other.

On the very top of Breidden Hill is Rodney's Pillar, a Doric
column in honour of Admiral Rodney, more oddly land-locked
than the Naval Temple at Monmouth. The monument was set
up by the voluntary action of local farmers and it was later
renovated by both the gentry of Powys and Shropshire.
Admiral Rodney had no association with either county, and it
seems that the subscribers were aroused by his action of buying
timber from the area for the Navy rather than by his victories
of Cape St Vincent and Dominica.

Breidden is one of several sites where Caractacus (Caradoc)
is said to have gathered his tribesmen for his last stand against
the Romans under Ostorious Scapula.

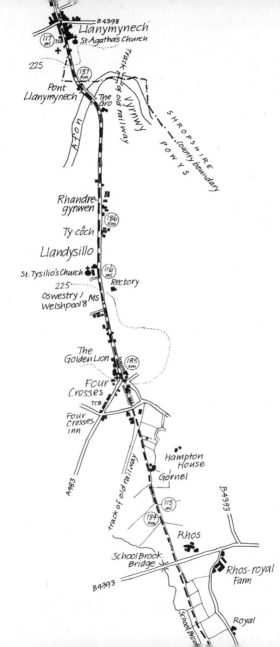

The Severn to Four Crosses

At Rhydescyn the immediate view of Breidden Hill is marred by the quarrying operations which are slowly eating the hill away, causing it to lose its shape and beauty. The quarrying ought to be stopped, and the spider web network of the nearby wireless station in the foreground adds to the vertical contrast in this flat valley.

Just north of Rhydescyn we leave the Severn at the flood control gates and join the Dyke again. The Dyke begins on the bank of the river, high above the summer level of the water. It is cut by the 'New Cut' and between this channel and the Bele Brook it is a broad and low (+ 2 ft) but quite definite ridge, which illustrates the characteristic dyke construction planed off by floods. Since it is in the direct alignment of a known stretch further north there is no reason to doubt its antiquity, and it asserts the tradition, and the OS map, of recording the Dyke as extending to the Severn.

The New Cut, an otherwise impassable watercourse, is crossed by Derwas Bridge, and the Path crosses the Bele Brook by a new footbridge. At this point the flood embankment of

Llanymynech Hill

the brook meets the Dyke. The flood bank has changed the alignment of the Dyke slightly, but then it is a shapeless mound 3 ft high forming the E hedge boundary of the trackway leading from the river meadows to Neath Farm.

Beyond the road the Dyke is a broad flat bank extending across open level pasture, at first forming part of the Neath Brook floodbank, then a hedge boundary, forming a narrow steep-sided ridge as it approaches B4393. On the far side of the road it is a broad shapeless ridge up to the disused railway. The alignment through the disused Cambrian Railway sidings and station is preserved by a footpath but no traces of the Dyke survive. A massive stretch of Dyke appears in the meadows beyond – a broad grassy ridge with definite traces of a ditch – leading right up to the junction of B4393 and A483 at Four Crosses.

Four Crosses to Llanymynech

The busy main road runs along the course of the Dyke between Four Crosses and Llanymynech, a long stretch of 1½ miles, relieved at first by a footpath to Llandysilio church. The old Cambrian Railway running parallel to the road might have offered an alternative path, but the bridges were pulled down and the gaps wired up before the idea of a footpath had been considered. Is it not yet too late to make this line a substitute footpath? The Offa's Dyke Association proposes a diversion along the towpath of the Montgomery Canal between Four Crosses and Llanymynech, and either way would be more satisfactory than the road.

There is a gap of nearly 1 mile in the Dyke between the church of St Tysilio at Llandysilio and Llanymynech's church of St Agatha, and it is possible that the River Vyrnwy formed a loop extending across the alluvial flat from church to church, as it nearly does today, and this would serve as an adequate boundary. That there is no trace of the Dyke cannot be regarded as surprising, for the whole alluvial flat is subject to floods and may have been, in the 8c, a marshy jungle full of pools and crossed by half-silted water-courses. It seems at first inconsistent that the Dyke should be present on the very bank of the Severn yet intermittent here at the Vrynwy, but the difference in treatment seems to have a geological basis. The Severn is deeply entrenched, cutting its way through glacial deposits of stony clay, and the banks, though at times

Offa's Dyke at Four Crosses, looking N

flooded, are normally dry – very different from the water-meadows of the Vyrnwy.

As the causeway from the bridge, built in 1826, to the church is modern, and as the church stands on a knoll, Fox believed that at the time the Dyke was built the Vyrnwy flowed at the foot of the church knoll. He thought it probable that the wall of St Agatha's churchyard was built on the bank of the Dyke, as the road on its western side is on the line of the filled-in Ditch.

Description of the route continues on p 256.

Llanymynech

The church of St Agatha stands on the southern side of Llanymynech village. It was built in 1845 by R K Penson and is quite interesting. Built in grey rubble stone with an elaborate buff terra-cotta brick trim, it is a crazy demonstration of the

Llanymynech Hill

St Agatha's

Afon Vyrnwy

neo-Norman fashion. Norman revival buildings were rare in
19c but this replica of the French style is remarkably accurate
in its detail. The NW tower has a porch under, with big angle
buttresses and pyramid roof. There are elaborate compositions
of windows and arcadings on the W and N ends, the E window
having stained glass in 5 equal lights, with a monogram of
Wailes, and a date 1855.

Tall gaunt Victorian houses line the main street of the village,
which here forms the boundary between England and Wales.
Both pavements are in Powys, but the houses on the eastern side
are in Shropshire. The border runs right through the Red Lion –
its front rooms are in Wales and its back rooms in England – but
the old advantage of the side entrance to an oasis for thirsty
Sunday travellers from a 'dry' Wales no longer has any
significance.

The village nestles under Llanymynech Hill, the carboniferous
limestone of which is rich in minerals, resulting in large-scale
quarrying which, although it led to the growth of the village,
has disfigured the landscape for a considerable area. The canal
and several railways also made the village a communications
centre, but the Potteries and North Wales Railway failed for
want of subscribers and all are now gone: the village has lost
the original reason for its existence.

Llanymynech, Afon Vyrnwy and Llanymynech Hill

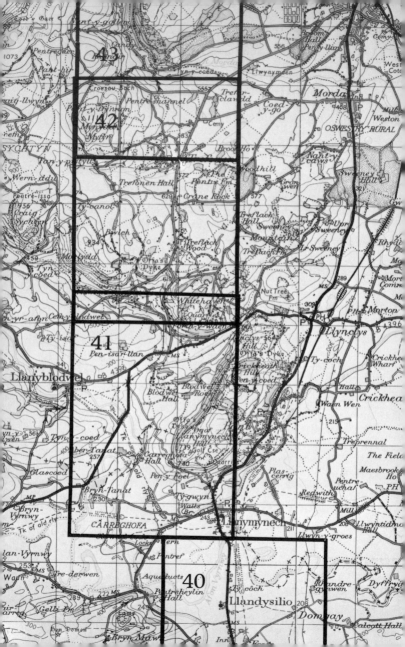

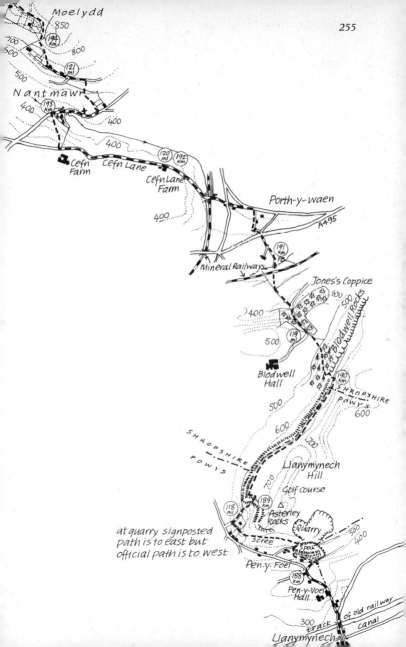

Moelydd

850

194
km

700

800

500

121
ml

500

N a n t m a w r

193
km

400

400

400

120
ml

192
km

Cefn
Farm

Cefn Lane

Cefn Lane
Farm

Porth-y-waen

A495

400

191
km

Mineral Railways

Jones's Coppice

400

Blodwell Rocks

119
ml

500

Blodwell
Hall

190
km

SHROPSHIRE
Powys

500

600

SHROPSHIRE

600

POWYS

Llanymynech
Hill

700

Golf course

118
ml

189
km

Asterley
Rocks

Quarry

at quarry signposted
path is to east but
official path is to west

scree

500

400

Pen-y-Foel

188
km

Pen-y-Voel
Hall

300

track of old railway

canal

Llanymynech

Llanymynech to Trefonen

There are no traces of the Dyke along the road through
Llanymynech or up the deep lane to Pen-y-voel Hall. The
county boundary remains coincident with the Dyke to the
foot of the scarp slope but at this point the two part. The
Dyke disappears in the old quarry, but it is fairly certain that
Offa's boundary clung to the edge of the hill. The official
Path goes up W of the quarry, but the signposted path goes up
E: they both soon join to cross the S face of the hill under the
limestone cliff, the Path becoming overgrown, to reach a
metalled lane with bungalows. This lane becomes a path,
making an easy ascent up to the head of the re-entrant to the
edge of the golf course on the top of Llanymynech Hill.

Llanymynech Hill is honeycombed with the shafts and
galleries of mines which were sunk to extract copper, silver,
zinc and lead. The Romans were drawn to this area by its
mineral resources: in 1965 a party of schoolboys exploring
one of the shafts known as Ogof's Hole found a hoard of 33
silver Roman denarii which are now on display in Oswestry
library. Several unguarded shafts to other Roman galleries can
be seen on the golf course.

A vast ancient hill fort once enclosed the plateau and the
Path follows Offa's boundary along the western rampart. In
fact, the western escarpment of Llanymynech Hill is practically
unscaleable and takes the place of Offa's earthwork: it was just
convenient for Offa to use the earthwork of the earlier defences.
Later the Earls of Shrewsbury built the Castle of Carreghofa
here, and up to 1213 it figured prominently in Welsh border
warfare and in royal silver-mining projects, but it has
disappeared so completely that no-one knows where it stood.

From the top of the plateau there are vast views across the
Shropshire plain on one side and the intricate valleys leading
up into the Berwyns on the other. The upland is a strange and
wild country with a luxuriant flora and woods of scrub birch
and yew growing out of the old quarries.

The Path follows the escarpment and leaves Powys just
before the Blodwell Roaks, then zig-zags down the steep face
through a mature beech wood, then through a young fir
plantation, to the Blodwell Hall track. The Path crosses a

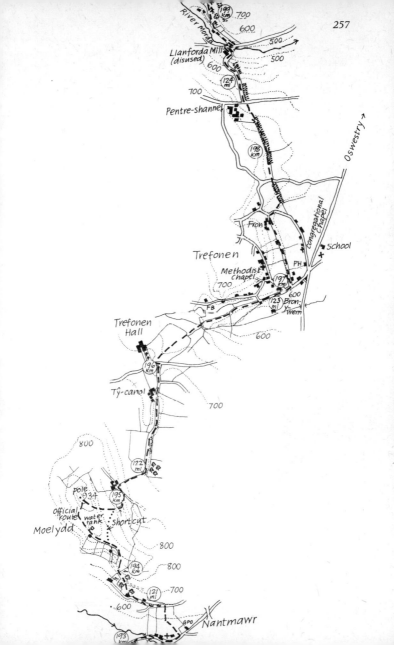

River Mon...

Llanforda Mill
(disused)

Pentre-shannel

Oswestry →

Fron

Congregational Chapel

Trefonen

School

Methodist
chapel

PH

Bron-
y-Wern

F.B.

Trefonen
Hall

Tŷ-canol

Moelydd

pole
934

official
route

water
tank

shortcut

Nantmawr

BPO

mineral railway line and a brook to reach A495 at Porth-y-waen.

Between Llanymynech Hill and Trefonen the Dyke crosses an undulating and agricultural countryside and it has been much damaged. Between Porth-y-waen and Treflach Wood old limestone quarries have extensively destroyed parts of it, and the road from Treflach Wood to Trefonen is in places on the line of its ditch. The Path therefore avoids the direct road link along this quarried and broken line and takes a route westwards through Nant-mawr and over Moelydd Hill.

The little village of Trefonen has both a Welsh Calvinistic Methodist and a Congregational chapel and a parish church. This was built in grey stone between 1821 and 1828 with a low, broad nave with pediment-like gable. The church was enlarged in 1876 by the building of the chancel and apse, the bellcote was renewed, and the windows 'gothicised'.

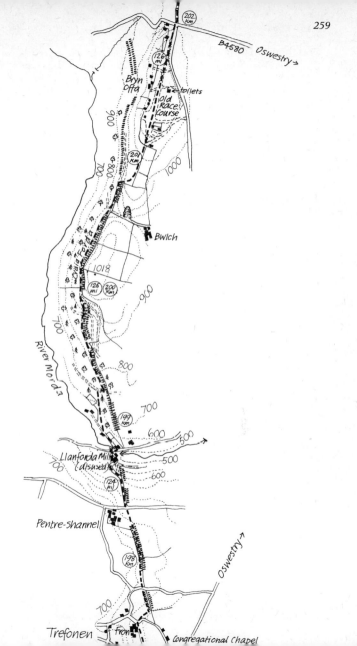

B4580 Oswestry →

126 mi

Bryn Offa

toilets

Old Race Course

201 Km

1000

900

800

700

Dyffryn Offa

1018

126 mi   200 Km

900

700

800

River Morda

700

199 Km

600   500 →

Llanforda Mill (disused)

500

124 mi

600

Pentre-Shannel

198 Km

Oswestry →

700

Trefonen   Iron

Congregational Chapel

Trefonen to Bakers Hill

The Dyke is picked up again just N of Trefonen village, the Path following alongside, and then on top of, a superb stretch of Dyke, the first full-scale and undamaged example that we have seen for 15 miles. This fine earthwork leads up to a road junction just E of Pentre-shannel farm, where at one time the ditch was widened and deepened to form a duck pond. Although this pond no longer exists the corner of the field here is very muddy after rain.

Where the Dyke runs alongside the road from Pentre-shannel to Llanforda Mill it is a magnificent work of normal character. The road follows the line of the ditch, dropping steeply to the pleasant valley of the River Morda and the less-pleasant pig-farm of Llanforda Mill.

From the ford of the Morda brook the Dyke is aligned directly to the crest of the steep W-facing slope of Craig Forda,

300 ft above. The choice of so dominant an alignment for the great earthwork is notable, influencing conclusions as to its purpose and significance.

The Dyke makes a fairly sharp ascent from the valley floor, diagonally up the hillside through natural woodland scarred with disused limestone quarries. At first the hillside is so steep that we follow a bridle-path up to a point where a gap in the Dyke admits its passage. After passing through the woodland the Dyke forms the boundary between hill pasture and beech woods. For $\frac{1}{2}$ mile the course is level at 950 ft, save at the end of the third field where a track to Bwlch farm (and the Vrynwy aqueduct) pass through the Dyke. After one more field the Dyke enters the plantations again and it can be seen running along the steep hillside of Craig Forda as a berm or platform cut into the hill scarp for a distance of 600 yds at a level of 950 ft. Try and find the quaint stone seat which was

built upon the Dyke in this section.

The Dyke continues its line through the pinewoods on the steep scarp of the Craig, but we have to leave it to take the Path over the common and along the old racecourse. (The Dyke takes a diagonal course down a steep slope of a re-entrant ravine, beside the stream of which runs an ancient trackway from the Oswestry road to the River Morda. There is no trace of the Dyke on the precipitous N flank of the ravine rising up to the Oswestry road).

The old racecourse is a common, with short cropped turf between the bracken, gorse and heather. From the open summit of this long flat-topped ridge there are most magnificent views. To the E roll the green farmlands of the Shropshire Plain, in which the pyramid of The Wrekin stands, 30 miles away. The faint crest of Wenlock Edge lies to the SE and the humped Breiddens lie further to the S. Westwards lie the Berwyns, with the jagged peaks of Cader Idris beyond.

We have come 7 or 8 miles along the Path from Llanymynech to Oswestry's old racecourse and the next 8 miles of good walking to the Dee may be too much for the rest of the day. It is a pleasant walk down B4580 into Oswestry if you want to find accommodation and do some exploration there.

Description of route continues on p 267.

Oswestry

The history of Oswestry is much more interesting than the town itself. It is named after St Oswald, Christian King of Northumbria, who was slain here in a battle by the Mercian King Penda in AD 642. A field across the road from the grammar school was the site of the battle; Oswald's body was hung, drawn and quartered and nailed to a tree. Tradition has it that an eagle carried off the remains but a part of the saint's body fell to the ground near the school and water gushed from the spot, which is now called St Oswald's Well.

Old Oswestry is a huge earthwork 1 mile N of the present town, on the line of Wat's Dyke, and it is probable that the settlement moved from here to the present site when an early monastery was created to commemorate Oswald's death. A settlement became established around the church, and later a castle was built on the nearest glacial mound to the church.

Offa's Dyke on Craig Forda (p 260)
Offa's Dyke on Craig Forda, looking N to Baker's Hill (p 261)
M *Oswestry (p 263)*

The Normans fortified the town with a castle and walls. Henry I granted the land to the Fitz Alans, and a charter to hold markets at 'The Cross' between the church and the castle. The town was burnt by King John in 1216 and by Llewelyn in 1234, and it was only then that the town centre moved from the church to the castle. The town walls were built between 1257 and 1300 but enclose only parts of the town around the castle, leaving the church settlement well outside. The Fitz Alans, now Earls of Arundel, were seldom present in their castle, the townspeople were already being

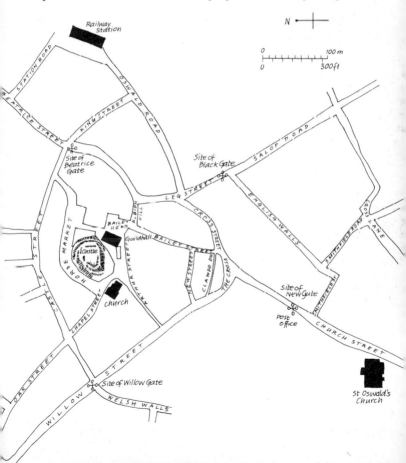

allowed to build in the castle bailey and the great days of the
castle were soon over.

There are few ancient buildings in the town, but there is a
preponderance of glazed red brick and some poor architecture.
The chief buildings are: the parish church of St Oswald, partly
17c but gutted and re-furnished in 1872–3 when it was
restored by G E Street; the grammar school next door was
founded in 1407, a few years before Agincourt. Although the
present buildings are not medieval there stands near the church
an old gabled house said to have been the original school. The
Rev William Archibald Spooner (1844–1930) renowned for his
Spoonerisms, was educated here. (One of his best was: 'Sir,
you have deliberately tasted two whole worms; you have
hissed all my mystery lectures and have been caught fighting
a liar in the quad; you can leave Oxford by the next town
drain.') The best of the old houses in the heart of the town is

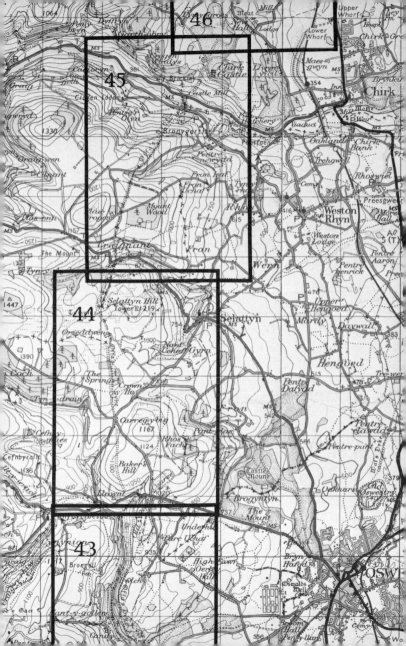

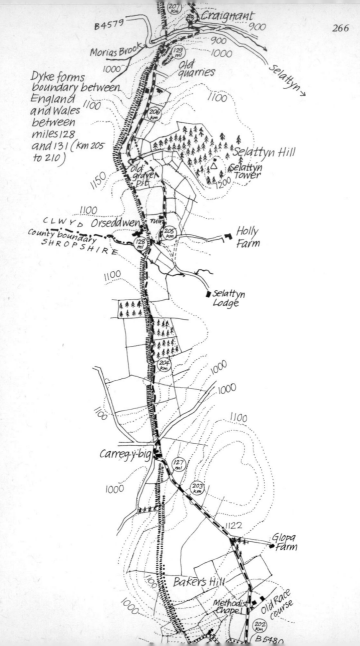

B4579

(207) Km

Craignant

900

900

1000

Selattyn →

Morias Brook

(129 ml)

1000

Old quarries

Dyke forms boundary between England and Wales between miles 128 and 131 (km 205 to 210)

1100

1100

(206) Km

Selattyn Hill

Selattyn Tower

1150

Old gravel pit

1200

1100

CLWYD Orseddwen

ruin

(205 ml)

Holly Farm

County boundary SHROPSHIRE

(128 ml)

1100

Selattyn Lodge

1100

(204) Km

1000

1000

1100

1100

Carreg-y-big

1000

(127 ml)

(203) Km

1122

Glopa Farm

Baker's Hill

1000

1000

Methodist Chapel

Old Race course

(202) Km

1000

B5480

the Lloyd or Llwyd Mansion, a black-and-white house with fine window tracery.

The castle ruins are a municipal park from which there is a grand view of the town and of the surrounding country.

Bakers Hill to Chirk Castle

The Dyke is built on a massive scale over Baker's Hill, but you will have to be content with the view from the road to the E leading to Carreg-y-big. It was proposed that the Path should follow the fine stretch of the Dyke over this hill, but this was opposed and the Minister decided in favour of the objectors. Nevertheless, you should make a detour to see part of it. A path leaves the Oswestry-Llawnt road 150 yds W of three sharp bends at a hidden stile. In its ascent the Dyke is its usual fine character: the Dyke can be seen rising up the opposite flank of the lateral ravine and its course is visible through the woods on Craig Forda. When the Dyke emerges on the moorland top of Bakers's Hill (1100 ft) it is seen as a magnificent monument. On the descent it passes an old quarry where it has been considerably damaged, but this is the disputed stretch of the path. As it leads to Carreg-y-big the Dyke is present as a low rounded ridge.

From Carreg-y-big the ground begins to rise. From the crossroads the Dyke is very fine, steep scarped and with pines growing on its crest: the ditch and bank are perfect. There is a gap in the Dyke where a footpath crosses, probably original since a spring rises here. From the spring the ditch is over-deepened by serving as a drainage channel. The ditch contains a marsh or pools and is wet in several places. The Dyke crosses moorland country, in places afforested, and crosses a stream to the isolated farmhouse of Orseddwen.

The Dyke changes direction through 40 degrees and ascends a gentle slope from Orseddwen Farm across the easy westward facing slopes of Selattyn Hill, its exact course being determined by the contours of this hill. The Path runs to the E of this magnificent stretch on a rough track winding through gorse to the salient of Selattyn Hill.

From Orseddwen to the River Ceiriog the boundary between Clwyd and Shropshire follows the line of the Dyke.

On Baker's Hill, looking S to Craig Forda (p 264)

Selattyn Hill seems to have been one of Offa's sighting points because the Dyke has followed a straight alignment from the S until here, when it swings over to the head of the Vale of Llangollen. The tower on the top of the hill was built in 1847 by a Mr West, a clergyman, to mark the site of a battle between the Saxons and the Britons, but its ruins are being quickly submerged by a young spruce plantation.

The Dyke crosses open ground – pasture and moorland – as a grassy bank with steep scarp and well-defined ditch: the Path

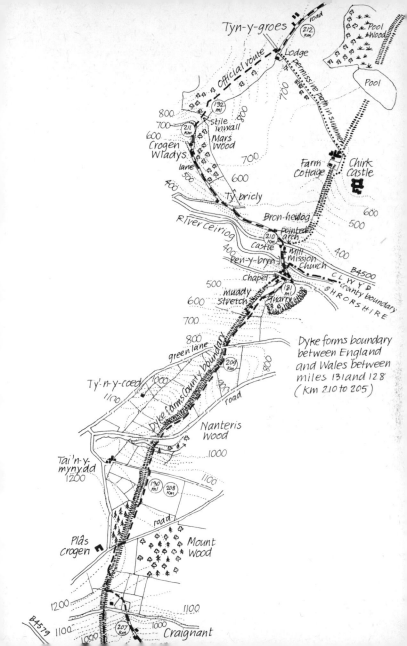

runs parallel to it on a rough track leading down to B4579 in the valley of the Morlas Brook at Craignant. The Dyke runs through Craignant Wood on the E side of a small re-entrant, the wall bounding the wood being on the bank. Where the track carrying the Path meets this wall the earthwork can be seen in the woodland dropping down the steep slope diagonally to Craignant road, the old turnpike road between Oswestry and Glyn Ceiriog.

The position of the Dyke in the valley of the Morlas Brook is marked by a stone tower, inscribed 'Offa's Dyke' standing on the road B4579. It is one of two 19c markers along the Dyke, the other being at the summit of the road to Presteigne. Between the road and the brook the Dyke is definite, though of small scale.

On the narrow ribbon of flat land, subject to floods, which here forms the floor of the valley, the Dyke is not present, but it begins on a steep slope on the far side of the brook. The earthwork is perfect and of normal dimensions. The ditch has become the bed of a streamlet and this is over-deepened on the steep slope. The Dyke climbs the hillside too steeply to be followed so the Path follows a rough road past a quarry and through Craignant farm.

Across the road the slope of the hill eases and the Path crosses pasture to re-join the tree-clad Dyke. As it rises to Plas Crogen the slope becomes more gradual and the earthwork passes through open moorland at about the 1200 ft contour: here the ditch is perfect, marshy, but the bank has been damaged.

On the level moorland around Plas Crogen the Dyke is constructed of earth and is overgrown with bracken and gorse. The dry-stone wall on the bank is not original. The ditch is marshy and forms a watercourse. The earthwork here is less impressive than the stretch just to the north. The Path keeps to the top of the Dyke, through high bracken, across rough moorland, to the crossing of an overgrown green lane. N of this, on the steep drop to the Nant Eris ravine the Dyke presents a remarkable appearance. Descending at a steep angle down the wooded scarp the earthwork has an immense

Offa's Dyke on Baker's Hill, looking N to Selattyn Hill (p 271)
Offa's Dyke on Baker's Hill, looking N to Selattyn Hill (p 271)
Offa's Dyke Path on Selattyn Hill, looking S (p 272 top)
Offa's Dyke Path on Selattyn Hill, looking N (p 272 below)
Offa's Dyke Memorial, B4579, near Craignant (p 273)

Selattyn Hill

Selattyn Hill

Carreg-y-big

V-shaped ditch on the W side, leading right to the edge of the brook. This ditch is another example of over-deepening due to water action, a very wet and overgrown dingle.

On the far side of the Nant Eris ravine there is a steep climb to a road, and between the 1100 and 1000 ft contours the Dyke is cut through limestone: the bank thus has a steep slope and the ditch maintains its angular contours. On this upland the ground is moorland pasture and both bank and ditch are undamaged save by time. At about 900 ft the upland is left,

and the Dyke is continually present as it drops diagonally down the steep hillside. In places the Dyke is of striking profile, and throughout this stretch it is either well-wooded or covered in bracken, sometimes so overgrown that it is better to keep to the fields below. On the slope the adjacent fields, now mostly pasture, have formerly been under cultivation and the ditch is in places ploughed in.

From the Dyke there are magnificent views up the Ceiriog valley and occasional glimpses of Chirk Castle perched like a picture-book fortress on the hill across the valley.

The Path joins a track at an old quarry then takes a path between cottages to join a road in Pen-y-bryn hamlet. There are traces of the Dyke on the steep scarp between this road and the river, but the Path follows the road into the valley of the River Ceiriog. There are no traces of the Dyke here, nor could one expect that any indications of its presence would have survived on this flood-swept valley floor. The valley is known as Adwy'r beddau – the gap of the graves – due to the tradition of the ambush and defeat of Henry II's expedition by the Welsh in the Battle of Crogen in 1165. There is no adequate authority to confirm the association of this gap with the tradition, nor evidence to show that the slain were buried in the hollow trenches of Offa's Dyke near the present Castle Mill.

Selattyn Hill

Offa's Dyke

There are remarkably fine stretches of the Dyke through the grounds of Chirk Castle, and you can, between April and September, use a sign-posted permissive path partly along the Dyke and visit the Castle at the same time.
Description of route continues on p 278.

Description of route continues on p 278.

Chirk Castle/Castell y Waun
Home of Lt Col Ririd and Lady Margaret Myddleton.
Hours of Admission
Easter Saturday and Sunday, thereafter each Sunday in April from 14.00–17.00, and then every Tuesday, Thursday, Saturday and Sunday from May-September 14.00–17.00.
Holiday Mondays 11.00–17.00
Fee for castle and grounds. Lunches, teas and refreshments.

The castle is a late baronial stronghold built on lands taken from the Welsh princes of Northern Powys after the final conquest of Wales in 1282. The castle was built in 1310 by one of the Marcher Lords, Roger Mortimer, who had been granted the lands of Chirk by Edward I as a reward for his part in bringing about the downfall of Llywelyn, the last of the native Princes of Wales.

It was an extremely strong fortification. Rectangular in plan, its heavy red-sandstone walls have massive drum towers at each corner. The north front is 250 ft long, and its central gateway leads into a massive quadrangle, 150 ft long by 100 ft wide, from which lead off various store rooms, guard rooms and stables. The battlements around the castle are laid out so that at least two persons could walk abreast when watching the defences.

The exterior of the castle is unique, an almost unaltered example of a border castle of Edward II's time. The castle still retains its appearance of a stronghold, but it has been so extensively repaired so as to be almost rebuilt. In the SW wing may still be seen traces of the original work. Adam's Tower, the oldest part of the castle, still retains its deep dungeon.

Owain Glyndwr's activities must have placed the castle in great peril, commanding as it does the valleys of Ceiriog and Dee, important entrances to turbulent Wales. The Lord of Chirk was also the Earl of Arundel, and he fought in many battles against Owain and his ally Hotspur.
Offa's Dyke at Plas Crogen, looking S

The castle suffered in the Wars of the Roses. It fell into the hands of Sir William Stanley, one of those who summoned the Earl of Richmond from France and placed an army of Welshmen at his back in order to gain the crown of England. After the victory of Bosworth Field, where the Earl became Henry VI, Sir William received many rewards and was reputed to be the richest man in England. In 1495 Sir William was executed for taking part in Perkin Warbeck's rebellion; on this occasion he had mistaken the course of events and Chirk remained in the hands of the Crown for a while.

The fortress was bought in 1595 by Sir Thomas Myddleton, who was later to become Lord Mayor of London in 1613. His son, also Thomas, found his castle seized by the Royalist forces at the start of the Civil War in 1642. The castle was cleverly obtained for the King by Colonel Ellis in January 1643, and John Watts was made Governor. Sir Thomas had been appointed Sergeant Major – General of North Wales and in December 1644 he besieged his own castle, not with ordnance but with firearms. His attempt to recover it failed.

After the end of the War Sir Thomas threw in his lot with the Parliamentarians and managed to acquire his castle again. He took up the cause of Charles II in 1659, but this change of allegiance did him no good because he found himself besieged by General Lambert, commanding the Parliamentarian forces under Richard Cromwell in August of that year. The Cromwellian artillery did considerable damage in the siege, and many of the walls were breached. Sir Thomas surrendered.

The castle had to be largely rebuilt after the Civil Wars, so that it is now more of a stately home than a medieval castle. It has a great deal of architectural and historic interest in its chambers and great rooms. There are some fine Stuart portraits, including those of Charles I and Charles II, his illegitimate son the Duke of Monmouth, and Dutch William and his wife Mary.

One curiosity in the collection of pictures is one by Richard Wilson, a landscape and portrait painter of the early 1700's. His picture of the 'Waterfalls at Pistyll Rhaiadr' includes ships sailing over dry land. The story is that he was invited to include a flock of sheep on the hills, but he misunderstood the request: his Welsh patron may have had difficulty in pronouncing the English word, and the artist would have heard 'ship' for 'sheep'. Nevertheless the presence of ships in the

Chrik Castle Gates, made 1718–21
Chirk Castle from Tyn-y-groes

IN VERITATE TRIVMPHO

1719

coat of arms may account for the intentional inclusion of ships in the picture.

Chirk Castle has been occupied since 1310 when it was built by Roger Mortimer, and since 1595 it has been the home of the Myddleton family. The present owner is Lt Col Myddleton, and he was recently given a grant of £52,000 under the 1953 Historic Buildings Act – one of the main recipients of government assistance to private owners of stately homes – in order to keep it in complete repair.

The main entrance gates to the castle park are a remarkable example of artistic wrought-iron work. In 1718 Sir Robert Myddleton commissioned two Welsh brothers, Robert and John Davies to make great lodge gates to his park. Their handiwork, completed in 1721, is a design of striking complexity and dedication. The Wolf of the Myddletons is incorporated many times in the design. The brothers Davies won fame as craftsmen and ironmasters and their splendid iron gates add distinction to many of the churches and mansions in the area around Bersham, near Wrexham, where they had their workshop.

The Dyke through Chirk Castle Park

The Dyke may be followed through part of Chirk Castle Park by a permissive path from Castle Mill to Farm Cottage, before it turns away to a public road at Tyn-y-gross.

On the slope rising from the Ceiriog valley the Dyke is on the full scale. A steep scarp fronts the valley above the road B4500 and the Dyke is not at first present, but a little higher it can be seen following the eastern flank of a small re-entrant. At the bottom of the gradient the re-entrant is a deep ravine which has eroded the bank of the Dyke and at one point the ditch co-incides with the streamlet which created the re-entrant. The Path follows the fine Dyke to 'The House on the Dyke', and its crest is here marked by stag-headed oak trees.

The Dyke is destroyed by the estate office enclosures. It can be seen going across the parkland to the Pool, and in dry seasons it can be seen on the floor of this artificial lake.

The River Ceiriog to River Dee

It is better to follow the permissive path through Chirk Park if you are passing this way between April and September, but at other times you have to use the official Path, which passes outside the park to the W.

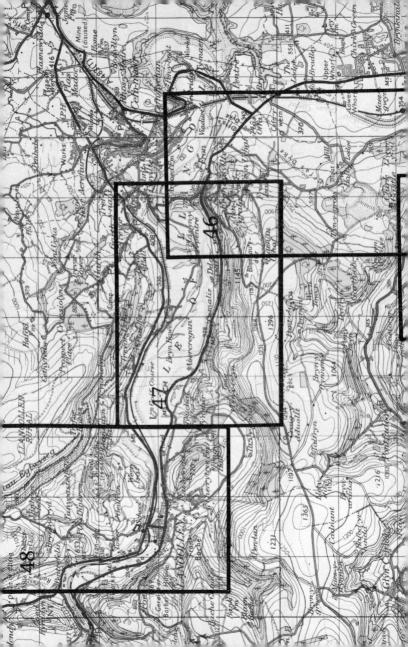

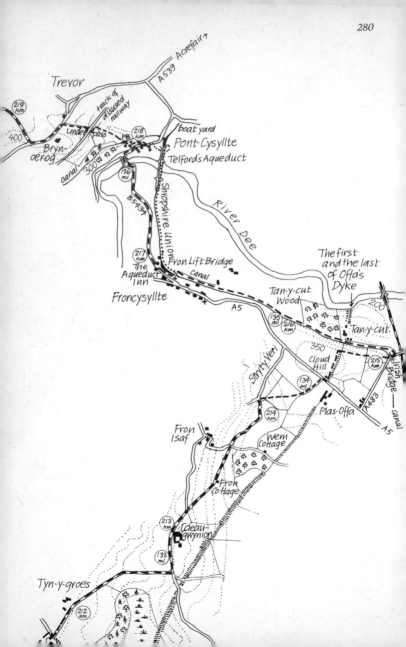

Trevor

A539 Acrefair →

219 Km

400

track & disused railway

under pass

218 Km

boat yard

Pont-Cysyllte

Telford's Aqueduct

Bryn oerog

canal

300 300

136 ml

B5434

A Shropshire Union canal

River Dee

217 Km

Fron Lift Bridge

The first and the last of Offa's Dyke

The Aqueduct Inn

canal

Froncysyllte

A5

Tan-y-cut Wood

200

135 ml

216 Km

Tan-y-cut

350

Cloud Hill

215 Km

1750 Bridge — canal

Sirhy veri

134 ml

A483

214 Km

Plas-Offa

A5

Fron Isaf

Wern Cottage

Fron Cottage

213 Km

Caeau-gwynion

133 ml

Tyn-y-groes

212 Km

From the Castle Mill on B4500 a narrow track ascends
diagonally up the valley side to Crogen Wladys, then turns a
sharp corner to go up a re-entrant across fields on a faint track
to the road at Tyn-y-Groes. Here the permissive path comes in
on the R from Chirk Castle Park. The Path follows the road to
the junction at Caeau-gwynion and turns N along another lane
called Stryt-y-Veri.

From the Path the Dyke is discernible with difficulty,
following an almost parallel course 200 yds to the E. Near
Caeau-gwynion it is an imposing work, crowned by old trees,
with a well marked W ditch. As it approaches Wern Wood it
can be picked out by the field boundary hedge on its bank.
Beyond Wern Wood the Dyke is very fine, with old oaks on
its bank, but it is damaged in the neighbourhood of Plas Offa
Farm, and between the farm and the main road A5 the line is
shown by the ditch forming a water channel.

Beyond A5 — Telford's Holyhead Road — the ditch is especially
well marked being in use as a pathway. The earthwork continues
in good condition and as it approaches the Shropshire Union
Canal it is on the full scale. This is the last surviving stretch of
Offa's Dyke that we will see. The construction of the canal and
the adjoining light railway have obliterated the earthwork, but
beyond it continues to the S bank of the Dee. The river flows
at the foot of a precipitous scarp as it widens its alluvial plain,
and many yards of the earthwork have been destroyed by river
erosion.

The Vale of Llangollen

Through Clwyd Offa's Dyke passes close to a succession of
grubby industrial towns such as Acrefair, Trevor, Cefn, Ruabon,
Wrexham, Buckley, Flint, and Holywell.

The devastation of the landscape of this region is due not
only to the presence of a large coalfield but also to the
occurrence of lead and other minerals and the use of stone in
the manufacture of cement, coarse pottery and chemicals. The
alignment of the Dyke through this region cut off from Wales
the southern shore of the Dee estuary and the rich mineral
deposits of the Halkyn Mountain. These economic advantages
suggest that Mercia was the dominant partner in the arrangement
that resulted in the partial construction of the Dyke in this area.

The Offa's Dyke Path therefore leaves the line of the Dyke
to follow a scenic alternative above the valley of the Dee and

then along the range of Clwydian Hills to Prestatyn.

The Offa's Dyke Path follows the towpath of the Shropshire Union Canal from Irish Bridge on A483, as it clings to the hillside above the Dee. The scenery and views are an indication of the delights of the Vale of Llangollen which lie ahead.

In the closing years of the 18c the borderland region saw the development of canals in an attempt to realise a dream of a waterway connection between the Mersey, the Dee and the Severn. A beginning was made by an Act of 1793 for the Ellesmere Canal, a scheme to link the Dee at Chester with the Severn at Shrewsbury. It was to run by way of Wrexham to tap the coal of Denbighshire, then through Chirk and past Ellesmere and Weston to Shrewsbury. One of its major feeders was the Montgomery Canal, which we have followed near Welshpool, and a branch to Llangollen, the section we are following now.

The section from Weston to Chirk was cut without difficulty, but the section between Chirk and Wrexham was more difficult because it involved the crossing of the deep valleys of the Ceiriog and Dee. Thomas Telford was called in to construct his famous and impressive aqueducts at Chirk and Pontcysyllte in 1795.

Passing the village of Froncysyllte the canal launches out into the deep valley of the Dee on a massive embankment, then crosses the river on the breathtaking Pontcysyllte Aqueduct, Telford's greatest civil engineering masterpiece, described by Sir Walter Scott as the most impressive work of art he had ever seen.

Telford realised that such a high crossing of the Dee was inevitable if time and water-wasting locks were to be avoided, and it was obvious to him that a conventional brick or stone aqueduct would be quite unsuitable. His plan was to build a cast-iron trough laying along the top of a row of stone piers, an entirely new concept for an aqueduct and the first time in the world that iron was used on the major scale. Telford's plan was at first greeted with derision, but work began in 1795 and it was completed 10 years later, opened in 1805. Its construction cost £47,018 – 'a very moderate sum' Telford said.

The length of the bridge is 1007 feet and it stands 121 feet above the turbulent river, carrying the canal in a channel nearly 12 ft wide. There are 18 majestic masonry piers, with very thin joints between the blocks. The mortar between them

River Dee with Cysylltau Bridge and Pont Cysyllte aqueduct

is the original mixture used by Telford, believed to be made of ox-blood and lime. The span of each arch is 48 ft and the length of embankment at the southern end of the bridge is 1500 feet.

One can hardly imagine the utter amazement felt by the people at that time as they witnessed boats moving easily across this tall, beautiful and unique structure. The excitement to be derived from crossing the aqueduct by boat is partly due to the fact that one side of the canal is completely unprotected from about 12 inches above the water level. The towpath on one side is safely fenced off with iron railings, but those with no head for heights on this 'concessionary' path will be able to admire the aqueduct from the narrow stone bridge over the Dee, which is the route taken by the Official Path.

When the aqueduct was opened it was clear that the whole canal project was doomed because the connection to Wrexham and Chester was not to be completed. Barges still floated across the valley up to the beginning of the 1939–45 War and a

passenger service operated between Chirk and Llangollen. Today the aqueduct remains as built, apart from recent renewals of balustrading and the towpath structure. The masonry is apparently in prime condition and the dovetailed joints in the iron trough hardly leak at all. The side plates of the trough are all wedge shaped, like the stones in a masonry arch. It is easily the most famous and spectacular feature in the whole canal system, a masterpiece, one of the major monuments to the industrial architecture of its time.

At Pontcysyllte wharves and basins were built in expectation of heavy traffic, but as the canal ended $\frac{1}{2}$ mile away at Cefn Mawr the optimism was hardly justifiable.

What was originally intended to be solely a water feeder from the Dee at Llantysilio – where water was fed into the system by Telford's graceful Horseshoe Falls – was turned into a canal branch to serve Llangollen. Today, now that many canals have become little more than reed-filled ditches, it is an irony of fate that the uneconomic Llangollen branch canal should have survived until this age of leisure when recreational pursuits, rather than commercial interests, are needed to ensure the survival of canals. The Llangollen branch canal has become one of the more popular stretches of water on the Shropshire Union Canal system, for not only does the narrow boat enthusiast have the thrill of a passage across the Chirk and Pontcysyllte aqueducts, but he also has superb views through one of the most beautiful valleys in the country.

The walker may follow the canal towpath through the valley to Llangollen and beyond, but our Official Path climbs high above to obtain magnificent panoramic views from the Precipice Walk. Passenger boats also travel this 3 mile stretch of water in the season. If for some reason you want to get to Llangollen quickly bus services are more frequent on the N side of the valley. Do not wait to catch a train! The Vale of Llangollen has been used to catering for tourists for a long time and there are better facilities here than anywhere else along our route, other than the Lower Wye valley.

The Path leaves A539 Ruabon-Ruthin road and goes diagonally up and across the spur of a hill through woods above the ruins of Trevor Hall. The line of the Official Path is shown on maps to run at a much lower level across the hillside, but no such path exists. The more obvious path through the Forestry Commission plantation climbs higher and joins the Precipice

47 *The Vale of Llangollen*

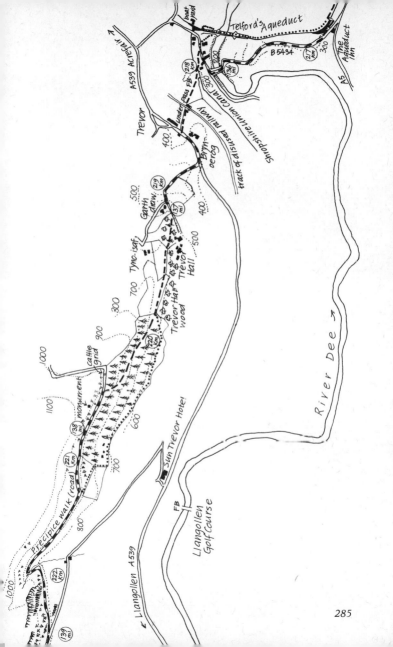

Walk at a stile and Offa's Dyke Path signpost. It seems that there have been difficulties on this stretch: perhaps it was an act of defiance to the long-distance path that hereabouts the signposts are in Welsh and the acorns hang upside down!

The Precipice Walk is a disappointment to those who expect to find a pleasant footpath. It is instead a metalled road and popular for the weekend motorists; rightly so, for it is a fine bit of scenic engineering, giving wide views down the Vale and across the Berwyns. The Pontcysyllte Aqueduct can be seen in one direction and Llangollen in the other, and at this place we will make a break in our journey. From below the limestone escarpment of Trevor Rocks we can drop down into the valley by lanes and paths past Castell Dinas Bran into Llangollen. *Description of route continues on p 293.*

Precipice Walk, Trevor Rocks and Castell Dinas Bran
Trevor Rocks and Castell Dinas Bran

Llangollen stands in the sheltered valley of the River Dee – Afon Dyfrdwy – one of the best known rivers of Wales, and the scenery through which it passes is among the most beautiful in the country. Ruskin said 'The Vale of Llangollen is a true valley between ranges of grandly formed hills . . . and the village of Llangollen is one of the most beautiful in Wales or anywhere else.' (ECD Thursday. MD Tuesday.)

Llangollen was the headquarters of George Borrow during the first stage of his visit to Wales and in his 'Wild Wales' he has much to say about the town and its vicinity.

In recent years the town has become famous as the centre of the International Eisteddfod, the contest for folk dancers and singers held annually in July. There are no records of any important early Eisteddfod in Clwyd, but it was at Llangollen that the idea of a really National Musical Festival in the present sense originated. There had been a successful Eisteddfod in Llangollen in 1789, but it was the Great Eisteddfod held in 1858 at which a committee was set up to plan for the future National Eisteddfodau. The present International Music Festival was inaugurated in 1947, and has been held every summer since.

The early history of Llangollen centred around the hill fort of Castle Dinas Bran, and it was not until 1284 that the settlement in the valley began to develop, when Roger Mortimer obtained a royal grant of market and fairs. Though it later became the centre of slate quarrying, the countryside around is largely unspoilt by industrial development.

The town is built principally on the S bank of the Dee, and it is approached by a bridge which is regarded as one of the Seven Wonders of Wales. These are, according to the old rhyme:

Pistyll Rhaiaidr and Wrexham steeple
Snowdon's mountain without its people
Overton yew trees, St Winefride's wells
Llangollen bridge and Gresford bells.

The stone bridge has four irregular pointed arches, said to have been originally built in the reign of Henry I, and widened in 1345 by Dr John Trevor, Bishop of St Asaph and Chancellor of Chester. In later days an additional arch was erected under which the railway passed and the bridge was enlarged to double its former width. When the bridge was widened in 1873 the workmen found on a stone in one of the arches the date 1131.

N *Llangollen*

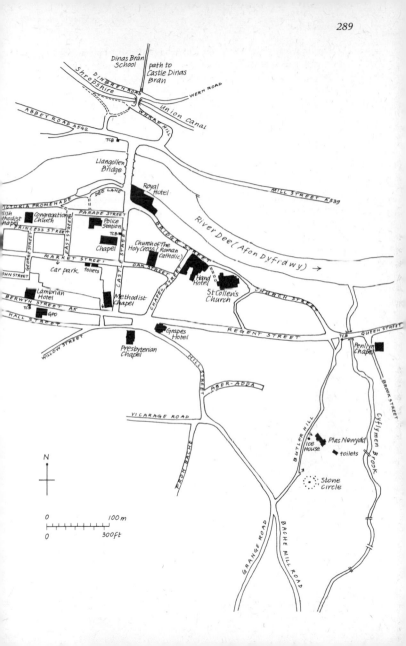

There are fine views from the bridge, both upstream and downstream, especially when, as Tennyson wrote:

The south-west, that blowing Bala Lake
Fills all the sacred Dee.

On such occasions the water may rise in a few hours to the height of the bridge, and these floods sometimes occur in the finest weather, when there has been neither rain nor thaw. The river is a good trout stream and also yields salmon: just below the bridge is a salmon leap and one may often see fish and white-water canoeists negotiating the rocky channels.

The town contains many stone-built Victorian buildings and there is an irregular layout of streets between the bridge and the church.

The parish church is dedicated to St Collen, from which the town derives its name. The fine building is mainly a 12c structure and it was considerably enlarged in 1861 by the then vicar, whose son, A G Edwards, became the first Archbishop of Wales. There is a splendid carved roof of intricate design, said to have come from the Valle Crucis Abbey. It is illuminated

for visitors and shows angels, flowers and animals. There are numerous excellent marble monuments: a monument in the churchyard is to the 'Ladies of Llangollen.'

The place to visit in Llangollen is Plas Newydd, the former home of the 'Ladies of Llangollen.' To get there take the hill road by The Grapes Hotel on the A5 road, or go up Butler Hill on the SE side of the town.

Plas Newydd

	Weekdays	Sundays
Open 1 May – 30 September	*10.30 – 19.30*	*11.30 – 16.00*

Admission charge to house.
Gardens open all year round without charge.

Plas Newydd was from 1779 1831 the home of Lady Elanor Charlotte Butler and Miss Sarah Ponsonby, two independent-minded Irish aristocrats, generally known as the 'Ladies of Llangollen'. They were both unhappy in Waterford and they left home; after travelling around Wales for several months they obtained the tenancy of Plas Newydd. At that time it was a plain, stonebuilt house, set in farm land, but the ladies set to work on creating a garden and embellishing the house with the carved porches over doors and windows. (The black-and-white effect was added by later owners.)

The ladies were as irregular in their dress as in their way of life, and were considered by many to be eccentric. Their hair was short, powdered but uncurled. Each wore a man's hat and neck-tie, and a blue riding jacket. Their mannish looks attracted a great deal of attention, but their reputation for wit and hospitality was widespread. During their time Llangollen was on the stage coach road between London and Holyhead and consequently they were visited by many celebrated persons of their time – the playwright Sheridan, the statesman Burke, Castlereagh and Canning, the Duke of Wellington, Sir Walter Scott, Browning, Tennyson and William Wordsworth being the most notable.

The house contains a vast amount of delicate carving, allegedly stolen or bought by the ladies from old churches and houses in the neighbourhood. The ladies also collected much stained glass and Cordovan leather, all of which remain today making Plas Newydd an interesting place to visit.

The grounds of the house extend to 12 acres, including a

Llangollen. Plas Newydd and Castell Dinas Bran

magnificent glen of the Cyflymen stream. It is crossed by rustic bridges, and the whole area gave the ladies scope for ambitious plans in landscape gardening. They planted beech, willow and poplar, lilacs and laburnums, and syringas, white broom and moss roses.

Lady Elanor died in June 1829 aged 90 and Miss Ponsonby died in December 1831 aged 76. Both were buried in the churchyard of St Collen, where also stands a three-sided tombstone erected by the ladies on the death in November 1809 of their valued Irish maid 'Mrs' Mary Carryl, known as 'Molly the Bruiser' after having thrown a candle-stick at a fellow servant.

In later years E and W wings were added to the house and the gardens were laid out in a formal manner with shrubberies and topiary. In front of the house there is a stone circle erected for the Gorsedd ritual of the Royal National Eisteddfod of Wales in 1908. After several changes in ownership, Llangollen UDC acquired the property in 1933, and in 1963 both wings of the house were demolished to leave the house exactly as it was when the ladies lived there. It is now regarded as one of the finest examples of black-and-white domestic architecture in all Britain.

21 Llangollen to Llandegla (main route)

On the N side of the Dee above Llangollen the official Offa's
Dyke Path goes past Castell Dinas Bran and follows a route
beneath the Elwyseg Rocks to World's End and then across
Llandegla Moor to Llandegla.

The Countryside Commission in their descriptive leaflet
recommend an alternative route to use in bad weather that
avoids the crossing of Llandegla Moor, but for other reasons
which will be given later the alternative is more practical. This
route leaves the Eglwyseg Glen before World's End and passes
S of Llandegla Moor near the Horseshoe Pass and joins the
main route just before Llandegla village.

The main route will be described in this chapter and the
alternative route will be given in the next. You could combine
either with a visit to Valle Crucis Abbey and Eliseg's Pillar,
both in the valley of the Eglwyseg to the NW of Llangollen,
particularly if you have a half day to spare or spend two
nights in Llangollen.

Llangollen to Castell Dinas Bran

From the Dee bridge at Llangollen go up Wharf Hill and over
the canal by the Siambr Wen Bridge to a path beside the school
which will lead you by lanes and paths back to the Offa's Dyke
Path, which runs below the carboniferous limestone escarpment
of Trevor Rocks. Without too much of a diversion paths will
take you up the steep slopes of an isolated conical hill of hard
Silurian shale to the hill-fort of Castell Dinas Bran.
Description of route continues on p 296.

Castell Dinas Bran

The Hill Fort of Bran was built on the oval summit 1062 ft
above sea level, towering 750 ft above the valley of the Dee.

The name and traditions of Dinas Bran suggest that it was
the site of a stronghold of Eliseg, Prince of Powys, whose
ancestry is commemorated on the Pillar of Eliseg. Apparently
the original Celtic system of fortifications consisted of ditches
and eath mounds topped by wooden palisades.

The primitive character of the architecture suggest that the
foundations of the existing ruins were laid down in the reign
of Henry III, probably by Madoc ap Gruffydd Maelor, ruler
of Northern Powys from 1191–1236. When he died he was
buried in the abbey of Valle Crucis, which he had founded in

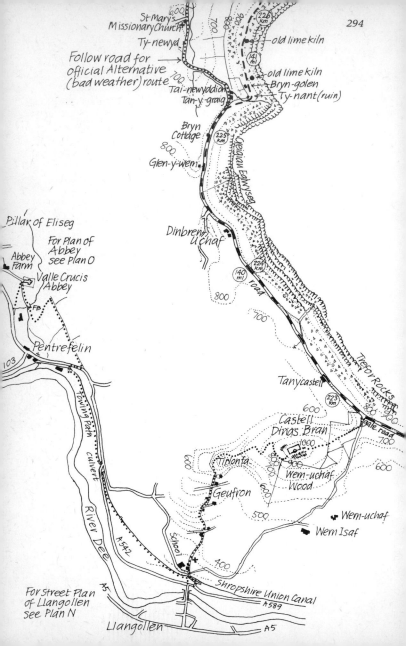

St Mary's
Missionary Church
Ty-newyd

old lime kiln

Follow road for
official Alternative
(bad weather) route

old lime kiln
Bryn-golen
Ty-nant (ruin)
Tai-newyddion
Tan-y-graig

Bryn
Cottage

Glen-y-wern

Creigiau Eglwyseg

road

Dinbren
Uchaf

Pillar of Eliseg

For Plan of
Abbey
see Plan O

Abbey
Farm
Valle Crucis
Abbey

FB

Pentrefelin

103

Trefor Rocks

Tanycastell

Castell
Dinas Bran

Towing Path

culvert

Tirionfa

Wem-uchaf
Wood

Geufron

Wem-uchaf

Wern Isaf

River Dee

A542

School

Shropshire Union Canal

A589

For Street Plan
of Llangollen
See Plan N

A5

Llangollen

A5

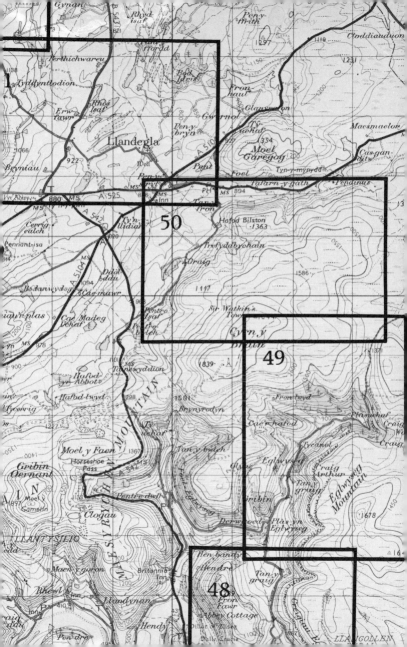

1201. His eldest son Gruffydd Madoc was driven out by Llywellyn in 1257, but they shortly became allies and Gruffydd died in possession of Dinas Bran in 1260. His son Madog was deprived of his castle in Edward I's campaign of 1276 against Llywellyn, and he died soon after it was restored to him in 1277.

The Welsh of Northern Powys joined the great Welsh rising of 1282 and after Welsh independence had been crushed the lands N of the Dee were granted to the Earl of Surrey, John Warenne, and the castle was neglected.

Dinas Bran is not known to have played any part in Owain Glyndwr's rebellion, and in 1540 Leland found it 'all in ruin.' Ever since the castle had been established the markets were held down by the church of St Collen in the valley. The steep hillside was too inaccessible for a borough, and the trading centre became established as the site for the new town of Llangollen.

Castell Dinas to World's End

The Vale of Llangollen coincides with a complex series of faults, with the result that the limestone forming the Eglwyseg escarpment on the N side of the valley has been displaced 2 or 3 miles to the W compared with the comparable outcrop on the S side at Froncysyllte.

The smooth, steep grassy slopes of the valley contrast with the bare limestone scree and boulders, culminating in the enormous terraced cliffs along the crest of the scarp. The general height of this stepped and broken formation is from 800 ft–1400 ft and in places juniper and gorse bushes grow out of pockets among the boulders. At the top of the scarp there is an open plateau, bare open moorland covered with heather and bilberry, reaching 1678 ft to form the summit of Eglwyseg Mountain.

Seen in evening light, with the almost horizontal rays of the setting sun playing directly on the scalloped western face of Eglwyseg Mountain, the bare limestone crags take on a strange pinkish glow, and an impression of a barren wilderness is heightened by the shadows in the deep re-entrant valleys.

Offa's Dyke Path follows the road below the cliffs as far as Tan-y-craig, and a track continues along the same level over open ground for 1½ miles towards World's End. If you wish to take the official alternative route keep on the road past St Mary's church to a junction in Eglwyseg Glen at Plas-yn-Eglwyseg.

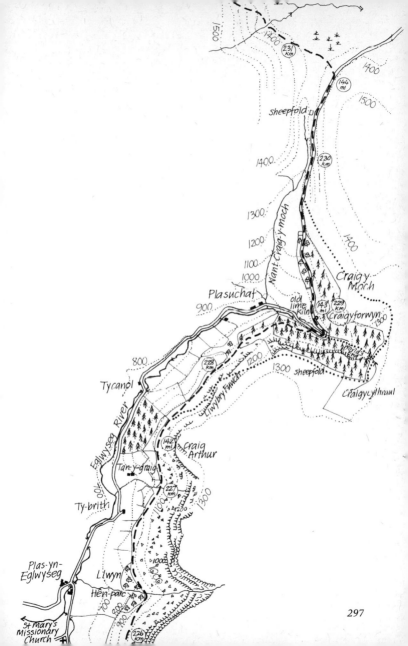

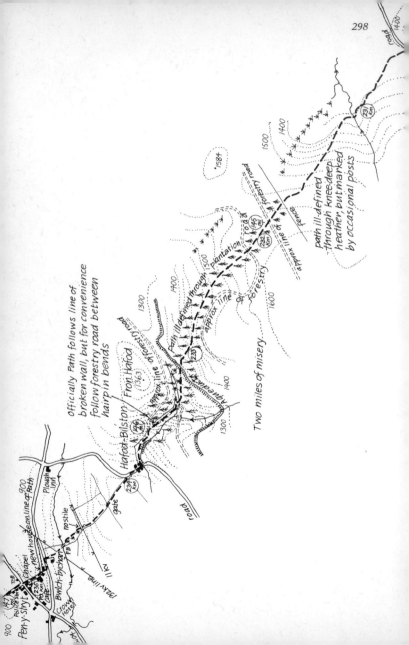

Officially Path follows line of broken wall, but for convenience follow forestry road between hairpin bends

Path ill-defined through plantation

approx line of forestry

approx line of forestry road

approx line of forestry road

path ill-defined through knee-deep heather, butmarked by occasional posts

Two miles of misery

1584

1500

1400

1400

1300

1300

1400

1500

1600

1363

Hafod-Bilston

Fron Hafod

new house on line of path

Plough Inn

nostile

FB

gate

road

Pen-y-Stryt

Chapel

Bwlch-bychan

Crown Hotel

132 km line

900

900

road

1400

1400

road

Police Sta

PO

Lane

TB

The main Path continues below the gleaming white crags of Eglwyseg on an old drove track below Craig Arthur. The path is very narrow and tends to fade in places, but provided you keep some distance above the tree-line no difficulty should be encountered. The official Path continues to traverse the hillside, across scree slopes, but the obvious path is the terraced Llawybr y Fuwch, gradually climbing to a gap in the rock-face. The official Path continues immediately above the line of trees and below the scree slope, and it can be easily lost as it contours the hill. The Path enters a wood to emerge on to the road at a hairpin at the foot of the valley of World's End. (If you follow the way by Llawybr y Fuwch there is a difficult descent off the bluff of Craig-yr-adar – directly above the isolated, half-timbered manor house of Plas Uchaf – but if you have come this way it is better to continue to the head of World's End.)

World's End is a picturesque little valley, formed by a meeting of the heights of Craig-yr-adar and Craig-y-forwyn. It contains abandoned mine workings, and there is a spring of cold water beside the steep path leading down from Craigcythraul.

World's End to Llandegla

The Path follows the road northwards and upwards through the plantations, but it is easier to go round the head of World's End above the plantation on the 'Nature Trail' over Craig-y-Moch. There is still nearly a mile of road across the moor before the Path strikes off NW across Llandegla Moor.

Moorland-lovers will not care for the route over Llandegla Moor to Hafod Bilston. The Path is ill-defined, and although some waymarking has been done map and compass work may be needed in mist and rain to get you across the knee-deep heather. This is the only part of the Path where game-keepers have been encountered maintaining a vigil against unauthorised disturbers of the grouse.

But this is only just the start of your troubles. From the top of the plateau to Hafod Bilston the Path has been deliberately obstructed by a new forestry plantation, and the hillside is coursed by drainage channels and forestry roads. Anyone with orienteering experience will find this an interesting exercise; most will find it a frustrating one.

48 *Llangollen, Castell Dinas Bran and Valle Crucis Abbey (p 294)*
49 *Eglwyseg and World's End (p 297)*
50 *Llandegla Moor (p 298)*

The official alternative path comes in at Hafod Bilston, but even then the main Path to A525 at Llandegla is not easy to find and follow. There is a direct path, but until this has been more clearly defined by the erection of signs and stiles by the Clwyd authorities it may be better to continue along the road to the Plough Inn on A525, then by path between A525 and A5104 to Pen-y-Styrt and Llandegla.

The quiet village of Llandegla offers some hospitality after a stretch of rather dull country. 'The Crown' once earned distinction by providing afternoon tea for Mr and Mrs Gladstone who were touring in this countryside. Now it caters principally for travellers on one of the main roads from Chester to North Wales.

Description of route continues on p 309.

Because the route over Llandegla Moor through the forestry plantation to Hafod Bilston is difficult to follow, and because the path from the Esclusham Mountain road is not easy in bad weather, the Countryside Commission have recommended in their descriptive leaflet an alternative route avoiding this high ground. It is not waymarked, nor is it shown in detail on my $2\frac{1}{2}$ inch sketch maps.

The alternative route leaves the main route at Tan-y-graig and follows the road down to the River Eglwyseg at Plas-yn-Eglwyseg. A cart track follows a stream up through a wood, then on a path diagonally up the steep side of the valley to the foot of the spoil heap of Aber-gwern quarry. A faint path through fields leads to the ruins of Cae'r-hafod, and then an open moorland track keeps above a steep drop, crossing the private road to the radio station on Cyrn-y-Brain. The 'Ponderosa Café' stands to the W on the summit of the famous Horseshoe Pass road, where the A542 crosses Maesyrych Mountain. The alternative path continues NW then N to Pentre-bwlch on A542, then takes the tarred and gated road NE past Graig to join the main route at Hafod Bilston.

(A practical alternative on this route, avoiding both the 2 miles of road between Pentre-bwlch and Hafod Bilston, and the unsatisfactory path between Haford Bilston and Pen-y-Stryt, is to take field paths N of Pentre-bwlch across the River Alyn to A5104 at its junction with A525 at Pen-y-Stryt).

If you intend to use the alternative route S of Llandegla Moor it is well worth extending this diversion to include a visit to Valle Crucis Abbey and the Pillar of Eliseg. On the other hand you might find time to visit these two places of interest on a rest-day or an afternoon whilst staying at Llangollen, and then take the alternative route after you have visited Castell Dinas Bran and the main Path below the Eglwyseg Rocks.

Llangollen to Valle Crucis Abbey

A pleasant way from Llangollen to Valle Crucis Abbey which avoids the busy A542 is to follow the canal along the towing path, a pretty tree-shaded walk to Pentre-felin. There was formerly a wharf here for shipping slates, and a little further to the W is Telford's picturesque Horseshoe Falls where the Dee falls over a crescent-shaped weir to form the feeder for the Llangollen Canal.

From Pentre-felin you can still avoid the Horseshoe Pass

road by crossing the canal bridge and taking an old metalled
road which serves the rifle range, crossing the Eglwyseg river,
through a camp site to Valle Crucis Abbey.

Valle Crucis Abbey/Abaty Glyn y Groes
In the care of the Department of the Environment.

Hours of Admission	Weekdays	Sundays
March, April and October	*09.30–17.30*	*14.00–17.30*
May to September	*09.30–19.00*	*09.30–19.00*
November to February	*09.30–16.00*	*14.00–16.00*

Small charge for admission.

The Abbey of the Vale of the Cross (i.e. the 9c Pillar of Eliseg
nearby which gave the little valley its name) is a majestic
and picturesque ruin, considered to be the most attractive and
interesting example of its kind in North Wales.

The Cistercian abbey was founded in 1201 by the Prince of
Northern Powys, Madoc ap Gruffydd Maelor, as a daughter
house of Strata Marcella, whose blank site by the Severn we
have passed near Welshpool, in Southern Powys. The monastic
buildings were in Elizabethan times used as a farm house,
but these have now been cleared out to show the Abbey as
it was.

The monastic church follows the normal cruciform plan,
built in the Early English style and consisting of an aisled nave
of five bays, a choir and a presbytery, flanked by two
transepts, each of which has two chapels. After a disastrous
fire in the middle of the century the E end of the church was
completed, the central aisle and nave rebuilt, together with a
greater part of the W front. The lack of ornament and
decoration is characteristic of all early Cistercian churches, the
church relying for its effect on good proportions, simple lines
and bold detail.

The W front has a central doorway, deeply recessed and
with a richly moulded arch. Above it is the great W window,
six lights grouped in pairs within a single arch; in the head
of each pair is a circular opening, octafoil in the damaged
centre window, and hexafoil on either side. Above the lofty
window is the rose-window of eight trefoiled lights.

The E end of the church is well preserved, the upper parts
of the walls being built after the great fire. The presbytery is
lighted by three fine lofty lancet windows with arched heads,
Vale Crucis Abbey

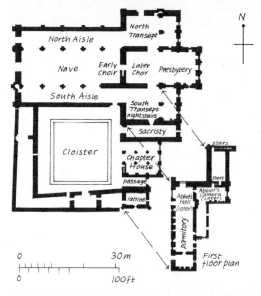

N

North Transept

North Aisle

Nave

Early Choir

Later Choir

Presbytery

South Aisle

South Transept nightstairs

Sacristy

Cloister

chapter House

passage

latrine

Stairs

Stairs

Abbot's Hall (later)

Abbot's Camera (later)

parlour

First floor plan

0   30 m

0   100 ft

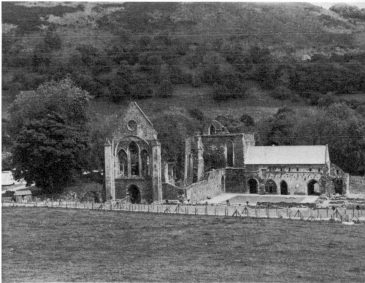

with two smaller lancets above with pointed heads.

The transepts each have two chapels with E windows. The S transept wall is pierced by a doorway to the sacristy, while in the SW corner is a doorway which stood at the head of the night stairs leading to the dormitory. The sacristy extends the full width of the transept and its main door leads off the cloister.

The monastic buildings lie to the S and E of the church, around the remains of the cloister. The chapter house occupies the E side and is a square building of late 14c or early 15c date. It has nine bays with groined vaults, the ribs of which spring without capitals from the piers or from corbels set in the walls. The central doorway from the cloister is flanked on one side by a screen of elaborate tracery, and on the other by a small door, from which stairs, in the thickness of the wall, lead up to the dormitory above.

S of the chapter house is a vaulted passage leading through the E range to Llyn Eglwystl, a large fishpond fed from the stream and where the abbot's house would normally lie.

The dormitory is a single hall, covered by a modern roof, occupying the space above the chapter house and sacristy. In the 15c the dormitory underwent revolutionary changes. A large fireplace was built in the E wall and a doorway was made in the wall facing the cloister, presumably reached by wooden stairs near the traceried chapter house window. A new room was built upon the E part of the sacristy and chapter house, and also provided with a fireplace. It seems that part of the dormitory was converted to provide the abbot's hall and chamber.

After the suppression of the monastery by Henry VIII the abbot's hall was adapted as a farmhouse, but only a few minor alterations of this remain. Excavations carried out in 1847 removed the farmhouse from the site, and restoration and consolidation of the remains followed in 1950 when the abbey ruins were conveyed to the Ministry of Works for permanent preservation.

In a field near to Valle Crucis Abbey is Eliseg's Pillar. It lies just to the N of Abbey Farm, close to the A542.

The Pillar of Eliseg/Colofon Eliseg
The pillar is a 9c memorial to Eliseg, Prince of Powys, and the
The Pillar of Eliseg

remains of the inscribed stone cross stand on a tumulus.
Together they form the most important surviving Dark Age
monuments in the Welsh borders.

The artificial mound on which the pillar stands was excavated
in 1779 and found to contain the remains of a body laid in a
rough stone coffin, and it is considered that the tomb dated
from the 5c or early 6c, before churchyard burial became a
general practice.

The pillar was set up on the tumulus about AD 850 and was
originally about 12 ft high. It had been thrown down, broken
and mutilated by the Roundhead soldiers in the Civil War.
Feelings ran high against the Papists as well as against the
King and the Puritan zealots despoiled the cross as some form
of Popish idolatry. In 1696 the long Latin inscription was
recorded by Edward Llwyd, the Celtic scholar and lexicographer.
The upper part of the pillar was re-erected in 1779 by Mr
Lloyd of Trevor Hall after the excavations of the tumulus, the
rest of the shaft and cross-head having gone missing.

The shaft now remaining stands 8 ft high and the inscription which Llwyd recorded is on one of the four faces near the base. The Latin inscription recorded the ancient glories of the royal house of Powys and consisted of about 31 lines each with 30 letters, forming a series of phrases. Some of the phrases have defied all attempts at restoration and interpretation, but the popular translation begins:

> *Cyngen, son of Cadell, Cadell son of Brochwel, Brochwel son of Eliseg, Eliseg son of Gwylog,*
>
> *Cyngen therefore, the great-grandson of Eliseg, erected this stone in honour of his great-grandfather Eliseg,*
>
> *It was Eliseg who united the inheritance of Powys (which had lain waste for nine years) from the hand of the English with fire and sword . . .*

This opening pedigree records the ancestors of the kings and princes of Powys, back from Cyngen, who died in Rome on a pilgrimage in 854, through his father Cadell, who died in 808, to Eliseg, contemporary of Offa, to Vortigern and his wife, daughter of the Roman commander Magnus Maximus. (Magnus Maximus had killed the Emperor Gratian in an attempt to make himself Emperor of Rome at the head of the British forces, but he in turn was murdered by Theodosius in 383). The princes of Powys could therefore connect themselves with the early British rulers and claim a continuity which was almost unique in Europe.

Valle Crucis Abbey to Llandegla

From the bridge over the River Eglwyseg at Valle Crucis Abbey you can take paths and tracks up the narrow steep-sided valley past Abbey Cottage and Hendre to join the official alternative route at the junction of roads near St Mary's Missionary Church. From here it is only a short way to the bridge over the river at Plas-yn-Eglwyseg and the route over Cyrn-y-Brain as described at the beginning of this chapter.

Alternatively you may either take the path up the side of Eglwyseg Glen to World's End or return to Llangollen by the Precipice Walk.

Eglwyseg Rocks, looking S

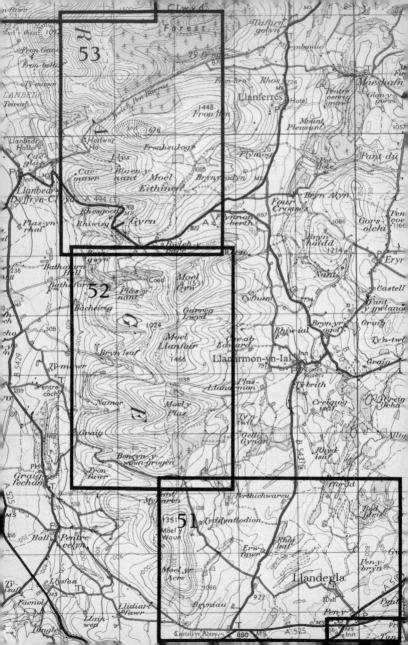

North of Llandegla you join the ridge of the Clwydian Hills,
a range of heights of striking and varied outline, with open
crests and little summits. Although they look like mountains –
and their traverse involves several steep ascents and descents
which add to this illusion – you do not in fact climb higher
than 2,000 ft. There is a series of six fortified hill-forts along the
range of hills and these add interest to the scenic value of the
route.

The hills belong to the Silurian age and in form and
vegetation they contrast strongly with the typical limestone
scenery to the NE and the Triassic New Red Sandstone of the
Vale of Clwyd to the W.

The chain of hills is broken by two main and two minor gaps:
the major gaps are those of Bwlch-y-Parc, crossed by the Mold-
Ruthin highway A494, and the valley of the River Wheeler at
Bodfari, 7 miles N, used by the Mold-Denbigh road A451.
Between these two passes are minor roads crossing Bwlch-
Pen-Barras and the col near Moel Arthur.

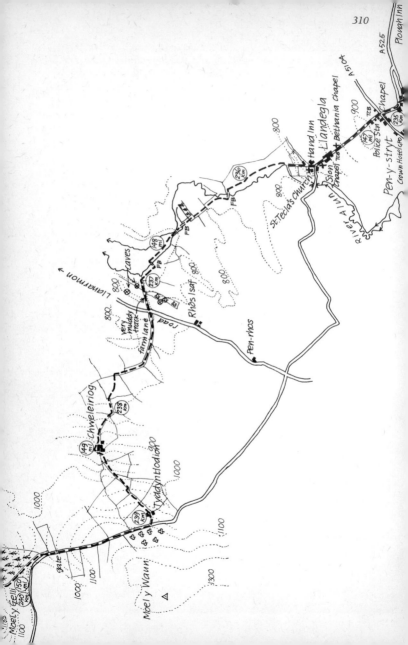

310

Although it may be possible to traverse this range of hills between Llandegla and Prestatyn in one day – the range of hills is 22 miles long and has 9 summits over 1,000 ft high – the stretch is divided into two sections to enable the walker to explore the towns in the Vale of Clwyd – Ruthin, Denbigh, St Asaph and Rhuddlan – and to find accommodation.

Llandegla to Moel Famau

Llandegla stands in a gap separating the high ground around Llangollen from the Clwydian Range, and it is crossed by busy main roads between the semi-industrial regions on one side and the agricultural region on the other. The gap is in fact a broad saddle of high ground, inclined to be moorland rather than pasture, and the Path crosses a confused terrain of fields and woods to avoid a direct route by roads before meeting the hills.

Beyond Llandegla you follow field paths marked out across the River Alyn and, although the Path has been improved, parts may be difficult to follow. The only recognisable features of historic interest on this stretch are the small caves in the low limestone ridges beside the track near the B5431 road. A complicated group of prehistoric burials were found in them when they were excavated a century ago.

Across the Llanarmon road a cart-track climbs up to Tyddyntlodion on a road below the eastern shoulder of Moel-y-Waun, 1351 ft, whose mile-long moorland crest terminates in Moel-y-Acre, the southernmost termination of the Clwydian Range.

You leave the road above Pant Myharen at a junction of lanes and beyond the dip go over Moel-y-Gelli behind a plantation and on the W side of Moel-y-Plas, obtaining a glimpse of Llyn Gweryd down on the R in a rim of forestry.

From the bwlch N of Moel-y-Plas a lane runs down to the pleasant little village of Llanarmon-yn-Ial, with its fine large church and a little castle mound. The black beamed 'Raven Inn' dating from 1722, is an unspoilt place and provides accommodation.

One mile of heathery ridge links the top of Moel Llanfair, 1466 ft, to the OS cairn on Moel Gyw, 1531 ft, but this ridge – including Moel Llech, Moel Llanfair, Boncyn Banhadlen and Moel Gyw – forms a bird sanctuary. Therefore the Path

Offa's Dyke Path on Llandegla Moor, looking NW (p 309)
51 *Llandegla and the River Alun (p 310)*

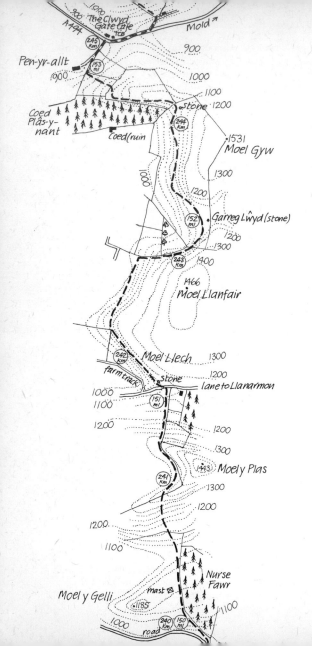

Mold ↗

The Clwyd
Gate Cafe
A494   TCB
(245 Km)

Pen-yr-allt
(153 mi)

900

900

1000

Coed
Plâs-y-
nant

Coed (ruin

stone   1200
(244 Km)

• 1531
Moel Gyw

1300

1200

• Garreg Lŵyd (stone)
(152 mi)

1200

1300

(243 Km)   1400

1466
Moel Llanfair

(242 Km)   Moel Llech   1300

farm track   stone   1200

1000   lane to Llanarmon

1100   (151 mi)

1200   1200

1300

• 1443 Moel y Plas

(241 Km)   1300

1200

1200

1100

Moel y Gelli

• 1185   mast ⌕   Nurse
Fawr

1000   road   1100

(240 Km) (150 mi)

continues at the same level as before, contouring round the western slopes of these hills. At the col between the two main summits you pass a grey boulder, the Carreg Lwyd, which marks an old way down to Llanarmon.

One or two bungalows straddle the pass of Bwlch-y-Parc and make it impossible to follow the direct line between the hilltops, so the Path keeps to the W flank of Moel Gyw and down beside a plantation of conifers on a spur to a farm lane, leading to the summit of the main road A494 at Clwyd Gate. There is a large restaurant in the pass, the Clwyd Gate Café, but unfortunately it is not always open.

Down in the Vale of Clwyd, $3\frac{1}{2}$ miles away, is the picturesque medieval town of Ruthin.

Ruthin

The ancient houses of Ruthin cluster in Market Street, Clwyd Street and Record Street on the slopes of the small plateau by the castle, church and market square. The late-Victorian broach spire of the church of St Peter's can be seen from some distance. The church is basically 14c, but parts of the building were demolished after the Dissolution, and restoration was carried out during 18c and 19c. Over the N aisle, the original nave of the church, is a magnificent carved and panelled roof, presented by Henry VII. There are brasses and monuments including one by Sir Richard Westmacott.

Lordship Court House is a half-timbered house built in 1404. At one time gallows were part of the house, as shown by a gibbet which projects from the façade. Nantclwyd House is a 13c mansion in Castle Street, with a half-timbered front and a gabled portico. The main features of the interior are a baronial hall, oak carvings and wainscotting. In the gallery are pre-Tudor heraldic emblems. The house is open by appointment only.

Bwlch-y-Parc is a high pass, 944 ft, and its deep v cleft divides the southern third of the Clwyds from the central section. To the N are heather-clad slopes of Gyrn and Moel Eithinen neighbouring the steep-sided, camp-crowned Foel Fenlli. The Official Path follows the hedge and fence over the top of the ridge, but the local farmer has erected misleading maps and signposts which guide the unwary walker below the E flank of Moel Eithinen.

Foel Fenlli's summit is 1676 ft and is topped by the most impressive of the Clwydian hill-forts. It is the southernmost of the six Iron Age hill forts, covering an area of 24 acres and measuring $\frac{3}{4}$ ml across. The defences consist of a single ditch and an earth bank, which in places measures 35 ft from bank top to ditch bottom. On the more gradual E side of the hill the ramparts have triple defences. Two entrances – one S and one W – both have returned entrances to give a narrow entry into the fort. There is a spring near the centre of the fort, around which was an embankment, portions of which still remain. Thirty-five hut circles were discovered within the defences of the fort, but they produced little save some pieces of 5c Romano-British pottery and some Roman coins, and nothing to show that they were ever occupied again after Roman times.

The view from the top of Foel Fenlli is magnificent, stretching N along the slopes of Moel Famau and W down into

Penycloddiau   Moel Arthur   Moel Famau

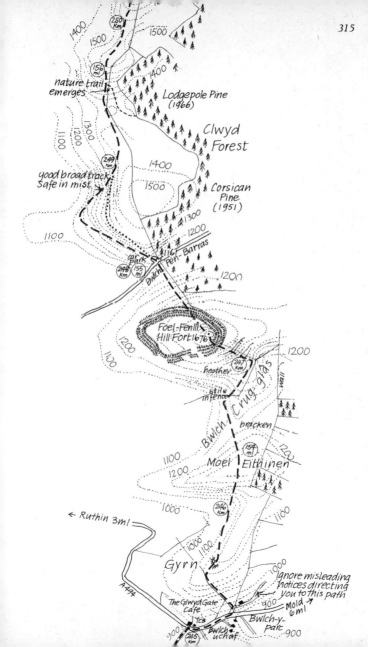

250 Km

1400

1500

1500

156 ml

nature trail
emerges

Lodgepole Pine
(1966)

Clwyd
Forest

1400

1300

1100

1200

249 Km

1400

good broad track
safe in mist

1500

Corsican
Pine
(1951)

1300

1200

1100

1200

car
park

116

248 Km   155 ml

Bwlch Pen-Barras

1200

Foel-Fenlli
Hill Fort 1676

1200

247 Km

heather

1200

Bwlch Crug-glas

wall

1200

stile
in fence

1100

1200

bracken

154 ml

Moel   Eithinen

1100

1200

1200

1000

246 Km

1100

← Ruthin 3ml

1000

1000   1100

Gyrn

Ignore misleading
notices directing
you to this path

1000

1000

Mold
6 ml →

A494

The Glwyd Gate
Cafe

TCB

245 Km

900

Bwlch
uchaf

Bwlch-y-
parc

900

900

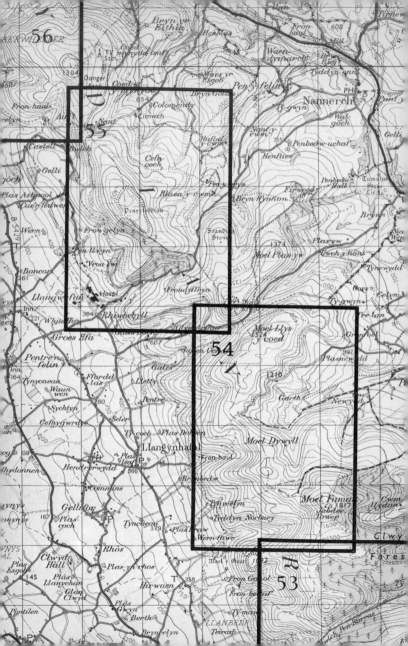

the Vale of Clwyd. The Vale of Clwyd is a rift valley, with the steep wall of the Clwydians bounding the single major fault on the E side. The lowland of the valley floor is a rich glacial drift and is intensively farmed, and from here it appears as a chequer-board of browns and greens, frequently dotted by woods and villages. On the W side of the vale are a series of stepped faults, the moorland of the Hiraethog which extends unbroken to the Conway valley.

A very steep descent of 500 ft through knee-deep heather brings you down to a road in the pass of Bwlch-Pen-Barras. This wide straight valley was the obvious route for the main turnpike road between Mold and Ruthin, but its height (1161 ft) and steepness of ascent meant that it had to be superceded by the more gradual road to the S over Bwlch-y-Parc.

To the N is the summit of Moel Famau, and it can be reached by a broad path ascending from the car park at the bwlch by an easy gradient, a steady climb for 1½ miles. The Path keeps to the W side of the broad ridge, and on the ascent you see little of the forestry plantation of Coed Clwyd which surges up along the eastern flanks of the hill to within 100 ft of the top. The lower slopes – up to 1,200 ft – were planted with Corsican pine in 1951, but the higher slopes near the ridge were planted with Lodgepole pine in 1966. From the top of the hill you can look down on a vast area of artificial 'forest' bisected with forestry roads and rides: accepted that commercial plantations are necessary, but the upper reaches of this fine range of hills is not the proper place. The remainder of the hill is clothed in grass and hundreds of acres of bilberry, and this is how it should be, open and accessible.

At 1820 ft Moel Famau (The Mother Mountain) is the highest summit in the Clwydians and its Jubilee Tower is a recognised landmark from Merseyside and Cheshire. The Jubilee Tower was designed in the Egyptian style by a Mr Harrison of Chester and was erected by the people of Clwyd to commemorate the 50th year of George III's reign. The pyramid of stone was 60 ft square at the base and it was to rise to a height of 150 ft, but the tower was never completed. It lay damaged by storms and vandals over the years until 1970 when the lower part, the only bit remaining, was extensively repaired and restored by volunteers in European Conservation Year.

Placed at four points of the compass on the tower platform are large identity plates, illustrating the places to be seen and how far away they are: the most magnificent views are to the S and W. To the S is a view of Llantisilio Mountain, and moving round to the SW and W are great mountain massifs in

the distance; the southernmost of these are the twin peaks of
Aran Fawddwy and Aran Benllyn at the head of Bala Lake;
next comes Arenig near Bala, and between and beyond these
two groups Cader Idris appears, 40 miles away. Westerly, after
a wide interval, comes the extensive Snowdonia group – Moel
Siabodd, Snowdon itself, 35 miles distant, distinguished among
the satellite peaks by its sharp summit, Tryfan and the
Glyders, and the smooth bulky Carnedds. In the western
foreground is the Vale of Clwyd with the Denbigh and
Hiraethog moors billowing behind. To the N lies Prestatyn,
14 miles as the crow flies, and to the eastward you look across
the Dee with its industrialised fringe, the Dee estuary itself,
the Wirral peninsula, and the estuary of the Mersey. Beneath
the smoke-pall lies Liverpool and industrial S Lancashire. In
very clear weather the Isle of Man, Blackpool tower and even
the hills of the Lake District can be seen.

Moel Famau to Bodfari

Moel Famau stands on the boundary between the Clwyd
districts of Glyndwr and Delyn and this line is followed by the
Path along the crest of the hills for several miles. After a steep
drop off the top of Moel Famau a path, sometimes indistinct,
gives pleasant walking for 3 miles along the undulating ridge,
first NW over Moel Dywyll, then N and NE nearly to the top

Moel Famau   Foel Fenlli   Moel Dywyll

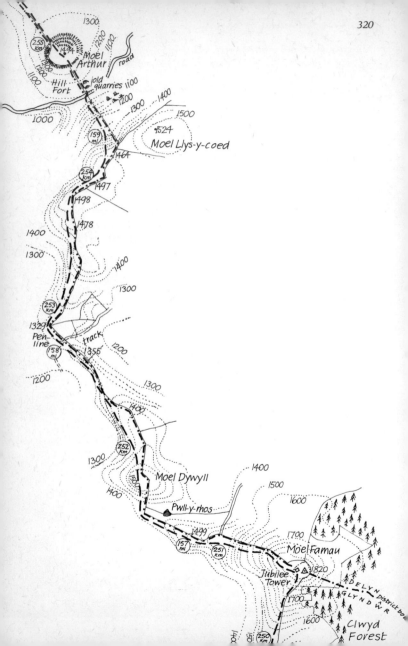

Moel Arthur

Hill Fort

road

(253 Km)

(144)

old quarries 1100

1300

1200

1100

1000

1200

1300

1400

1500

(159 mi)

1524

Moel Llys-y-coed

1464

(254 Km)

1497

1498

1478

1400

1300

1400

1300

(253 Km)

1329

Pen-line

track

(158 mi)

1355

1200

1200

1300

1400

(252 Km)

1300

Moel Dywyll

1400

1400

Pwll-y-rhos

1500

1600

1499

(157 mi)

(251 Km)

1700

Moel Famau

△ 1820

Jubilee Tower

DELYN

district bou

GLYNDWR

1700

Clwyd Forest

1600

(250 Km)

1400

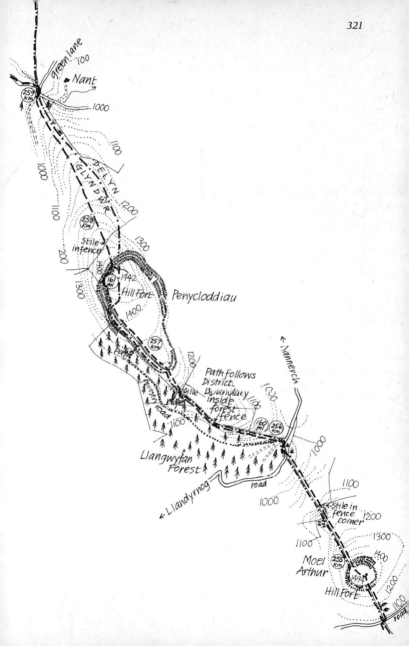

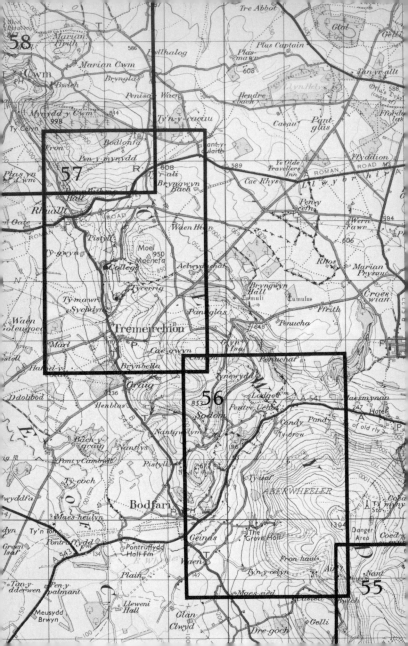

of Moel Llys-y-Coed, 1524 ft, before making sharp descent to a
road in the pass to the N.

Ahead is the small but powerfully defended hill-fort on
Moel Arthur, 1494 ft. Clwyd County Council have bought this
hill as a 'country park' so the Path goes straight over the top.
The steep climb to the top, like the sharp ascent of Foel
Fenlli, makes you realise why Iron Age man found these hills
popular for defensive purposes. The hilltop boasts an
impressive triple defence, and on all sides but the N the hill
is as steep as can be without actual cliffs.

There is a gradual drop down to a bwlch where a minor road
comes up from Nannerch, and the ridge continues to the next
summit of Penycloddiau, 1442 ft.

The SW flanks of this hill are also clad in a state forest:
this one is Llangwyfan Forest, whose conifers are clawing at the
very ramparts of a vast fort on the hilltop. The Path follows
the very edge of the forest along the crest of the ridge, but
open ground is reached when you come to the earthworks of
the hill-fort. The massive elliptical ramparts consist of a fine
triple vallum, and enclose an area of more than 50 acres. The
name Penycloddiau means 'The Hill of the Trenches'. Following
the rampart along the W side of the fort is rather like walking
some section of Offa's Dyke, the scale is so great and perfect.

A pleasant path runs down through the heather to a charming
bwlch where an old trackway from Ysceifiog crossed the range
to Bodfari. To the N is the conical hill of Moel-y-Parc, 1304 ft,
whose vast bracken and heather slopes are topped by bald
turf. Fortunately the TV mast and its clutter of buildings are
sited well below the summit.

The Path does not climb Moel-y-Parc but from the bwlch
(given a spot height of 1006 ft on 1 inch OS maps, but having
a height of over 1025 ft on 2½ inch OS maps) it takes green
lanes and paths below the W flank to Bodfari, where the
River Wheeler breaches the Clwydians.

This has been a fine stretch of open hill-walking for the
12–14 miles of ridge between Moel Llanfair and Moel-y-Parc. It
has contained the best day's walking in the Clwyds, even
perhaps along the whole of the Path, through the grass and

Moel Famau · · · Foel Fenlli

bracken and where gorse and heather spread a blaze of colour in the summer.

It will be perhaps too much to continue along the northern section of the range above Tremeirchion and Dyserth to Prestatyn in the same day, and it will be better to leave this stretch for your last day. If accommodation cannot be found in Bodfari then Denbigh is only a few miles away. In fact it is well worth paying a visit to this town to take a walk around the spectacular town walls and gaunt ruins of Denbigh Castle. You will need to spend some time to make a thorough inspection of the castle, but it would not be impossible to have a look at the castle on your final day before catching a bus out to Bodfari and continuing your walk to Prestatyn.

Description of route continues on p 339.

Denbigh

Denbigh is one of the few Welsh towns set on a hill, and may have been a defensive site before Dafydd ap Gruffydd, brother of Llywelyn the Last, established himself there in 1277, and precipitated the final war with Edward I in 1282. In October of that year his lands were captured and were granted by the king to Henry de Lacy, Earl of Lincoln, and he started building a great castle and fortified town in order to hold the area in subjection. However, the Welsh captured the town in 1294, but the rising was suppressed shortly afterwards and the Earl of Lincoln resumed work on the town and castle defences, making them incredibly strong, and the work was still unfinished when he died in 1311.

After Henry de Lacy's death Denbigh passed through several hands, and in 1399 it was the headquarters of Hotspur – Henry Percy. The town, which stood mainly outside the walls, was burnt by Owain Glyndwr in 1402 and again by Jasper Tudor, Earl of Pembroke, in 1468 while the castle was in the hands of the Yorkists during the Wars of the Roses.

When Leland visited the town in the 1540's he found the area within the walls derelict. A chapel of St Hilary, which had been built for the townspeople and garrison within the

fortified outer bailey of the castle, was in ruins. In 1563 the
castle came into the possession of the Earl of Leicester,
Robert Dudley, favourite of Queen Elizabeth I. He repaired the
castle and built a new hall, c1580, and began to erect a new
church in 1579 within the walls which was intended to replace
the humble Cathedral Church of St Asaph, but it was never
completed. There was no parish church or burial ground in the
town until the 19c.

During the Civil War the castle and the town walls were
held for the king, and Charles I stayed there for a few days in
1645. Late in 1646 the castle surrendered to the Parliamentarian
troops, but after the Restoration the castle was allowed to fall
into ruins. The best of the remains have been preserved by the
Secretary of State for Wales to illustrate the features of this
spectacular site, which includes a three-towered gate-house,
more complete than that at Caernarvon Castle.

Denbigh Castle

It was Edward I's custom, where town and castle were designed
to form a single unit, to build first a ring of outer defences,
using where possible the existing stronghold to protect the men

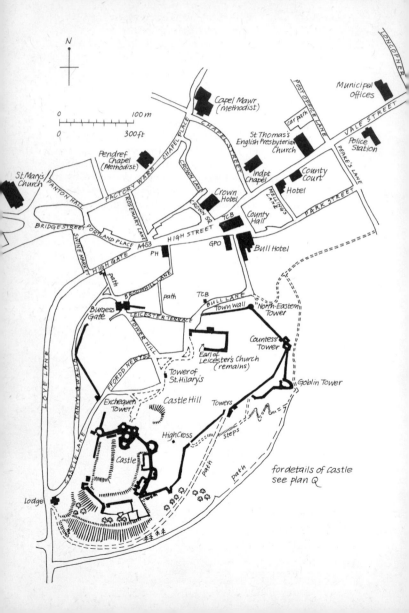

for details of Castle
see plan Q

engaged on the work, and there seems to be little doubt that this procedure was followed when he captured Denbigh in 1282. On the completion of these outer defences it was then the turn of building the castle within these walls, and at Denbigh the site chosen was the SW corner, the highest and least accessible point. When the castle was built the next stage was then to strengthen those parts of the town wall which formed part of the curtain wall of the castle. An elaborate system of defences was constructed on the outer faces on the S and SW, consisting of a mantlet with postern and sallyport. Finally the E salient of the town walls were strengthened, and the Goblin Tower, Countess Tower and Burgess Gate date from this later period – work undertaken by Henry de Lacy after the suppression of the 1294 revolt. Our tour will follow these stages of development once we have entered the castle.

A Tour of the Castle

Hours of admission	Weekdays	Sundays
March	09.30–17.30	14.00–17.30
April	09.30 17.30	09.30–17.30
May to September	09.30–19.00	09.30 19.00
October	09.30–17.30	14.00–17.00
November to February	09.30–16.00	14.00–16.00

The castle is entered through a massive gatehouse, outside which once stood a barbican and a ditch spanned by a drawbridge. The gatehouse consists of three octagonal towers, one placed on either side of the gatehouse – the Prison Tower and the Porter's Lodge Tower – and the other, the Badnes Tower, behind them and within the inner bailey. These towers enclosed a central octagonal hall, and the entrance to this was guarded by a drawbridge and two portcullises. Behind the counterpoise pit for the drawbridge was a door, and there was finally another door at the entry of the hall. The exit from the hall into the inner bailey is between the Prison and Badnes Towers, and was guarded by a door and a portcullis.

The central octagonal hall was vaulted in stone, and above it was a chamber of similar plan, which was entered from a

On Penycloddiau (p 328 top)
On Penycloddiau, looking SE (p 328 below)
Denbigh Castle. The Gatehouse (p 329)
P *Denbigh (p 330)*

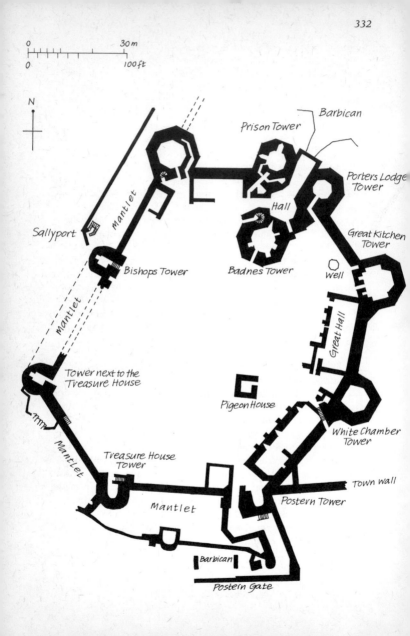

0   30 m

0   100 ft

N

Barbican

Prison Tower

Porters Lodge Tower

Hall

Great Kitchen Tower

Sallyport

Mantlet

Bishops Tower

Badnes Tower

Well

Great Hall

Mantlet

Tower next to the Treasure House

Pigeon House

White Chamber Tower

Mantlet

Treasure House Tower

Mantlet

Postern Tower

Town wall

Barbican

Postern Gate

stair in the Badnes Tower.

The Prison Tower is entered by a vaulted passage on the N side of the inner entry to the courtyard. On the L is a small toilet, and from this chamber can be seen the elaborate arrangement by which the chutes from five different toilets discharged into a common cesspit. On the LHS of the adjoining passage can be seen the manner by which rainwater was led from the roof to the cesspit by a curving pipe in the thickness of the wall. The tower had three storeys and the prison occupied the basement, entry to which was by a trapdoor in the floor of the ground floor room.

The Porter's Lodge Tower is much ruined, but it resembles the Prison Tower in general design. It had no basement and the entrance to the ground floor was by a passage, protected by two doors, which led directly from the courtyard.

The Badnes Tower is also much ruined, but it too had three storeys above a cellar. The ground floor was entered through a porch from the courtyard and on this side of the room there were also two windows. On the N side a window looked into the main entrance hall, and in the E wall was a fireplace and a toilet. The upper floors were approached by an octagonal staircase in the thickness of the walls, and the entry to this stair is from the courtyard adjoining the inner entry, through a porch with an outer and inner door. On the first floor, above the main entrance passage between the Prison and Badnes towers is a small chamber into which the portcullises were raised when not in use. This chamber was reached from wall-passages from both towers, and other passages also led from these towers to the curtain wall on both sides of the gatehouse. This essential feature of the Edwardian castle enabled the defenders to pass from one tower to the other without entering any of the residential rooms, and it was also possible from this level to make a complete circuit of the wall tops. Today the only portion of the curtain wall which retains its wall-walk is that between the Badnes Tower of the gatehouse and the Great Kitchen Tower.

To the W of the gatehouse is the Red Tower which dates from the same period. It is octagonal in plan. On the E side is a wall passage leading to a similar passage in the town wall. The upper floors of the tower were reached by a circular stair in the SW angle.

The towers on the W and S sides of the courtyard – Bishop's

*Q *Denbigh Castle*

Tower, Tower-next-the-Treasure House, Treasure House Tower and Postern Tower – are all of similar design and belong to the original town wall. Each has an added stair on the inner side to provide access to the wall-walk.

Across on the E side of the courtyard is the Great Kitchen Tower, next in line along the curtain from the gatehouse, and its most notable features are two great fireplaces in the N and S walls on the ground floor. The only light to this room was from two small windows in the W wall, one on either side of the entrance. The tower was of three storeys and the upper floors were reached directly from the courtyard by a stair in the NW angle of the tower.

The next tower in the curtain is the White Chamber Tower, now mostly in ruins. The basement was reached by a flight of steps down from the courtyard, and access to the upper floors was by a circular stair in the SW corner of the tower.

The Postern Tower was one of the original towers of the town wall and stands at the point where the town and castle walls meet. When the castle was remodelled after 1294 the tower was considerably altered because of the elaborate system of defences which were then constructed on the castle's S and W sides. Adjoining the tower on the W a gatehouse, the upper gate, was built. It had a drawbridge – the two pits can still be seen – though the gatehouse has almost entirely disappeared. Running S from the tower and gatehouse were built two walls, flanking a steep passage leading to the lower or postern gate. This passage originally had steps for pedestrians on one side and a ramp on the other for horses. The postern gate protected the point where the passageway takes a right-angled turn towards the W. This gate is much ruined, but the drawbridge and counterpoise pits still remain. Beyond, to the W, are fragmentary remains of a barbican.

The final stage of development of de Lacy's castle can be seen in the mantlet and sallyport. The mantlet formed an additional line of defence outside the walls on the S and W sides, but the only portion that remains in fairly complete condition is that between the Postern and Treasure House Towers. Midway along the retaining wall in this section is a projecting bastion to command the entrance to the barbican below.

The sallyport lies to the NW of the Bishop's Tower. It is small but elaborately planned, and consists of a narrow winding stair and passage leading down and out through the face of the mantlet. The passage was defended at the foot of the stair by a portcullis and an inner door, and between this and the entrance were two openings through which missiles could be dropped on assailants below.

On the inside of the curtain on the E side of the courtyard are buildings which probably date from the middle 14c. Between the Great Kitchen Tower and White Chamber Tower are the foundations of the Great Hall, which contained a buttery and a pantry, and between the White Chamber Tower and the Postern Tower was a building with chambers at ground and first floor levels.

Before leaving the castle examine the postern which was cut through the curtain by the SW corner of White Chamber Tower. The main purpose of this postern appears to have been to provide access to the well in the Goblin Tower of the town wall, as the supply from the well in the castle courtyard had proved inadequate. At the top of the stairs leading down to the postern is a small chamber where the pitchers of water were stored after they were brought up from the well.

The Town Walls

Hours of Admission	*Weekdays*	*Sundays*
March to April	09.30–17.30	14.00–17.30
May to September	09.30–19.00	14.00–19.00
October	09.30–17.30	14.00–17.30
November to February	09.30–16.00	14.00–16.00

Visitors wishing to examine the town walls should consult the custodian at the castle pay-desk. The Burgess Gate is at the W end of the northern stretch of town wall. It consists of a vaulted entrance passage with gates at each end and a portcullis, originally approached by a bridge crossing a ditch. The entrance is flanked by projecting towers, the western containing a vaulted guardroom, the eastern having a stair in the thickness of the wall leading to an upper room which extended over the whole of the gatehouse.

The northern wall runs eastward to the North-East Tower and then SE to the Countess Tower, at which point the N end of the salient joins the original town wall. This tower consists of two angular turrets with added rooms, but there is little else of interest. The curtain linking the Countess and Goblin Towers has a double series of embrasures, the upper reached by a narrow wall-walk, the lower from the pathway between the two buildings.

The Goblin Tower forms a bastion projecting from the face of a limestone cliff. It is of two storeys with a narrow stairway descending to the well. The pathway leading down from the Countess Tower enters this tower on the lower floor by a flight of steps.

The salient wall joins the original town wall again SW of the Goblin Tower at a point where there are remains of a postern gate, but no details can be seen except a drawbridge pit.

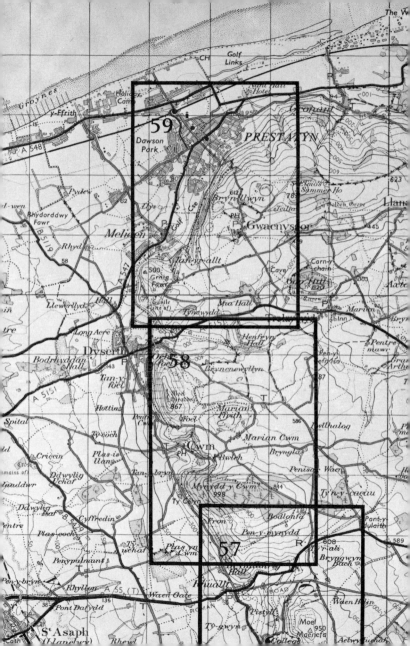

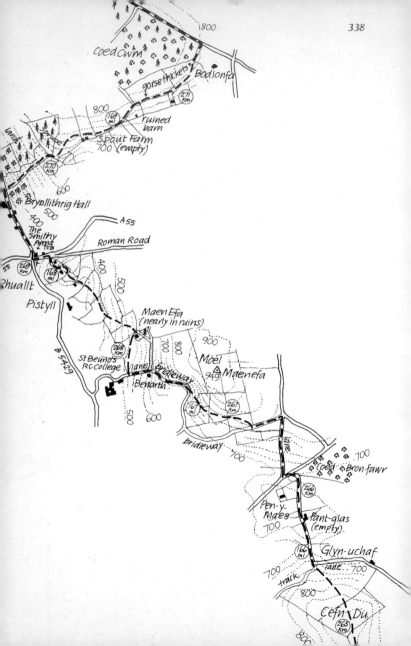

Bodfari to Rhuallt

The northernmost section of the Clwydians still show the characteristic formation of the range — steeply scarped on the W with innumerable little re-entrant valleys, with larger and gentler slopes on the E. Some of the hills still have individual tops and hill-forts, but they are nothing like those to the S.

Bodfari church, with its conspicuous striped slate roof, stands at the foot of camp-crowned Moel-y-Gaer, 672 ft, and although there is a path uphill from this place our Path ascends a steep and narrow lane opposite the Downing Arms on the main road A541.

The Path continues by pleasant paths and lanes over Cefn Du and Moel Maenfa, 950 ft. This small hill has a rough open top and still manages to give views over the Vale of Clwyd. A path drops down the W slope to Rhuallt.

The Roman road from Deva (Chester) to Canovium in the Vale of Conway comes over the hills here and is joined in the gap at Rhuallt by the busy A55 — the busiest of the roads over the Clwyds, carrying the main route from Merseyside to the North Wales resorts.

Rhuallt to Dyserth

The route of a path through Coed Cwm on Mynydd y Cwm, 998 ft, was opposed by forestry interests, and so our Path goes

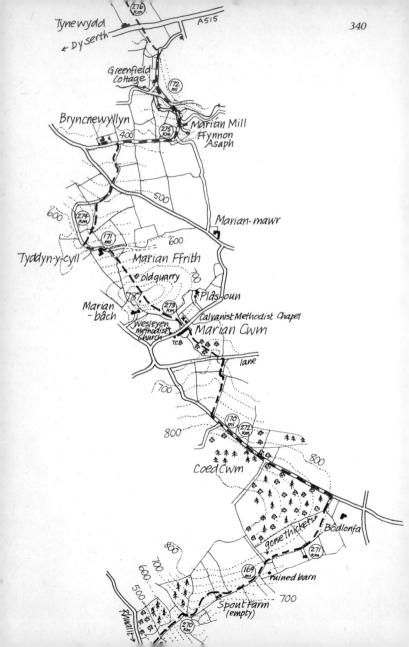

S and E of the forested hill by paths and lanes through pasture land.

Marian Cwm is a tiny hamlet with two chapels below the pleasant little hill of Marian Ffrith, 787 ft. The Path on the top commands good views down to Rhuddlan on one side and Gop Hill on the other. Moel Hiraddug, 867 ft, in the foreground has a hill-fort, but it is gradually being eaten away by quarrying. You pass the powerful spring Ffynnon Asaph which powered the now derelict Marian Mill and then come to the Dyserth road A5151, the last of the four main roads that crosses the Clwyds.

Description of route continues on p 343.

Gop Hill and Offa's Dyke

The hump of Gop Hill, 820 ft, lies 1 mile E of the Path and is just N of the main road between Dyserth and Trelawnyd. With the odd pimple of its huge burial cairn, the largest prehistoric cairn in Wales, it rises prominently over the rolling plateau forming the NE extension of the Clwydian Hills. It is over 60 ft high and when it was partly excavated in 1866 it was found to be built entirely of dry-stone. Here Offa's Dyke ends or begins, for on its lower slopes the last, or first, dimly recognisable stretches of the earthwork are to be found.

In the vicinity of Gop Farm the Dyke is of uniform style, consisting of a bank between two ditches, averaging 50 ft wide. There are two short stretches of earthwork to the W of Gop Hill, and these suggest that the hill was included within the alignment of the Dyke to give visual control over Welsh territory.

The Dyke fades out on Gop Hill in a form which suggests that it was never completed, but the direction of the alignment when it is lost is strongly in favour of the frontier having gone on to reach the coast near Prestatyn.

One suggested and possible route of the Dyke from Gop Hill was through the Dyserth gap to the crossing of the River Clwyd by a ford at Rhuddlan, which was the site of an important crossing of the river during the border warfare of the 8c. Such a termination would have agreed with Asser's statement that the Dyke went *di mare usque ad mare* – from coast to coast – for Rhuddlan marsh, now reclaimed, was essentially part of the

57 *Rhuallt (p 338)*
   The Prestatyn Hills from Marian Ffrith, looking N (p 339)
58 *Rhuallt to Dyserth (p 340)*

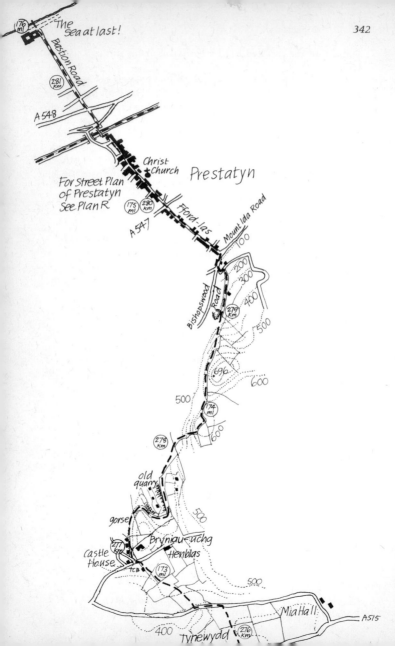

The Sea at last!

176 ml

Bastion Road

281 Km

A 548

For Street Plan
of Prestatyn
See Plan R

Christ
Church

Prestatyn

175 ml   280 Km

Ffordd-las

A 547

Mount Ida Road

100

Bishopswood Road

200

300

279 Km

400

500

696

600

500

174 ml

278 Km

600

old
quarry

500

gorse

Bryniau-uchg

277 Km

Castle
House

Henblas

173 ml

TCB

500

Mia Hall

A 515

400

Tynewydd   276 Km

coastline, and the river was crossed at the head of the tidal estuary immediately below the Norman castle.

Tradition has it that Offa died at Rhuddlan in 798, 3 miles away from his frontier, presumably in border warfare, and his work was never completed. There can be no doubt that this suggested line did have possibilities, but there is no evidence to sustain that remains of Offa's Dyke existed on this line.

Bishop Asser of St Davids, writing within 100 years of Offa's death, stated that the line of the Dyke was marked out to the sea, and there are one or two clues which suggest that the line to be taken by the frontier led to Prestatyn. It looks as though the two short stretches of earthwork near Gop Farm were marking-out trenches for the Dyke, left unfinished when the directing hand was withdrawn. The existence of a straight road – Fford Las – sweeping down from the cliffy scarp of the upland directly above Prestatyn, now the main street of the town leading to the sea, and passing ½ mile W of the site of Prestatyn castle, seems convincing. These shreds of evidence led Fox to conclude that this is the line of the final stretch of the Dyke in its long march *di mare usque ad mare*.

Dyserth to Prestatyn

From the Dyserth road to Tan-yr-allt stiles lead you at first into ploughed fields with no traces of a path, but the way ahead is obvious, leading you to the hills above Prestatyn. Here you meet the full force of the winds blowing in from Liverpool Bay, and you notice how the hawthorns and shrubs grow away from the wind. The Path follows the crest of the steep scarp slope, where brambles and gorse grow freely. It has been cleared in places and waymarked by the familiar small concrete slabs and by white paint: do not confuse these marks with the yellow paint-splashes of a nature trail.

It might have been better if the Path had kept a little further to the E of Prestatyn and ended on the empty sand dunes beyond the golf links. As it is the Path drops down the face of the steep scarp slope right into the town.

Prestatyn

Prestatyn is a popular holiday resort with plenty of entertainment and sport and 4 miles of fine beaches. It is also a small market town, and was in the 18c a busy industrial centre for the lead-mining district of NE Wales. Its bus and

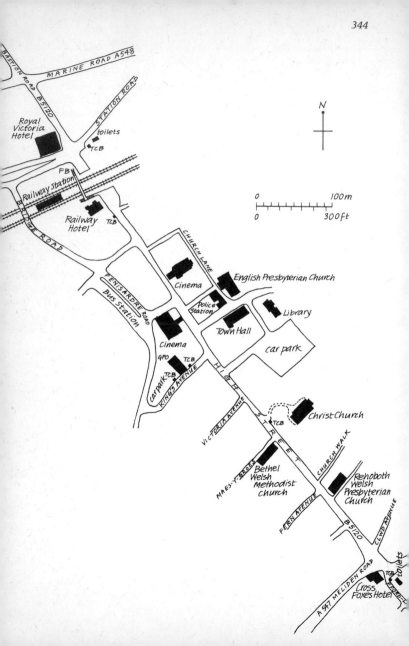

railway stations have connections to the coastal resorts and to Chester, where other connections can be made to take you home. (ECD Thursday.)

The last 'acorn' of the long-distance footpath is sited where the Path joins the steep zig-zags of the roads on the S edge of the town. The Path surely cannot end here? It is known that Offa did not construct his Dyke entirely to the coast at Prestatyn, and it is obvious why the Countryside Commission have stopped their Path short of the built-up area of the town. Nevertheless, having come so far it is only a further 1½ miles to the shore.

Follow the long sweeping line of Fford Las – 'The Green Road' – becoming High Street and Bastion Road, carving its way through the straggling resort. Ignore the stares of puzzled holidaymakers as you stand in the surf having completed your walk from coast to coast.

R *Prestatyn*

E G Bowen (editor), *Wales – A Physical, Historical and Regional Geography* (Methuen, 1957).

F V Emery, *The World's Landscapes – Wales* (Longmans, 1969).

H L V Fletcher, *Herefordshire – County Book Series* (Robert Hale, 1948).

Sir Cyril Fox, *Archaeologia Cambrensis, vols 81–86* (Cambrian Archaeological Association, 1926–31).

Sir Cyril Fox, *Antiquity, Vol III, pp 135–154* (Publisher not known, 1929).

Sir Cyril Fox, *Offa's Dyke – A Field Survey* (Oxford University Press and the British Academy, 1955).

W J Gruffydd, *North Wales and the Marches* (Collins, 1951).

W J Gruffydd, *South Wales and the Marches* (Collins, 1951).

Her Majesty's Stationery Office, *Forest Park Guide: Dean Forest and the Wye Valley* (HMSO, 1956).

Her Majesty's Stationery Office, *Brecon Beacons National Park Guide* (HMSO, 1967).

G Hogg, *And Far Away* (J M Dent/Phoenix House, 1946).

Miss Maxwell Fraser, *West of Offa's Dyke – North Wales* (Robert Hale, 1958).

Miss Maxwell Fraser, *West of Offa's Dyke – South Wales* (Robert Hale, 1958).

Miss Maxwell Fraser, *Welsh Border Country* (Batsford, 1972).

R Milward and A Robinson, *The Welsh Marches* (Macmillan, 1971).

Ministry of Works, *Illustrated Regional Guide to Ancient Monuments – North Wales* (HMSO).

Ministry of Works, *Illustrated Regional Guide to Ancient Monuments – Midlands* (HMSO).

Ministry of Works, *Illustrated Regional Guide to Ancient Monuments – South Wales* (HMSO).

F Noble, *Shell Book of Offa's Dyke Path* (Queen Anne Press, 1969/72).

Ordnance Survey, *Britain in the Dark Ages* (Ordnance Survey, 1955).

W T Palmer, *The Verge of Wales* (Robert Hale, 1942).

W T Palmer, *Odd Corners in North Wales* (Steffington, 1946).

N Pevsner, *Shropshire – Buildings of England Series* (Penguin, 1958).

J Piper and J Betjeman, *Shell Guide to Shropshire* (Faber & Faber, 1951).

W Plomer (editor), *Kilvert's Diary* (Cape, 1964).

W Rees, *An Historical Atlas of Wales* (Faber & Faber, 1951).

T A Ryder, *Portrait of Gloucestershire – Portrait Series* (Robert Hale, 1966).

W V Thomas and A Llewelyn, *Shell Guide to Wales* (Michael Joseph, 1969).

P Thoresby Jones, *Welsh Border Country* (Batsford, 1938/49).

Edmund Vale, *Shropshire – County Book Series* (Robert Hale, 1945).

David Verey, *Gloucestershire – Buildings of England Series* (Penguin, 1970).

David Verey, *Shell Guide to Herefordshire* (Faber & Faber, 1955).

David Verey, *Shell Guide to Mid Wales* (Faber & Faber, 1960).

Vincent Waite, *Shropshire Hill Country* (Dent, 1970).

Ward Locke, *North Wales – Red Guide* (Ward Locke, 1971).

Ward Locke, *The Wye Valley – Red Guide* (Ward Locke, 1970).

Alfred Watkins, *The Old Straight Track* (Methuen, 1925).

A West and D Verey, *Shell Guide to Gloucestershire* (Faber & Faber, 1951–70).